Appendix A

X TOOLKIT DATA TYPES

The most commonly used Xlib and toolkit data types are described in this section. This is not an exhaustive reference to all X data structures; the header files are always the final arbiter. Listings in this section adhere to the following format:

Data Type   (Intrinsics version)

`<Header>`
The header file in which the data type and related information is specified, per the X11R6 distribution. Vendor-specific implementations of the Intrinsics may define these data types elsewhere.

Description of the data type and its purpose, situations in which the data type is used, and (where applicable) warnings about proper usage and version mismatches

Arg, ArgList   (R3)

`<X11/Intrinsic.h>`

`Arg` is a structure associating a resource name with a value. An `ArgList` is a pointer to an array of `Args`.

```
typedef struct {
    String     name;
    XtArgVal   value;
} Arg, *ArgList;
```

`ArgLists` are passed to all routines that set or query resource values. An array of `Args` is usually declared statically; values are filled in with repeated calls to `XtSetArg`.

Atom   (R3)

`<X11/X.h>`

`Atom` is a 32-bit ID used to reference a character string stored in the X server. `Atoms` are used rather than the actual strings because they fit conveniently in event packets. The server assigns the value for `Atoms`, guaranteeing that every unique string receives a unique `Atom` value, and that the mapping between an `Atom` and a string will remain invariant for the lifetime of the server.

The Atom for a specified string is returned by the Xlib routine XInternAtom. The inverse transform is carried out with XGetAtomName. X predefines certain widely-used Atom values in <X11/Xatom.h>. Atoms are used to identify window properties and toolkit selections, and in synthetic ClientMessage events to implement inter-process communications protocols.

Boolean   (R3)

<X11/Intrinsic.h>

Boolean is a datum containing a zero (false) or non-zero (true) value. The exact representation of this data type is implementation-dependent. Unless explicitly stated, clients should not assume that the non-zero Boolean value returned by a routine is equal to the symbolic value True (see *XtEnum*)

caddr_t   (R3O)

/sys/h/types.h (on most UNIX-based systems)

caddr_t is a datum large enough to contain the largest of a char*, int*, function pointer, structure pointer or long value. A pointer to any data type or function, or a long value, may be converted to a caddr_t and back again and the result will compare equal to the original value. The exact representation of this data type is implementation-dependent. The type caddr_t is used to specify pointers to application-defined data which must be passed transparently by Xlib or the Intrinsics. caddr_t is superseded in the R4 Intrinsics by the data type XtPointer, and in the R5 Xlib by the type XPointer.

Cardinal   (R3)

<X11/Intrinsic.h>

Cardinal is an unsigned datum with a minimum range of 0 to 2^{16}-1. The exact representation of this data type is implementation-dependent. A Cardinal is used to specify a value representing a number of items.

Colormap   (R3)

<X11/X.h>

Colormap is a 32-bit ID referencing a Colormap resource maintained by the X server. The colormap is a table that is used to determine the mapping of pixel values to actual colors. The default colormap is shared by most programs, and matches the root window's depth and visual class. New Colormaps are allocated with the Xlib routine XCreateColormap.

Cursor   (R3)

<X11/X.h>

Cursor is a 32-bit ID referencing a Cursor resource maintained by the X server. Cursors are allocated with the Xlib routines XCreateBitmapCursor, XCreateGlyphCursor, or XCreateFontCursor. A cursor is bound to a window with XDefineCursor, or in some toolkits with a "cursor" resource.

Dimension   **(R3)**

`<X11/Intrinsic.h>`

Dimension is an unsigned datum with a minimum range of 0 to 2^{16}-1. The exact representation of this data type is implementation-dependent. Variables of type Dimension express a distance, such as a widget's width or height.

Display   **(R3)**

`<X11/Xlib.h>`

Display is a large data structure containing run-time information about an open connection to an X server. The internals of this data structure are rarely examined by ordinary applications, which instead pass a pointer to the structure to routines that require it.

A Display data structure is dynamically allocated when a connection to an X server is established with XtOpenDisplay (or one of the convenience initialization routines). The Display data structure is never accessed directly by an application, but many Xlib and Intrinsics routines accept a Display pointer as an argument. A display pointer is derived from a widget ID with XtWindow(widget).

Drawable   **(R3)**

`<X11/X.h>`

Drawable is equivalent to either a Window or a Pixmap. Most Xlib drawing function take a Drawable argument, implying that the function can be used in either.

EventMask   **(R3)**

`<X11/Intrinsic.h>`

EventMask is a bit mask used to specify which types of X events a client is interested in. Each bit in the EventMask represents a particular type or types of event. An EventMask must be specified when registering event handlers with XtAddEventHandler and related routines, and is usually constructed by ORing together the symbolic constants associated with the event types of interest (see Table 9-2):

```
    EventMask mask = ( PointerMotionMask | ButtonPressMask );
```

Font   **(R3)**

`<X11/X.h>`

Font is a 32-bit ID referencing a font resource loaded by the X server. Fonts are allocated with the Xlib routines XLoadFont and XLoadQueryFont.

GC   **(R3)**

`<X11/Xlib.h>`

GC is a pointer to an opaque data structure representing a collection of graphics attributes. This data structure in turn references the actual server object. A GC must be referenced in any Xlib drawing function calls. The Intrinsics routines XtGetGC, XtAllocateGC and XtReleaseGC allocate and free GCs.

KeyCode (R3)

`<X11/X.h>`

KeyCode is an 8-bit value in the included range 8-255. A KeyCode is a field in a Key event, and reports the physical key pressed on a given hardware keyboard. Because a KeyCode is hardware-specific, an incoming KeyCode is automatically parsed by a KeyCode-to-KeySym translator during translation management (see *KeySym*).

KeySym (R3)

`<X11/X.h>`

KeySym is a unique numeric identifier for a symbolic character defined in an alphabet such as ISO Latin-1 or Katakana. The value of this identifier need not map in any particular way to the the eight- or sixteen-bit encoding defined by a character set. Standard KeySyms are defined in the header file `<X11/keysymdef.h>`. Others may be defined by vendor-specific implementations, and are often contained in the file `/usr/lib/X11/XKeysymDB`. For each identifier, a symbolic constant is also defined which is used to identify the KeySym in "C" programs. Examples from `<X11/keysymdef.h>`:

```
#define XK_period    0x02e /* the symbol "." */
#define XK_0         0x030 /* the number "0" */
#define XK_1         0x031 /* the number "1" */
#define XK_Ccedilla  0x0c7 /* the letter "Ç" */
```

KeySym names are used to define key sequences in translation tables, since a KeySym is invariant and does not depend on the hardware implementation.

Modifiers (R3)

`<X11/Intrinsic.h>`

Modifiers is a bit mask used to report the state of keys that affect the mapping of KeyCodes to KeySyms. A value of type Modifiers is passed to Intrinsics routines that parse KeyCodes. A valid Modifiers value is constructed by ORing any of the modifier bit masks defined in `<X11/X.h>`: ShiftMask, LockMask, ControlMask, Mod1Mask, Mod2Mask, Mod3Mask, Mod4Mask, Mod5Mask. The mapping of physical keys to particular modifier bits is set with the xmodmap utility.

Object (R4)

`<X11/Intrinsic.h>`

Object is a pointer to the instance record for a toolkit windowed or windowless object. Objects are referenced by various toolkit routines; a valid Object value is returned by XtCreateWidget.

Opaque (R3O)

`<X11/Intrinsic.h>`

Opaque is a data type used to specify a pointer to a toolkit internal data object which is not defined in the scope of a normal application. The definition of Opaque depends on the definition of XtPointer, which is itself an implementation-dependent data type. The Opaque data type is not part of the standard and should no longer be used.

Pixel **(R3)**

`<X11/Intrinsic.h>`

`Pixel` is a 32-bit unsigned value specifying the contents of a location in the video frame buffer. This in turn is translated to a color value by the display hardware. The mapping from a `Pixel` value to a color depends on the `Visual` class and capabilities of the workstation hardware. By far the most common transform of a pixel value is to use it as an index into a color map (`Visual` type `PseudoColor`). A `Pixel` value is valid only if it has been allocated and initialized by the X server. This is done with the Xlib routines `XAllocColor`, `XAllocNamedColor`, `XAllocColorCells` and/or `XAllocPlanes`. Pixels (and sometimes arrays of `Pixels`) are used by the Xlib and Intrinsics routines that manipulate colors or color resources.

Pixmap **(R3)**

`<X11/X.h>`

`Pixmap` is a 32-bit value used to identify an offscreen drawing area allocated and maintained by the X server. A Pixmap usually contains a picture used as a pattern to fill areas, or as an icon or button label. A valid `Pixmap` value is assigned when a Pixmap is created with `XCreatePixmap`, `XCreatePixmapFromBitmapData` or `XCreateBitmapFromData`. A bitmap is a single-plane Pixmap.

Position **(R3)**

`<X11/Intrinsic.h>`

`Position` is a signed datum with a minimum range of -2^{15} to $+2^{15}-1$. The exact representation of this data type is implementation-dependent. The data type `Position` is used to define a location within a widget or window coordinate system, as an offset from the drawable's origin.

Region **(R3)**

`<X11/Xutil.h>`

`Region` is a pointer to an internal data type representing an area within a drawable. Regions are usually manipulated with the Xlib "X*Something*Region" routines.

Screen **(R3)**

`<X11/Xlib.h>`

`Screen` is a large data structure containing specific information about a physical screen maintained by a server. A Screen data structure is dynamically allocated when a server connection is opened with `XtOpenDisplay`. A client rarely examines the Screen directly; however, various Xlib information macros (see Table 12-2) require a pointer to the structure. The screen pointer associated with a widget is returned with `XtScreen(widget)`.

String   (R3)

`<X11/Intrinsic.h>`

String is a pointer to a NULL-terminated char array. The String data type may be used anywhere the declaration char* would be appropriate.

Substitution, SubstitutionRec   (R4)

`<X11/Intrinsic.h>`

SubstitutionRec is a data structure that associates a character to be searched for in a path definition with a string to be substituted for the character if it is found.   A Substitution is a list of SubstitutionRecs.   Substitutions are passed as arguments to the routines XtFindFile and XtResolvePathname.

```
typedef struct {
    char    match;
    String  substitution;
} SubstitutionRec, *Substitution;
```

Time   (R3)

`<X11/X.h>`

Time is a 32-bit unsigned value representing X server time, measured in milliseconds.   A timestamp is included in several types of Xevent to report when the event occurred. Timestamps are required by Xlib and Intrinsics routines that arbitrate possible race conditions between applications, including those involved in toolkit selection and grabs. A Time argument must usually be the timestamp provided by an actual event, but in some cases may be the symbolic value CurrentTime.

Visual   (R3)

`<X11/Xlib.h>`

Visual is a data structure which defines the color mapping by which Pixel values are translated to actual RGB colors on a particular screen. The pointer to a Visual may be specified as a resource to Shell widgets. Visual types are discussed in detail in the Xlib reference manual. Applications rarely examine the fields of the Visual structure, but instead examine the fields of the related XVisualInfo struct.

Widget   (R3)

`<X11/Intrinsic.h>`

Widget is a pointer to a widget instance record. Since each instance record occupies a different place in memory, a Widget value constitutes a unique identifier for a particular instance, and is sometimes referred to as a "widget ID".   A unique widget ID is returned by the routines XtCreateWidget, XtCreatePopupShell, XtAppCreateShell, XtAppInitialize or XtOpenApplication (R6), and is a required argument to most Intrinsics routines. A widget data structure should not be accessed directly by application routines.

WidgetClass   **(R3)**

`<X11/Intrinsic.h>`

`WidgetClass` is a pointer to a widget class record, the contents of which are defined when the class is compiled. A one-time class initialization is also performed when the first widget of a given class is created. Application programs never deal directly with the contents of a widget class record, but must pass the publicly-declared class pointer to any Intrinsics routine that creates or checks the class of a widget. The `WidgetClass` of an existing widget is returned by the Intrinsics routine `XtClass`.

WidgetList   **(R3)**

`<X11/Intrinsic.h>`

`WidgetList` is a pointer to an array of `Widgets`. A widget list is passed to routines that operate on a number of widgets in a single call, including `XtManageChildren` and `XtChangeManagedSet` (R6).

Window   **(R3)**

`<X11/X.h>`

`Window` is a 32-bit value used to refer to a particular window maintained by an X server. A `Window` is a required argument to Xlib drawing routines and many Xlib resource management routines. After realization, every `Widget` has an associated `Window`, the ID of which is returned by `XtWindow(widget)`.

XEvent   **(R3)**

`<X11/Xlib.h>`

An `XEvent` is a union of 31 different data structures, each of which defines a type of event that can be delivered by an X server. Applications must cast a generic `XEvent` structure to the appropriate type before inspecting the detail fields. The first field in any `XEvent` structure declares the type of the `XEvent`. A pointer to an `XEvent` is returned by various Intrinsics event loop functions, including `XtAppNextEvent`. Event pointers are always passed as arguments to event handlers and action procedures, and sometimes to callback routines (via the *call_data*).

XFontSet   **(R5)**

`<X11/Xlib.h>`

An `XFontSet` is a data structure describing the collection of fonts required by a locale. An `XFontSet` is a required argument to multibyte string rendering routines, and is used as the font resource for internationalized widgets in the Athena widget set. A pointer to an `XFontSet` is returned by `XCreateFontSet`.

XFontStruct   **(R3)**

`<X11/Xlib.h>`

An `XFontStruct` is a data structure describing a Font resource loaded by the X server. Fields in the `XFontStruct` describe the valid character range and spatial metrics of the font. A pointer to an `XFontStruct` is returned by `XLoadQueryFont`.

XGCValues   (R3)

`<X11/Xlib.h>`

`XGCValues` is a data structure used to specify the values of graphics attributes to be set in a GC creation or manipulation function. Details of its use are discussed in the Xlib reference manual.

XPointer   (R5)

`<X11/Xlib.h>`

`XPointer` is a datum large enough to contain the largest of a `char*`, `int*`, function pointer, structure pointer or `long` value. A pointer to any data type or function, or a `long`, may be converted to an `XPointer` and back again and the result will compare equal to the original value. The exact representation of this data type is implementation-dependent. `XPointer` replaces the data type `caddr_t` which was used in R4 and earlier Xlib. `XPointer` is used in various Xlib structs that pass data transparently. In this context it may refer to a single long value, or a pointer to an application-defined data structure.

XrmDatabase   (R3)

`<X11/Xresource.h>`

`XrmDatabase` is a pointer to an X internal data structure representing a resource database. An `XrmDatabase` is passed to Xlib and Intrinsics routines that query resource databases, and may be manipulated directly with Xlib "Xrm" functions. The database associated with a given display is returned by the Intrinsics routine `XtDatabase`. The database sepecific to a screen is returned by `XtGetScreenDatabase` (R6).

XrmOptionDescList, XrmOptionDescRec   (R3)

`<X11/Xresource.h>`

`XrmOptionDescRec` is a data structure associating a command-line argument string with a widget or application resource. An `XrmOptionDescList` is a pointer to an array of `XrmOptionDescRec` structures. An `XrmOptionDescList` is passed to `XtOpenDisplay`, `XtAppInitialize`, or `XtOpenApplication` (R6) to specify application-specific command-line options, which are then automatically parsed by the Intrinsics.

```
typedef struct {
    char           *option;     /* Option abbreviation in argv     */
    char           *specifier;  /* Resource specifier              */
    XrmOptionKind argKind;      /* Which style of option it is     */
    XPointer       value;       /* Value provided if XrmoptionNoArg */
} XrmOptionDescRec, *XrmOptionDescList;
```

XrmOptionKind   (R3)

`<X11/Xresource.h>`

`XrmOptionKind` is an enumerated type with possible values shown below. It is used in the definition of an `XrmOptionDescRec` to determine how the value of a command line option is derived from *argv*, and how the *value* field of the `XrmOptionDescRec` is interpreted.

```
typedef enum {
    XrmoptionNoArg,       /* Value is specified in value field      */
    XrmoptionIsArg,       /* Value is the option string itself      */
    XrmoptionStickyArg,   /* Value is chars immed. following option  */
    XrmoptionSepArg,      /* Value is next argument in argv          */
    XrmoptionResArg,      /* Resource+value are next argument in argv */
    XrmoptionSkipArg,     /* Ignore this option and next arg in argv */
    XrmoptionSkipLine,    /* Ignore this option and the rest of argv */
    XrmoptionSkipNArgs    /* Ignore option + next value args in argv */
} XrmOptionKind;
```

XrmValue, XrmValuePtr   (R3)

<X11/Xresource.h>

XrmValue is a structure that describes data to be passed to or from a resource conversion routine. The first field is the size, in bytes, of the value to be passed. The second field is a pointer to a buffer where the actual value is stored.

```
typedef struct {
    unsigned int    size;
    XPointer        addr;
} XrmValue, *XrmValuePtr;
```

In cases where the XrmValue data structure is used to receive a resource conversion result, the application is responsible for making sure that *addr* points to a large enough buffer to hold the conversion result. An XrmValuePtr is a pointer to a structure, or an array of structures, of type XrmValue.

XSetWindowAttributes   (R3)

<X11/Xlib.h>

XSetWindowAttributes is a data structure containing fields that specify the attributes of a window, and is used by Xlib and Intrinsics routines that manipulate windows directly. The appropriate use of the XSetWindowAttributes structure is discussed in the Xlib reference manual.

XtAccelerators   (R3)

<X11/Intrinsic.h>

XtAccelerators is a pointer to a toolkit internal data object representing a compiled accelerator table. It is used to bind actions defined in one widget to events received in another. The accelerator table is first prepared in its plaintext translation table representation and is then parsed to the internal compiled format with XtParseAcceleratorTable.

XtActionList   (R3)

<X11/Intrinsic.h>

XtActionList is a pointer to an array of XtActionsRec defining an action table. Action tables are registered with the toolkit by the routine XtAppAddActions.

XtActionHookId   (R4)

`<X11/Intrinsic.h>`

`XtActionHookId` uniquely identifies an action hook *procedure/client_data* pair registered with `XtAppAddActionHook`. The value of an `XtActionHookId` is assigned by the Intrinsics when the hook is registered, and must be referenced to unregister the procedure with `XtRemoveActionHook`.

XtActionsRec   (R3)

`<X11/Intrinsic.h>`

`XtActionsRec` is a data structure associating an action name with a pointer to a compiled action procedure. It is used to register new action procedures, which are invoked through translation management.

```
typedef struct _XtActionsRec{
    char         *string;
    XtActionProc proc;
} XtActionsRec, *XtActionList;
```

XtAppContext   (R3)

`<X11/Intrinsic.h>`

`XtAppContext` is a pointer to a toolkit internal data structure which describes the state of the application. Information maintained by the application context includes the lists of open displays, work procs, timers, input sources, signal callbacks, global action procedures, action hooks, block hooks, and the grab list for event processing.

A new application context is created with either `XtCreateApplicationContext`, `XtAppInitialize` or `XtOpenApplication` (R6) and is a required argument to most routines that deal with event loop management, including `XtAppNextEvent`, `XtAppMainLoop`, `XtAppAddInput`, etc. These routines all start with the letters "XtApp" to distinguish them from their pre-R3 counterparts which operate upon a default application context. An application context can be derived from a widget ID with `XtWidgetToApplicationContext(widget)`.

XtAddressMode   (R3)

`<X11/Intrinsic.h>`

`XtAddressMode` is an enumerated type with possible values shown below. This is used to specify how the *address_id* field of an `XtConvertArgRec` structure is interpreted by the Intrinsics.

```
typedef enum {
    /* address mode       address_id interpretation */
    XtAddress,            /* address of required value             */
    XtBaseOffset,         /* offset from widget base address       */
    XtImmediate,          /* constant                              */
    XtResourceString,     /* Resource name - convert to req. value */
    XtResourceQuark,      /* Resource name in internal toolkit form */
    XtWidgetBaseOffset,   /* offset from windowed ancestor base    */
    XtProcedureArg        /* procedure to invoke to return value   */
} XtAddressMode;
```

XtArgVal   **(R3)**

`<X11/Intrinsic.h>`

XtArgVal is a datum large enough to contain the largest of an XtPointer, Cardinal, Dimension or Position value. The exact representation of this data type is implementation-dependent. An XtArgVal is used to specify a resource value to be passed to a widget in an ArgList. The Intrinsics provide the convenience macro XtSetArg for assembling ArgLists.

XtBlockHookId   **(R6)**

`<X11/Intrinsic.h>`

XtBlockHookId uniquely identifies a block hook *procedure/client_data* pair registered with XtAppAddBlockHook. The value of an XtBlockHookId is assigned by the Intrinsics when the hook is registered, and must be referenced to unregister the procedure with XtRemoveBlockHook.

XtCacheRef   **(R4)**

`<X11/Intrinsic.h>`

XtCacheRef represents a reference to a cached resource type conversion result. A value of type XtCacheRef is returned by a type converter, and must be passed to XtAppReleaseCacheRefs to free the cached result.

XtCacheType   **(R4)**

`<X11/Intrinsic.h>`

XtCacheType is a value used to specify how the results of a type conversion should be cached, and is specified when a new type converter is registered with XtAppSetTypeConverter. Possible values are defined by the symbolic constants XtCacheNone, XtCacheAll, XtCacheByDisplay, which may be modified by ORing with the modifier XtCacheRefCount.

XtCallbackList, XtCallbackRec   **(R3)**

`<X11/Intrinsic.h>`

XtCallbackRec is a structure associating a callback routine with *client_data* to be passed to the routine when it is executed. An XtCallbackList is a pointer to a NULL-terminated array of XtCallbackRecs:

```
typedef struct _XtCallbackRec {
    XtCallbackProc    callback;
    XtPointer         closure;
} XtCallbackRec, *XtCallbackList;
```

An XtCallbackList is supplied to the routines XtAddCallbacks or XtRemoveCallbacks, and may also be specified as the value of a widget's callback resource at creation time. After creation, callback lists are compiled to an internal format and cannot be set or queried with XtSetValues/XtGetValues.

XtCallbackStatus   (R3)

`<X11/Intrinsic.h>`

An enumerated type with possible values `XtCallbackNoList`, `XtCallbackHasNone` and `XtCallbackHasSome`. An `XtCallbackStatus` is returned by the Intrinsics routine `XtHasCallbacks` to indicate whether a specified callback list has any routines.

XtCheckpointTokenRec, XtCheckpointToken   (R6)

`<X11/Intrinsic.h>`

An `XtCheckpointTokenRec` is a structure that defines the state of a session manager operation. An `XtCheckpointToken` is a pointer to an `XtCheckpointTokenRec`, and is passed as *call_data* to callback routines invoked by the SessionShell widget. Additional checkpoint tokens are acquired with `XtSessionGetToken` if an application needs to continue some interaction with the user or other applications before it can decide how to respond to a session manager directive. A checkpoint token is returned with `XtSessionReturnToken` when the application has decided how to respond.

```
typedef struct _XtCheckpointTokenRec {
    int         save_type;
    int         interact_style;
    Boolean     shutdown;
    Boolean     fast;
    Boolean     cancel_shutdown;
    int         phase;
    int         interact_dialog_type;   /* return */
    Boolean     request_cancel;         /* return */
    Boolean     request_next_phase;     /* return */
    Boolean     save_success;           /* return */
    int         type;                   /* implementation private */
    Widget      widget;                 /* implementation private */
} XtCheckpointTokenRec, *XtCheckpointToken;
```

XtConvertArgList, XtConvertArgRec   (R3)

`<X11/Intrinsic.h>`

`XtConvertArgRec` is a structure used to define supplemental arguments passed to resource converters at the time they are invoked. An `XtConvertArgList` is a pointer to an array of `XtConvertArgRecs`.

```
typedef struct {
    XtAddressMode   address_mode;
    XtPointer       address_id;
    Cardinal        size;
} XtConvertArgRec, *XtConvertArgList;
```

The *address_mode* field is expressed in the enumerated type `XtAddressMode`, which determines how the *address_id* field is interpreted. The *size* field specifies the length, in bytes, of the data pointed to by *address_id*. An `XtConvertArgList` may be specified when a new type converter is registered with `XtAppSetTypeConverter`.

XtEnum   **(R4)**

`<X11/Intrinsic.h>`

XtEnum is a datum large enough to encode 128 distinct values, two of which are the symbolic values True and False. The exact representation of this data type is implementation-dependent. You can't assume that 0 is False and 1 is True.

XtGCMask   **(R3)**

`<X11/Intrinsic.h>`

XtGCMask is a bit mask specifying which fields in an associated GC are to be set or modified. A valid XtGCMask is usually assembled by ORing together the GC bit masks defined in `<X11/X.h>`, and is identical to the valuemask supplied to the Xlib routine XCreateGC.

XtGeometryMask   **(R3)**

`<X11/Intrinsic.h>`

XtGeometryMask is a bit mask specifying which fields are set in an XtGeometry structure used in a geometry management request or reply. Possible values are defined by the bitwise inclusive OR of the "CW" bit masks defined in `<X11/X.h>`: CWX, CWY, CWWidth, CWHeight, CWBorderWidth, CWSibling, CWStackMode and XtCWQueryOnly.

XtGeometryResult   **(R3)**

`<X11/Intrinsic.h>`

XtGeometryResult is an enumerated type with possible values XtGeometryYes, XtGeometryNo, XtGeometryAlmost or XtGeometryDone. An XtGeometryResult is returned by widget class procedures that deal with geometry management.

XtGrabKind   **(R3)**

`<X11/Intrinsic.h>`

XtGrabKind is an enumerated type with possible values XtGrabNone, XtGrabNonexclusive or XtGrabExclusive. XtGrabKind is used to define whether a pop-up shell grabs the event stream, and is required by the Intrinsics routine XtPopup, and the callback convenience routines which pop up Shells.

XtInputId   **(R3)**

`<X11/Intrinsic.h>`

XtInputId is a value used to uniquely identify a file input source registered with XtAppAddInput or XtAddInput (obsolete). The value of an XtInputId is assigned by the Intrinsics when the source is registered, and must be referenced to unregister the source with XtRemoveInput.

XtInputMask   (R3)

`<X11/Intrinsic.h>`

`XtInputMask` is a mask returned by `XtAppPending` that identifies which types of input are waiting to be handled. An `XtInputMask` is also passed to `XtProcessEvent` to specify which type or types of input to handle. Acceptable values are formed by ORing any or all of the symbolic values `XtIMXEvent`, `XtIMTimer`, `XtIMAlternateInput` and `XtIMSignal` (R6) The symbolic value `XtIMAll` is the bitwise inclusive OR of all masks.

XtIntervalId   (R3)

`<X11/Intrinsic.h>`

`XtIntervalId` uniquely identifies a timer registered with `XtAppAddTimeOut` or `XtAddTimeOut` (obsolete). The value of an `XtIntervalId` is assigned by the Intrinsics when the timer is registered, and must be referenced to cancel the timer with `XtRemoveTimeOut`.

XtListPosition   (R4)

`<X11/Intrinsic.h>`

`XtListPosition` is an enumerated type with possible values `XtListHead` and `XtListTail`. This data type is used by the calls `XtInsertEventHandler` and `XtInsertEventTypeHandler` to specify the position of the newly-registered handler.

XtPointer   (R4)

`<X11/Intrinsic.h>`

`XtPointer` is a datum large enough to contain the largest of a `char*`, `int*`, function pointer, structure pointer or `long` value. A pointer to any data type or function, or a `long`, may be converted to an `XtPointer` and back again and the result will compare equal to the original value. In ANSI C environments it is expected that `XtPointer` will be defined as `void*`; however, the exact representation of this data type is implementation-dependent. `XtPointer` replaces the data type `caddr_t` which was used throughout the R3 and earlier Intrinsics. `XtPointer` is used in many routines to specify data which must be passed transparently by the Intrinsics. It may be a single long value, or a pointer to an application-defined data structure.

XtPopdownID, XtPopdownIDRec   (R3)

`<X11/Intrinsic.h>`

`XtPopdownIDRec` is a data structure passed to `XtCallbackPopdown`, identifying a Shell to be popped down and the "enable_widget" which caused it to be popped up in the first place. The *enable_widget* is set sensitive and the *shell_widget* is popped down.

```
typedef struct {
    Widget shell_widget;
    Widget enable_widget;
} XtPopdownIDRec, *XtPopdownID;
```

XtRequestId   (R4)

<X11/Intrinsic.h>

XtRequestId is an opaque data type used to identify a specific request for the toolkit incremental selection value.   The value is assigned by the Intrinsics, and is passed to a *convert_proc* registered with XtOwnSelectionIncremental to identify a particular selection transfer in progess.

XtResource, XtResourceList   (R3)

<X11/Intrinsic.h>

XtResource is a data structure defining the name, type, size, location and default value of a widget or application resource.   An XtResourceList is a pointer to an array of XtResource.   A resource list must be provided in widget implementation code to specify available widget resources, and in application code to define resources fetched with XtGetApplicationResources.

```
typedef struct _XtResource {
    String     resource_name;      /* Resource name            */
    String     resource_class;     /* Resource class           */
    String     resource_type;      /* Representation type      */
    Cardinal   resource_size;      /* Size of data in bytes    */
    Cardinal   resource_offset;    /* Byte offset from base addr */
    String     default_type;       /* rep. type of default     */
    XtPointer default_addr;        /* Address of default value  */
} XtResource, *XtResourceList;
```

The default value is automatically converted from the the specified default type to the required resource type at the time a resource is fetched.   If the value of the *default_type* field is XtRImmediate, it implies that the default value is in the *default_addr* field and requires no conversion.   If *default_type* is XtRCallProc, *default_addr* is the address of an XtResourceDefaultProc that is called to return the value.

XtSignalId   (R6)

<X11/Intrinsic.h>

XtSignalId uniquely identifies a *signal callback/client_data* pair registered with XtAppAddSignal or XtAddSignal (obsolete).   The value of an XtSignalId is assigned by the Intrinsics when a signal callback is registered, and must be referenced to cancel the callback with XtRemoveSignal.

XtTranslations   (R3)

<X11/Intrinsic.h>

XtTranslations is a pointer to a toolkit internal data object representing a compiled translation table. It is used to pass a compiled translation table in the routines XtAugmentTranslations and XtOverrideTranslations, which affect widget translation management.   The translation table is first prepared in its plaintext representation and is then parsed to the internal compiled format with XtParseTranslationTable.

XtValueMask   (R3)

`<X11/Intrinsic.h>`

A bit mask used to specify which window attributes are set in a call to `XtCreateWindow`. It is identical to the values mask used in Xlib window creation routines.

XtVarArgsList   (R4)

`<X11/Intrinsic.h>`

`XtVarArgsList` is a pointer to a toolkit data structure used to represent a variable-length argument list employed in "XtVa" resource management routines. A value of type `XtVarArgsList` is returned by the Intrinsics routine `XtVaCreateArgsList`.

XtWidgetGeometry   (R3)

`<X11/Intrinsic.h>`

`XtWidgetGeometry` is a data structure used to specify the desired or assigned geometry of a child widget. A pointer to an `XtWidgetGeometry` data structure is passed by toolkit routines which perform geometry management, and is never used by application programmers.

```
typedef struct {
    XtGeometryMask   request_mode;          /* Which fields are set    */
    Position         x, y;                  /* Geometry                */
    Dimension        width, height, border_width;
    Widget           sibling;               /* Sibling stacked rel. to */
    int              stack_mode;            /* Window stacking order   */
} XtWidgetGeometry;
```

XtWorkProcId   (R3)

`<X11/Intrinsic.h>`

`XtWorkProcId` uniquely identifies a *work procedure/client_data* pair registered with `XtAppAddWorkProc` or `XtAddWorkProc` (obsolete). The value of an `XtWorkProcId` is assigned by the Intrinsics when the work procedure is registered, and must be referenced to unregister the work proc with `XtRemoveWorkProc`.

Appendix B

X TOOLKIT CALLBACK PROCEDURE TYPES

This appendix is a reference to the public procedure types that may be registered by an application programmer. Widget internal methods and class procedures are not discussed. Descriptions follow the format described below.

ProcedureType   **(Version)**

The procedure typedef and the Intrinsics version:

        (RN)   Procedure type first supported in the Release N Intrinsics
        (RNO)   Release N procedure type superseded by a new type as of Release 6

SYNOPSIS

Summary of the procedure prototype binding.

ARGUMENTS

Description of input and output arguments of the procedure. Arguments defined as "in/out" represent values to be returned by side-effect. These arguments are pointers to storage in which returned values are to be placed. Note that even input arguments are often passed by reference and must be dereferenced before use.

DESCRIPTION

Brief description of the procedure's function and conditions under which it is called.

USAGE

How the procedure is registered, what it is expected to do, cautions, and practical uses.

XtActionProc   (R3)

SYNOPSIS

```
typedef void (*XtActionProc)( Widget, XEvent*, String*, Cardinal* );
        Widget                          widget;
        XEvent                          *event;
        String                          *params;
        Cardinal                        *num_params
```

ARGUMENTS

widget	in	The widget that called the action procedure.
event	in	Pointer to the event that triggered the action; if invoked by translation management, this is the last event in the translation event sequence.
params	in	Pointer to a list of strings that the action procedure may use as arguments, or NULL if no arguments are passed.
num_params	in	Pointer to value specifying the number of strings in *params*.

DESCRIPTION

An XtActionProc is invoked when a widget receives an event or sequence of events matching an entry in its translation table. An action procedure may also be invoked explicitly by a call to XtCallActionProc. The action procedure is expected to respond to the input as it sees fit.

USAGE

Action procedures carry out most of the internal event processing in widgets. Each widget class supplies a list of action procedures that handle user-interface events, and a default translation table that references them. Programmers can supplement these by registering additional action procedures with XtAppAddActions; this declares the names by which the actions are referenced in translation tables. The Intrinsics reserve all action names and parameters starting with the letters "Xt".

Events are mapped to actions by a translation table, which may be specified as a widget's XtNtranslations resource in a resource file (see Appendix D). The compiled procedures are actually bound when a widget is realized, so any name referenced in a widget's default translations (including any translations defined in a resource file) must be registered before the widget is realized. After realization, translation tables may be modified explicitly with XtOverrideTranslations or XtAugmentTranslations. Actions provided by a widget are made available to its descendants and subclasses. In resolving references to an action name, the Intrinsics first search action tables supplied by the widget, its superclasses and ancestors. Tables registered with XtAppAddActions are searched last.

An action procedure usually does something to the widget that is receiving events, and gets everything it needs from the *widget* and *event* arguments. Parameters defined in the translation table are passed as a list of NULL-terminated strings. When writing action procedures, always verify that the number of parameters is correct, since they could be modified in a resource file. Be similarly cautious about depending on type-specific fields in the *event*, which could also be changed. And since an action procedure may be invoked by accelerators, do not even assume that the calling widget is realized without checking.

Action procedures provided by a widget may operate directly on the widget's data structure, but those provided by an application should use public routines such as XtSetValues to update the widget's state. Action procedures do not receive a *client_data* argument, so often confine their operations to the widget that is calling. Data that must be shared with other procedures may be passed through global variables.

XtActionHookProc (R4)

SYNOPSIS

```
typedef void (*XtActionHookProc)( Widget, XtPointer, String, XEvent*,
    String*, Cardinal* );
        Widget              widget;
        XtPointer           client_data;
        String              action_name;
        XEvent              *event;
        String              *params;
        Cardinal            *num_params;
```

ARGUMENTS

widget	in	The widget whose action procedure is about to be called.
client_data	in/out	Application-defined data registered with the action hook procedure by XtAppAddActionHook.
action_name	in	Name of the action about to be invoked.
event	in	Pointer to the event which will be passed to the action procedure.
params	in	Pointer to a list of strings that the action procedure will receive as parameters.
num_params	in	Pointer to a value specifying the number of strings in *params*.

DESCRIPTION

An XtActionHookProc is called immediately before any named action is executed, and receives the name of the action that is about to be invoked, and the *widget, event, params* and *num_params* arguments that will be passed to it. The action hook is usually expected to report or journal this information. An action hook is called whether the action is invoked by translation management, or called explicitly with XtCallActionProc.

USAGE

A list of action hooks is attached to the application context. An action hook is added to the head of the list with XtAppAddActionHook and is removed from the list with XtRemoveActionHook. Just before any named action is executed, all action hooks on the list are called in order, from last-registered to first.

Action hooks are usually used to record actions and their parameters for later playback with XtCallActionProc. Applications of this feature might include journaling user input for crash recovery, providing "teach" or "demo" modes in an application, or building macro recording and playback facilities. Operations processed by event handlers do not invoke action hook procs, and cannot be journaled this way.

The *client_data* is supplied when the action hook is registered, and may be a single value or more commonly, a pointer to an application-specific data structure. It should be cast to the appropriate data type inside the action hook. It is usually used to convey information between the action hook procedure and the rest of a program. Action hooks should not modify the data pointed to by any of their arguments except *client_data*.

The widget ID is valid only for the lifetime of the current process; if the information is to be journaled for playback in a future instance of the application, the widget ID must be saved in some non-volatile format. One way would be to retrieve the name of the widget with XtName and then use XtNameToWidget to perform the appropriate mapping in a future invocation.

XtBlockHookProc (R6)

SYNOPSIS

```
typedef void (*XtBlockHookProc)( XtPointer );
        XtPointer                    client_data;
```

ARGUMENTS

client_data   in/out   Application-defined data specified when the block hook procedure is registered with XtAppAddBlockHook.

DESCRIPTION

An XtBlockHookProc is called just before XtAppNextEvent enters an implementation-dependent wait for input.

USAGE

A list of block hooks is attached to the application context. An XtBlockHookProc is added to the head of the list with XtAppAddBlockHook and is removed from the list with XtRemoveBlockHook. Just before the toolkit enters an implementation-dependent wait for events, all block hooks on the list are called in order, from last-registered to first.

Block hook procedures can be used perform a limited style of background processing. The main difference between a block hook and a work procedure is that all block hooks are called when the toolkit enters a wait, whereas only the latest-registered work procedure is called. Also, block hooks do not return a value and are not removed from the execution list automatically.

The *client_data* is supplied when the block hook is registered, and may be a single value or more commonly, a pointer to an application-specific data structure. It is used to convey information between the block hook procedure and the rest of a program, it is cast as type XtPointer when registered, and should be cast to the appropriate data type inside the procedure.

XtCallbackProc   (R3)

SYNOPSIS

```
typedef void (*XtCallbackProc)( Widget, XtPointer, XtPointer );
        Widget                    widget;
        XtPointer                 client_data;
        XtPointer                 call_data;
```

ARGUMENTS

widget	in	The widget that is calling back.
client_data	in/out	Application-defined data registered with the callback routine by `XtAddCallback(s)`.
call_data	in/out	Data supplied by the widget which is calling back.

DESCRIPTION

An `XtCallbackProc` is registered on a widget's callback list with `XtAddCallback`, and is called when the widget detects an "interesting" change in the state of the user interface. A callback procedure is expected to perform any application-specific processing in response to the condition.

USAGE

Callback procedures are registered with widgets by the application programmer, and sometimes by other widgets in a toolkit. Callback procedures are kept in lists attached to each widget; when a widget wishes to report a change in its condition, it calls the routines on one or more of its callback lists.

The callback lists supported by a widget depend on its class, and correspond to the conditions that the widget can detect. An `XtCallbackprocedure` is registered with `XtAddCallback` or `XtAddCallbacks`, and is canceled with `XtRemoveCallback` or `XtRemoveCallbacks`. The procedure may perform any toolkit or application function, up to and including destroying the widget that called. The only condition is that it must return quickly.

The *widget* argument may be used to derive information about the widget or the environment. This information can be gotten through toolkit information routines (Chapter 8, Table 8-2) Xlib Screen information functions (Chapter 12, Table 12-3), or by calling `XtGetValues` on the widget itself.

The *client_data* is specified when the callback is registered, and may be a single value or more commonly, a pointer to an application-specific data structure. It is used to transfer data between the callback procedure and the rest of a program, and may be NULL if everything the callback procedure needs to do its job can be derived from its other arguments. To avoid compiler warnings, *client_data* is cast as an `XtPointer` when registered, and should be cast back to the appropriate type inside the callback proc.

The *call_data* argument is supplied by the widget that is calling back; you will find it documented in the widget's manpage. In many toolkits it is a pointer to a class-specific data structure holding additional information about the state of the widget. A callback routine should not free any storage pointed to by *call_data*; however, sometimes you will be allowed to set values in the callback structure to return information to the calling widget. The *call_data* is also passed as type `XtPointer`, and should be cast appropriately inside the callback proc.

A callback procedure can call `XtLastEventProcessed` (R6) to retrieve the event that triggered the callback; however, you should not make assumptions about the type or detail of this event since the triggering condition could be modified if the user overrides translations in a resource file.

XtCancelConvertSelectionProc (R4)

SYNOPSIS

```
typedef void (*XtCancelConvertSelectionProc)( Widget, Atom*, Atom*,
    XtRequestId*, XtPointer );
        Widget                      widget;
        Atom                        *selection;
        Atom                        *target;
        XtRequestId                 *request_id;
        XtPointer                   client_data;
```

ARGUMENTS

widget	in	Identifies the widget which owns the selection.
selection	in	Pointer to an Atom identifying which selection was being transferred, e.g. XA_PRIMARY.
target	in	Pointer to an Atom identifying the target to which the selection was being converted, e.g. TEXT.
request_id	in	Pointer to an identifier for the incremental transfer that is being canceled.
client_data	in/out	Application data registered with XtOwnSelectionIncremental.

DESCRIPTION

An XtCancelConvertSelectionProc is an optional procedure registered by a toolkit incremental selection owner. It is called when the Intrinsics determine that the remaining segments of a selection transfer in progress are not required. The XtCancelConvertSelectionProc is expected to free any memory or other resources which had been dedicated to the transfer.

USAGE

An XtCancelConvertSelectionProc is registered when a client volunteers to own the selection with XtOwnSelectionIncremental. The XtCancelConvertSelectionProc may be called while an incremental selection transfer is in progress, and tells the sending application that any remaining segments of a transfer are not required. The usual reason for this is that a timeout forced the Intrinsics to cancel the selection transfer.

The selection owner should consider the transfer complete. The XtCancelConvertSelectionProc is expected to free any memory or other resources which had been dedicated to the transfer, and notify the application user, if necessary. Since multiple transfers could be in progress at the same time, the *request_id* uniquely identifies which one has been halted; this will match a *request_id* previously seen by an XtConvertSelectionIncrProc. Selection ownership is not surrendered, and only the transfer identified by *request_id* is affected.

The *client_data* is shared with the XtConvertSelectionIncrProc and is often used to pass the request IDs of transfers currently in progress, and the address of buffers that may be freed by the XtCancelConvertSelectionProc. The *selection* and *target* arguments are those specified by the selection requester, and may be used to identify which resources can be freed.

XtCaseProc   **(R3)**

SYNOPSIS

```
typedef void (*XtCaseProc)( Display*, KeySym, KeySym*, KeySym* );
        Display                       *display;
        KeySym                        keysym;
        KeySym                        *upper_return;
        KeySym                        *lower_return;
```

ARGUMENTS

display	in	Display with which conversion is associated.
keysym	in	Input keysym; it may be lower-case or upper-case.
upper_return	in/out	Pointer to storage into which the upper-case equivalent keysym is returned.
lower_return	in/out	Pointer to storage into which the lower-case equivalent keysym is returned.

DESCRIPTION

An XtCaseProc accepts an input keysym and returns the keysyms representing its lower-case and upper-case equivalents. Case procedures are automatically invoked by the translation manager when matching incoming Key events to case-sensitive translations (see Appendix D). A case procedure may also be called directly with the Intrinsics routine XtConvertCase.

USAGE

An XtCaseProc is expected to place the upper and lower-case equivalents of *keysym* in the locations specified by *upper_return* and *lower_return*. The Intrinsics register a default XtCaseProc named _XtConvertCase that handles all standard alphanumeric keysyms defined in the core protocol. This is sufficient for most applications, so you would rarely need to define a new case proc.

Application-specific case procedures may be registered with XtRegisterCaseConverter if some non-standard case conversion is required for a particular keysym range, or if non-standard keysyms have been registered in /usr/lib/X11/XKeysymDB. There is no routine to cancel a registered XtCaseProc; instead, an "identity" XtCaseProc can be registered which returns the same keysym that was supplied to it. If there is no case distinction between upper and lower case for a given keysym, a case procedure should copy the input keysym into both return locations.

XtConverter (R3O)

SYNOPSIS

```
typedef void (*XtConverter)( XrmValue*, Cardinal*, XrmValue*, XrmValue*);
        XrmValue                    *args;
        Cardinal                    *num_args;
        XrmValue                    *from;
        XrmValue                    *to_return;
```

ARGUMENTS

args	in	Pointe to a list of descriptors specifying additional arguments required for the conversion, or NULL if none are provided.
num_args	in	Pointer to value specifying the number of arguments in *args*.
from	in	Pointer to a descriptor which supplies the input value.
to_return	in/out	Pointer to a descriptor in which the converted value is returned.

DESCRIPTION

An XtConverter is an old-format (R3) type converter which converts an input value expressed in a source data type to an output value expressed in a destination data type. A converter is specific to a single source/destination type conversion, and is called automatically when the Intrinsics fetch resource values of the destination type from resource files. Old-format converters may also be invoked explicitly with the Intrinsics routines XtConvert or XtDirectConvert. XtConverter has been superseded by XtTypeConverter as of the R4 Intrinsics.

USAGE

An XtConverter is registered with XtAppAddConverter or XtAddConverter for a specific source/destination type conversion. When the toolkit is initialized, the Intrinsics automatically register built-in converters that accept strings and convert them to the major toolkit resource types. Converters for other source/destination combinations may be supplied by applications or widgets. Widgets register type converters for class-specific types when the first widget of a particular class is created, or when the class is initialized with XtInitializeWidgetClass. The existing converters are adequate for most purposes. If you write new converters, they should really be of type XtTypeConverter.

The value to be converted is pointed to by *from->addr*. A converter is registered only for a single source/destination type pair, so it must assume that the *from* data is of the appropriate type. The *args* argument supplies any additional data required by the converter - a converter that produces Pixel values, for example, might require the colormap of the widget for which the conversion is being undertaken. Values supplied in *args* are computed by the Intrinsics when the converter is called, based on the *convert_args* specified to XtAddConverter when the converter was registered. A converter should always check *num_args* to be sure that the appropriate number of arguments are present before attempting the conversion.

If the conversion is successful, a converter should return a pointer to the converted value in *to_return->addr* and the size of the conversion result in *to_return->size*. The address written to *to_return->addr* cannot be a pointer to a local variable, as this would be invalid after the converter returns; however, a pointer to static static storage may be used instead. The value will be copied by the caller. If the conversion is not successful, a converter should call XtStringConversionWarning or XtWarningMsg to log a message, and should leave *to_return* unmodified.

XtConvertArgProc   (R4)

SYNOPSIS

```
typedef void (*XtConvertArgProc)( Widget, Cardinal*, XrmValue* );
        Widget                  widget;
        Cardinal                *size;
        XrmValue                *value_return;
```

ARGUMENTS

widget   in   Widget for which resource conversion is being performed, or NULL if conversion was invoked by XtCallConverter or XtDirectConvert.

size   in   Pointer to the *size* field from the XtConvertArgRec, specifying the size of the required argument value in bytes.

value_return   in/out   Pointer to a descriptor in which the computed argument is returned.

DESCRIPTION

An XtConvertArgProc is called by the Intrinsics to supply a resource conversion argument that must be computed at the time a type converter is invoked.

USAGE

Type converters may require additional arguments that must be computed at run time. Because type converters are invoked implicitly by the Intrinsics while fetching resource values, an application has no opportunity to pass such arguments directly. Instead, the Intrinsics must be told how to compute any required values. This is done by specifying an XtConvertArgRec array when a converter is registered with XtAppSetTypeConverter. Each additional argument is represented by an XtConvertArgRec:

```
typedef struct {
    XtAddressMode  address_mode;
    XtPointer      address_id;
    Cardinal       size;
} XtConvertArgRec, *XtConvertArgList;
```

If the *address_mode* field is the symbolic value XtProcedureArg, the Intrinsics interpret *address_id* as a pointer to an XtConvertArgProc, which is called to supply the required argument. Convert arg procedures are actually pretty rare since the XtConvertArgRec also supplies other, usually better, ways to get a value to a converter.

An XtConvertArgProc is always specific to one particular type of argument; for example, you might register a procedure that always returns the colormap of *widget*. An XtConvertArgProc should return a pointer to the computed argument value in *value_return->addr*, specifying its size in *value_return->size*. The Intrinsics do not guarantee to copy the result, so the storage pointed to by *value_return->addr* must have a lifetime no less than that of *widget*. The *widget* argument can be used to derive instance-specific or display-specific data, such as the colormap or screen. The input argument *size* should be used to truncate the value if necessary.

XtConvertSelectionIncrProc (R4)

SYNOPSIS

```
typedef Boolean (*XtConvertSelectionIncrProc)( Widget, Atom*, Atom*,
    Atom*, XtPointer*, unsigned long*, int*, unsigned long*, XtPointer,
    XtRequestId* );
        Widget                          widget;
        Atom                            *selection;
        Atom                            *target;
        Atom                            *type_return;
        XtPointer                       *value_return;
        unsigned long                   *length_return;
        int                             *format_return;
        unsigned long                   *max_length;
        XtPointer                       client_data;
        XtRequestId                     *request_id;
```

ARGUMENTS

widget	in	Widget that owns the selection.
selection	in	Pointer to an Atom specifying which selection is being requested, e.g. XA_PRIMARY.
target	in	Pointer to an Atom identifying which information is requested about the selection, e.g. FILE_NAME, TEXT (see Chapter 10).
type_return	in/out	Pointer to an Atom in which a value is returned describing the data type used to represent the converted selection value, e.g. XA_STRING. This is not necessarily the same as the type specified in *target*.
value_return	in/out	Pointer to storage in which a pointer to the converted value is returned. Storage for the converted value itself should be allocated with XtMalloc.
length_return	in/out	Pointer to storage in which the number of data elements in *value_return* is returned.
format_return	in/out	Pointer to storage in which to return the size, in bits, of a data element; acceptable values: 8, 16, 32.
max_length	in	Pointer to a value specifying the maximum number of bytes that may be transferred at one time.
client_data	in/out	Application-defined data registered when client took selection ownership with XtOwnSelectionIncr.
request_id	in	Pointer to a toolkit-assigned identifier for this incremental request.

DESCRIPTION

An XtConvertSelectionIncrProc is registered by a selection owner and is called repeatedly when the selection value is requested. Each time it is called, an XtConvertSelectionIncrProc is expected to provide a new chunk of the selection value. It is similar to an XtConvertSelectionProc, but must provide for multiple simultaneous transfers.

USAGE

A toolkit selection owner registers an XtConvertSelectionIncrProc when ownership is asserted with XtOwnSelectionIncr. This procedure is called repeatedly by the Intrinsics when the selection is requested, each time supplying a new piece of the converted value.

Since multiple conversions to different targets or requesters may be in progress at one time, *request_id* identifies a particular selection transfer. On the first call with a new *request_id*, an XtConvertSelectionIncrProc should begin a new transfer of the requested *selection* and *target*. Each time the procedure is called thereafter with the same *request_id*, another segment should be transferred.

The XtConvertSelectionIncrProc is expected to allocate the storage for the converted selection value. The Intrinsics do not free memory associated with any intermediate segments of a transfer, so the procedure may reuse or free the storage allocated for a previous segment each time it is called.

To indicate the end of a transfer, the owner must pass a non-NULL value in *value_return* and a length of zero in *length_return*. Storage for the final zero-length transfer is automatically freed by the Intrinsics with XtFree if no XtSelectionDoneIncrProc is registered. This implies that a client could use XtMalloc to allocate a fixed transfer area of *max_length* bytes the first time that it is called with a new *request_id*, and reuse that area for all succeeding segments of a particular transfer, letting the Intrinsics free it when the transfer is complete.

If an XtSelectionDoneIncrProc is registered, then the Intrinsics do not free storage associated with the the final zero-length transfer, and it is up to the XtSelectionDoneIncrProc to do so. Sometimes, in fact, an owner may choose to pass selection segments in a statically-allocated buffer, so a selection done procedure should be registered expressly to keep the Intrinsics from trying to free the memory at the end.

After the final piece of a transfer is processed, the Intrinsics may reuse a *request_id* for a subsequent transfer. A selection owner must note when it has finished a transfer so that it will treat a subsequent call with the same *request_id* as a new request.

The *client_data* is shared with the XtCancelConvertSelectionProc, the XtLoseSelectionIncrProc, and the XtSelectionDoneIncrProc, and is often used to share the request IDs of transfers currently in progress, and the address of buffers that may be freed by these other procedures.

The procedure is expected to return True if a conversion to the requested target succeeded. If the conversion fails, it should return False and leave the return arguments unmodified. For details on how to treat other arguments, please see XtConvertSelectionProc.

XtConvertSelectionProc (R3)

SYNOPSIS

```
typedef Boolean (*XtConvertSelectionProc)(Widget, Atom*, Atom*, Atom*,
    XtPointer*, unsigned long*, int* );
        Widget                      widget;
        Atom                        *selection;
        Atom                        *target;
        Atom                        *type_return;
        XtPointer                   *value_return;
        unsigned long               *length_return;
        int                         *format_return;
```

ARGUMENTS

widget	in	Widget that owns the selection.
selection	in	Pointer to an Atom specifying which selection is being requested, e.g. XA_PRIMARY.
target	in	Pointer to an Atom identifying which information is requested about the selection, e.g. FILE_NAME, TEXT (see Chapter 10).
type_return	in/out	Pointer to an Atom in which a value is returned describing the data type used to represent the converted selection value, e.g. XA_STRING. This is not necessarily the same Atom specified by *target*.
value_return	in/out	Pointer to storage in which a pointer to the converted value is returned.
length_return	in/out	Pointer to storage in which the number of data elements in *value_return* is returned.
format_return	in/out	Pointer to storage in which to return the size, in bits, of a data element; acceptable values: 8, 16, 32.

DESCRIPTION

An XtConvertSelectionProc is registered by a toolkit selection owner and is called by the Intrinsics when the value of the selection is requested. An XtConvertSelectionProc is expected to convert the requested selection to the target representation specified by the requester.

USAGE

A toolkit selection owner registers an XtConvertSelectionProc when selection ownership is asserted with XtOwnSelection. This procedure is called by the Intrinsics when the selection is requested.

The *target* atom specifies what information is being requested about the selection; the *Inter-Client Communication Conventions Manual* lists a suggested set of targets and their interpretations (see Chapter 10). Most targets are not represented by predefined atoms, so the selection owner should intern atoms for targets it expects to support. These must be interpreted carefully, and are not always the value seen by the user as selected text, pictures, etc. converted wholesale.

For example, if the currently selected item is a block of text in an editor, the target FILE_NAME requests the name of the file being edited, even if the selected text looks like a file name. The targets TEXT, STRING or COMPOUND_TEXT all request the value of the selected text, but in different encodings. Most applications support the target TEXT, which means "the selected value expressed as text in the owner's choice of encoding", and/or the target STRING, meaning "the selected value expressed as ISO Latin-1 text". Other private targets may be worked out between cooperating applications.

The target TARGETS implies that the requester wants to know which targets the selection owner could provide. The selection owner should use *value_return* to return a list of Atoms representing targets into which the selection could be converted. The procedure need not respond to the types MULTIPLE or TIMESTAMP, which are handled automatically by the Intrinsics. A selection owner will see a request for the MULTIPLE selection target as a series of calls to the convert proc, each requesting a diferent target.

The *type_return* argument is used to return the representation type used for the converted value. This is not necessarily the same as the *target* value. Consider the targets TEXT and FILE_NAME; in both cases the representation type of the converted value would be a NULL-terminated character string, represented by the predefined Atom XA_STRING. Suggested return types for specific targets are listed in the *ICCCM* and in Chapter 10.

The XtConvertSelectionProc is expected to allocate the storage for the converted selection value. The returned value is a buffer of *length_return* elements, each of length *format_return*. The returned format may be 8, 16, or 32; in C, this implies a buffer of char, short or long values. The Intrinsics require this information in order to resolve possible byte-order differences between the selection owner and the requester.

If no XtSelectionDoneProc is registered, the Intrinsics automatically call XtFree to free storage for the selection value, so it must be in storage allocated with XtMalloc. If a selection owner does register an XtSelectionDoneProc when it asserts selection ownership, the storage for the returned value belongs to the selection owner. In this case it could be static storage, or dynamic storage that is freed by the selection done proc. If, in fact, the selection value is passed in a statically-allocated buffer, a selection done procedure should be registered expressly to keep the Intrinsics from trying to free the memory.

An XtConvertSelectionProc receives no *client_data* argument, so any additional information required to deal with the selection is often passed through global variables. This is a deficiency in the Intrinsics that must be worked around. Some toolkits (e.g. Motif, OLIT) provide for a "user data" resource that lets you attach arbitrary data to a widget instance. This can be retrieved with XtGetValues in routines that receive a widget ID but do not receive client data.

An XtConvertSelectionProc is expected to return True if a conversion to the requested target succeeded. If the conversion fails, it should return False and leave the return arguments unmodified.

XtCreatePopupChildProc (R3)

SYNOPSIS

```
typedef void (*XtCreatePopupChildProc)( Widget );
       Widget                          widget;
```

ARGUMENTS

widget   in   Widget ID of the Shell which is about to be popped up; it must be used as the parent for the pop-up child.

DESCRIPTION

An XtCreatePopupChildProc is registered with a Shell widget and is called just before the shell is mapped by XtPopup. The XtNcreatePopupChildProc is expected to create the Shell's pop-up child.

USAGE

An XtCreatePopupChildProc may be registered as the value of a Shell's XtNcreatePopupChildProc resource. This is usually done when the Shell is created. When the procedure is called, it should create the pop-up child using *widget* as the parent, and then set *widget*'s XtNcreatePopupChildProc to NULL. This defers creation of the pop-up child until it is needed. If the pop-up is never used, the pop-up child is never created, saving memory and time.

XtDestructor   (R4)

SYNOPSIS

```
typedef void (*XtDestructor)( XtAppContext, XrmValue*, XtPointer,
    XrmValue*, Cardinal* );
        XtAppContext          app_context;
        XrmValue              *to;
        XtPointer             convert_data;
        XrmValue              *args;
        Cardinal              *num_args;
```

ARGUMENTS

app_context	in	The application context in which the conversion was performed.
to	in	Pointer to a descriptor specifying the conversion result to be freed.
convert_data	in	Pointer to conversion-specific data stored by the converter when it was called.
args	in	Pointer to a list of additional conversion arguments that were supplied to the converter when it was called.
num_args	in	Pointer to a value specifying the number of arguments in *args*.

DESCRIPTION

An XtDestructor is called by the Intrinsics when a cached conversion result is no longer required. The destructor is expected to release any client or server resources allocated to the conversion.

USAGE

An XtDestructor must be registered with XtAppSetTypeConverter or XtSetTypeConverter, if a converter is registered in such a way that it caches its conversion results. A converter and a destructor are usually written together; the destructor is specific to the same destination data type, and is responsible for freeing the cached value when it is no longer required. The simple converters registered by most applications don't need to cache values, so will not require a destructor.

If the modifier XtCacheRefCount is ORed with any of the valid values for the *cache_type* argument to XtAppSetTypeConverter, a reference count is maintained for specific conversion from/to combinations. When the reference count for a particular conversion result drops to zero, its associated destructor is called. If a converter is registered with *cache_type* of XtCacheByDisplay, the destructor is called if the display is closed with XtCloseDisplay.

Args and *num_args* supply the same additional arguments that were passed to the converter when it was invoked, and may provide information necessary to release the resources associated with the conversion - for example, the colormap of a widget, if a pixel value is to be freed. The *convert_data* argument is whatever was returned by the converter (see XtTypeConverter).

The destructor is responsible for freeing any server resources or client storage associated with the conversion result specified in the *to* argument. If the resource were a pixel value, for example, *to->addr* would point to the pixel value and the destructor would call XFreeColors to release the server resource. Destructors are not responsible for freeing memory directly addressed by the *size* and *addr* fields of the *to* argument, or memory specified by *args*. However, if *convert_data* is used to pass more than a single value, it is a pointer to memory which should be allocated by the converter and freed by the destructor.

XtDoChangeProc (R6)

SYNOPSIS

```
typedef void (*XtDoChangeProc)( Widget, WidgetList, Cardinal*,
    WidgetList, Cardinal*, XtPointer );
        Widget                    parent;
        WidgetList                unmanage_children;
        Cardinal                  *num_unmanage;
        WidgetList                manage_children;
        Cardinal                  *num_manage;
        XtPointer                 client_data;
```

ARGUMENTS

parent	in	Parent of the widgets being managed/unmanaged.
unmanage_children	in	List of children that have been unmanaged.
num_unmanage	in	Pointer to a value specifying the number of widgets in *unmanage_children*.
manage_children	in	List of children that will be managed.
num_manage	in	Pointer to a value specifying the number of widgets in *manage_children*.
client_data	in/out	Application data supplied in call to XtChangeManagedSet.

DESCRIPTION

An XtDoChangeProc is invoked by the Intrinsics during a call to XtChangeManagedSet and is expected to make geometry changes on behalf of the new managed children.

USAGE

An XtDoChangeProc is specified in a call to XtChangeManagedSet, and is called right after *unmanage_children* have been unmanaged, but just before *manage_children* are managed. It is expected to effect changes on children while the Composite parent has the fewest widgets in its managed set. This usually means adjusting their geometry, taking advantage of the fact that a manager with only a few children is more likely to say yes, and that when a child is unmanaged, the Intrinsics internally grant any geometry it wants. Children that appear in both *unmanage_children* and *manage_children* may be resized with impunity when the XtDoChangeProc is called.

Geometry changes should be made by calling XtSetValues and setting the XtNx, XtNy, XtNwidth and XtNheight resources of the children. The final result, of course, depends on the parent's geometry management policy, as it could immediately resize the children when they are finally managed. However, this method works quite well for resetting the state of simple manager widgets like the XmBulletinBoard, since it tries to honor the initial sizes requested by its children.

XtErrorHandler   **(R3)**

SYNOPSIS

```
typedef void (*XtErrorHandler)( String );
        String                        message;
```

ARGUMENTS

message   in   Message to be displayed or logged.

DESCRIPTION

A procedure of type XtErrorHandler is invoked when a widget or application calls XtAppError, XtError, XtAppWarning or XtWarning, and is expected to display or log a message. Depending on whether it is registered to handle fatal or non-fatal conditions, the error handler is expected to return or exit after displaying the message.

USAGE

XtErrorHandler is registered for fatal error conditions with XtAppSetErrorHandler or XtSetErrorHandler, and for non-fatal warning conditions with XtAppSetWarningHandler or XtSetWarningHandler. The same procedure type is used for handling both fatal (error) and non-fatal (warning) conditions, but a handler registered for fatal conditions is expected to exit, lest the application try to continue on a severe error. An XtErrorHandler is unregistered by registering a new one which replaces it.

An XtErrorHandler must display or log the specified message, usually by calling printf(). It should then perform application-specific fixups, if any, and return or exit depending on the context for which it is registered.

The Intrinsics register default XtErrorHandlers named _XtDefaultError and _XtDefaultWarning, which print the error message to stderr and then exit or return, respectively. These work fine for most applications. Though it may be tempting to create an error handler that pops up a dialog box, it's not a good idea, since error handlers are often called for severe problems that may have destroyed the user interface or the server connection. If you do write a custom handler, you can perform any special cleanup that your program needs, and then call _XtDefaultError and _XtDefaultWarning directly to take further action.

XtErrorMsgHandler (R3)

SYNOPSIS

```
typedef void (*XtErrorMsgHandler)(String, String, String, String,
    String*, Cardinal*);
        String                      name;
        String                      type;
        String                      class;
        String                      defaultp;
        String                      *params;
        Cardinal                    *num_params;
```

ARGUMENTS

name	in	Resource name of message to be fetched.
type	in	Additional specifier of message to be fetched.
class	in	Resource class of message to be fetched.
defaultp	in	Default message to use if specified message cannot be found.
params	in	Pointer to a list of strings to be substituted into the message text.
num_params	in	Pointer to a value specifying the number of strings in *params*.

DESCRIPTION

An XtErrorMsgHandler is called to display or log a message. The currently-registered message handler is invoked when a widget or application calls XtAppErrorMsg, XtErrorMsg, XtAppWarningMsg or XtWarningMsg. An error message handler is expected to look up the message specified by the *name*, *type* and *class* arguments, incorporating detail supplied by *params*. Then it should display the message and return or exit, as appropriate.

USAGE

Error message handlers provide a high-level interface for displaying messages. In contrast to an error handler which simply accepts a message string, an error message handler is expected to look up its message in a database, and substitute parameters into the text to provide richer detail on the condition being reported.

An XtErrorMsgHandler is registered for fatal error conditions with XtAppSetErrorMsgHandler or XtSetErrorMsgHandler, and for non-fatal conditions with XtAppSetWarningMsgHandler or XtSetWarningMsgHandler. The same procedure type is used for handling both fatal (error) and non-fatal (warning) conditions, but a handler registered for fatal conditions is expected to exit, lest the application try to continue on a severe error. An error message handler is unregistered by registering a new one to replace it.

Message text is usually fetched with XtAppGetErrorDatabaseText from a database merged from the file /usr/lib/X11/XtErrorDB. The *params* argument supplies strings which are to be substituted into the message text. The most common way to perform the substitution is by using the message text as a format for printf(). The caller is expected to provide the right number of parameters for the corresponding message.

The Intrinsics register default error message handlers named _XtDefaultErrorMsg and _XtDefaultWarningMsg, which look up the error message, perform the parameter substitutions, and then call XtError or XtWarning to take further action, including displaying the message. These are sufficient for most applications.

XtEventDispatchProc   **(R6)**

SYNOPSIS

```
typedef Boolean (*XtEventDispatchProc)( XEvent* );
   XEvent                        *event;
```

ARGUMENTS

event   in   The event to be dispatched.

DESCRIPTION

An XtEventDispatchProc is called by the main loop to dispatch an event to a widget or other agent. The XtEventDispatchProc is expected to forward the event as appropriate to its type and detail, returning True if the dispatch succeeded, or False if it did not.

USAGE

When an event is received, it is dispatched to the toolkit by an XtEventDispatchProc. The Intrinsics register a default event dispatcher which handles all event types in the core protocol, and determines which widget should receive an event by inspecting the window ID in the event structure. This is sufficient for most applications.

Extension events, however, might not involve windows directly, or might need to be handled in other ways. If you write programs that expect to receive extension events not included in the core protocol, you should register an XtEventDispatchProc with XtSetEventDispatcher. This is rare.

An event dispatcher is expected to first decide if the event is of a type that should be dispatched to a widget. If it is, the event dispatcher should determine for which widget it is intended, and call XFilterEvent passing the event and the widget's window ID. If XFilterEvent returns True, the event dispatcher may assume that the event has been used by an input method and need not be processed further. If XFilterEvent returns False, the event should be dispatched to the destination widget with XtDispatchEventToWidget, which will deliver it to the appropriate event handlers, if any. If either XFilterEvent or XtDispatchEventToWidget return True, the event dispatcher should also return True.

If the event dispatcher decides that this type of event does not need to be dispatched to a widget, it is free to send it to whatever agent should handle it, and return True if the event was successfully dispatched, and False otherwise.

XtEventHandler (R3)

SYNOPSIS

```
typedef void (*XtEventHandler)(Widget, XtPointer, XEvent*, Boolean* );
        Widget                          widget;
        XtPointer                       client_data;
        XEvent                          *event;
        Boolean                         *continue_to_dispatch;
```

ARGUMENTS

widget	in	Widget to which the event handler is attached.
client_data	in/out	Application-defined data specified when the handler was registered.
event	in	Pointer to the event to be handled.
continue_to_dispatch	in/out	If False is returned in the location specified by this argument, the event will not be dispatched to event handlers following this one.

DESCRIPTION

An XtEventHandler is bound to a widget instance and called when a single event of a specified type is dispatched to the widget.

USAGE

An XtEventHandler is added to a widget with XtAddEventHandler and is removed with XtRemoveEventHandler. Each handler is registered with an event mask that selects for one or more X event types, and is called when a matching event is sent to the widget by XtDispatchEvent. Handlers may also be registered to respond to non-maskable events.

Event handlers are the first stop in processing events, and are called before the event is processed through translation management. Event handlers should only be used when it is necessary to respond to single events of a particular type with a minimum of overhead. Action procedures (see XtActionProc) or callbacks (see XtCallbackProc) offer more robust means of interacting with the user interface.

An event handler should check *event->type* and then cast the event pointer appropriately to access type-specific fields. However, it should not assume that the event was generated by *widget*'s window, as an event may have been dispatched to *widget* as the result of a remap.

Event handlers are placed in a list in which each unique handler/*client_data* pair occurs exactly once. the order in which handlers are placed on the list is undefined. A handler that wishes to be called before or after previously-registered handlers may be placed at the head or tail of the list with XtInsertEventHandler, but is subject to being reordered by successive calls to XtAddEventHandler and XtRemoveEventHandler.

By default, an event is dispatched to each handler that selects for it; if an event handler wishes to prevent the event from being passed to succeeding handlers, it may set the Boolean value pointed to by *continue_to_dispatch* to False. This is extremely non-portable, and demands a thorough understanding of the toolkit implementation on the development platform.

The *client_data* is supplied when the handler is registered, and may be a single value or more commonly, a pointer to an application-specific data structure. It is used to transfer data between the event handler and the rest of a program, and may be NULL if everything the handler requires to do its job can be derived from its other arguments. The *client_data* is cast to an XtPointer when registered and should be cast back to the appropriate type inside the event handler.

XtExtensionSelectProc (R6)

SYNOPSIS

```
typedef void (*XtExtensionSelectProc)( Widget, int*, XtPointer*, int,
    XtPointer );
        Widget                    widget;
        int                       *event_types;
        XtPointer                 *select_data;
        int                       count;
        XtPointer                 client_data;
```

ARGUMENTS

widget	in	The widget to which an event handler is added or removed.
event_types	in	Pointer to a list of event types to be selected.
select_data	in	Pointer to a list of additional data required to select the events, one for each event type in *event_types*.
count	in	Number of entries in *select_data* and *event_types*.
client_data	in/out	Additional data required by the selector and registered with XtRegisterExtensionSelector.

DESCRIPTION

An XtExtensionSelectProc is called when a widget is realized, if the widget has any event handlers registered for event types in the extension range. Otherwise, it is called when an extension event handler is registered with XtInsertEventTypeHandler or canceled with XtRemoveEventHandler. It is expected to ask the server to send the requested event types.

USAGE

The X protocol can be extended to allow servers to deliver new types of event. Each protocol extension is allotted a contiguous range of event type IDs. In R6, widgets can listen for extension events through event handlers. However, when the event handler is bound to a widget instance, the Intrinsics have to find the appropriate method to request the events from the server. Since extensions might not involve windows directly, each extension provides its own methods for controlling the delivery of its events. To allow events to be selected in a uniform way, an XtExtensionSelectProc should be registered for the range of event types specified by an extension. When the Intrinsics see that a widget wants to listen to extension events, they call the appropriate selector to request them. The XtExtensionSelectProc is expected to do whatever is required to ask the server to send the requested events.

Unless you write programs that need to process extension events, you will not register an XtExtensionSelectProc. Most extensions do not provide such a procedure directly. The extension selector procedure will usually be a wrapper around one or more extension-specific routines that actually select the events.

An XtExtensionSelectProc is established with XtRegisterExtensionSelector, which also registers the *client_data* that gets passed to the procedure. This *client_data* may be information computed at run-time that has bearing on how the events can be selected. The *select_data* is specified when an event handler is bound with XtInsertEventTypeHandler, and may supply more detail about the specific events to be selected.

XtFilePredicate   **(R4)**

SYNOPSIS

```
typedef Boolean (*XtFilePredicate)( String );
        String                          filename;
```

ARGUMENTS

filename   in   The filename to be checked.

DESCRIPTION

An `XtFilePredicate` is called repeatedly when `XtFindFile` or `XtResolvePathname` is used to search a path. Each time it is called, a new filename is presented. The file predicate is expected to return `True` if a proposed filename is appropriate, and `False` if it is not.

USAGE

An `XtFilePredicate` is specified as an argument to `XtFindFile` or `XtResolvePathname`, and is registered only for the duration of the call. The argument *filename* represents the complete path of a file; the file predicate is expected to return `True` if the proposed path is appropriate, or `False` if it is not.

The criteria used by an `XtFilePredicate` to determine if a path is correct are its own; a path could be considered "appropriate" if *filename* simply exists. The default predicate used by XtFindFile and `XtResolvePathname` is named `TestFile`, and returns `True` if the indicated file exists, is readable, and is not a directory.

XtInputCallbackProc   (R3)

SYNOPSIS

```
typedef void (*XtInputCallbackProc)( XtPointer, int*, XtInputId* );
        XtPointer               client_data;
        int                     *source;
        XtInputId               *input_id;
```

ARGUMENTS

client_data	in/out	Client data specified at the time the input callback procedure was registered.
source	in	Pointer to an integer specifying the file descriptor of the source.
input_id	in	Pointer to an identifier for this input source and conditions. Usually used by the callback procedure to cancel itself with XtRemoveInput when all data has been read or written.

DESCRIPTION

An XtInputCallbackProc is called by the Intrinsics when a read, write or exception condition is detected on a file descriptor. The callback is expected to read from or write to the source.

USAGE

An XtInputCallbackProc is registered with XtAppAddInput or XtAddInput (obsolete) and is canceled with XtRemoveInput. The condition and file descriptor for which the callback is invoked are defined when the callback is registered.

The *source* argument is a pointer to file descriptor, which is usually referenced in a read(2) or write(2) operation. A well-behaved input callback procedure reads or writes a little and returns quickly; since input callbacks are invoked by XtAppMainLoop in the course of processing events, failure to return in a timely way will impact the responsiveness of the user interface. Blocking reads should never be performed in an input callback. An XtInputCallbackProc will be called repeatedly as long as the read, write or exception condition exists on its file, so it does not have to handle all available data at once.

An input callback is often used to handle communications with other clients through sockets or pipes. Care should be taken if using an input callback procedure to read a physical disk file, since a physical file is readable and writeable regardless of whether there is any "new" data available. This can cause an XtInputCallbackProc to be called on every pass through XtAppNextEvent. To avoid this, an input callback reading from a disk file should call XtRemoveInput to cancel interest in the input source when an end-of-file has been detected.

The *input_id* argument is a pointer to an identifier assigned when the source is registered with XtAppAddInput. This is usually used by the procedure to remove the input source when an end-of-file is reached. In any case, the input source *must* be canceled with XtRemoveInput before a close() is performed on the associated file descriptor; otherwise, a lot of errors will be generated by XtAppMainLoop.

The *client_data* is supplied when the input callback is registered, and may be a single value or more commonly, a pointer to an application-specific data structure. It is cast to an XtPointer when registered and should be cast back to the appropriate type inside the callback proc. The *client_data* is used to transfer data between the callback procedure and the rest of a program.

XtKeyProc (R3)

SYNOPSIS

```
typedef void (*XtKeyProc)( Display*, KeyCode, Modifiers, Modifiers*,
    KeySym* );
        Display                     *display;
        KeyCode                     keycode;
        Modifiers                   modifiers;
        Modifiers                   *modifiers_return;
        KeySym                      *keysym_return;
```

ARGUMENTS

display	in	Display associated with the translation.
keycode	in	The keycode to be translated.
modifiers	in	Modifiers to be applied to the input keycode.
modifiers_return	in/out	If non-NULL, specifies an address where a mask should be returned representing the modifiers actually inspected to parse the keycode.
keysym_return	in/out	Address of variable into which the translated KeySym is returned.

DESCRIPTION

An XtKeyProc is invoked automatically whenever the Intrinsics parse a Key event through translation management, and is expected to translate a KeyCode plus modifiers to a KeySym. An XtKeyProc may also be called exlicitly with XtTranslateKeycode.

USAGE

The keycodes reported in Key events are hardware-dependent, and must be converted to a vendor-neutral encoding before they can be processed. This job is accomplished in toolkit programs by a keycode-to-keysym translator called an XtKeyProc.

An XtKeyProc is registered with XtSetKeyTranslator. The Intrinsics automatically register a default XtKeyProc named XtTranslateKey which uses Shift, Lock and group modifiers with the interpretations specified by the X protocol. In OSF/Motif programs this is replaced by a toolkit-specific key procedure that calls XtTranslateKey directly to perform the initial translation, and then consults its own internal tables to convert the standard keysyms to Motif-specific keysyms. These default procedures are sufficient for ordinary applications. You would register a new key procedure only if you needed to support alternate keyboard layouts without affecting the global keyboard mapping.

The input arguments *display*, *keycode* and *modifiers* are used to perform the translation. The usual way to convert a keycode to a keysym is to consult the mapping tables provided by the X server, which may be examined by calling XtGetKeysymTable. However, you are free to perform the mapping any way you like.

The translated keysym should be returned in the address provided by *keysym_return*. If *modifiers_return* is non-NULL, it defines an address where the procedure is expected to return the bitwise inclusive OR of any modifiers that were actually inspected in performng the translation. For a given key translator, this will be a constant.

XtLanguageProc   **(R5)**

SYNOPSIS

```
typedef String (*XtLanguageProc)( Display*, String, XtPointer );
   Display                       *display;
   String                        language_spec;
   XtPointer                     client_data;
```

ARGUMENTS

display	in	Display associated with the translation.
language_spec	in	Implementation-dependent language specification identifying the desired locale, or the empty string "" if none was found.
client_data	in/out	Application-specific data registered with XtSetLanguageProc.

DESCRIPTION

An XtLanguageProc is called whenever a display is initialized, and is expected to initialize locale-specific support for the new display.

USAGE

An XtLanguageProc is registered with XtSetLanguageProc, and is called whenever the toolkit opens a new display. The language procedure is expected to set the locale used to process information to and from the display, and return a string that is used to set the paths searched by XtDisplayInitialize for resource files (see XtDisplayInitialize, Appendix C).

Setting the locale consists of several parts: preparing the operating system to process locale-dependent data, preparing X to process internationalized input, and preparing X to accept internationalized output. Locale support is system-dependent, and usually depends on the setlocale(3) function to enable support for local-specific date, time, numeric and currency formats, collation sequences, etc.

The *language_spec* is determined by XtDisplayInitialize, and is the value of the application resource .xnlLanguage (class: .XnlLanguage) if this is defined, or the empty string "" if it is not. The language spec is implementation-specific. An XtLanguageProc is expected to use *language_spec* to enable language support. The Intrinsics register a default XtLanguageProc which calls:

```
setlocale(LC_ALL, language_spec);
```

to enable O.S. locale support; note that if *language_spec* is the empty string, this causes setlocale(3) to use the value of the LANG environment variable as the locale specifier. If this succeeds, XSupportsLocale is called to verify that X also supports the locale. If the locale is not supported, the default language procedure issues a warning and sets the locale to C. If the locale is supported, XSetLocaleModifiers is called, passing the empty string "". Finally, the default proc returns the string returned by a final call to:

```
setlocale(LC_ALL, NULL);
```

which queries the current locale. This is sufficient for most applications.

XtLoseSelectionIncrProc   (R4)

SYNOPSIS

```
typedef void (*XtLoseSelectionIncrProc) (Widget, Atom*, XtPointer);
        Widget                          widget;
        Atom                            *selection;
        XtPointer                       client_data;
```

ARGUMENTS

widget	in	Widget which just lost selection ownership.
selection	in	Pointer to an Atom specifying which selection was lost, e.g. XA_PRIMARY.
client_data	in/out	Application-defined data registered when incremental selection ownership was claimed with XtOwnSelectionIncr.

DESCRIPTION

An XtLoseSelectionIncrProc is an optional callback routine registered by a toolkit incremental selection owner to be called if ownership of the selection is lost involuntarily. The procedure is expected to remove any highlighting that indicated that a selection had been made, and free any resources that had been allocated to a potential transfer.

USAGE

An XtLoseSelectionIncrProc is an optional procedure registered when a client volunteers to own the selection with a call to XtOwnSelectionIncremental. If the XtLoseSelectionIncrProc is called it means that the selection ownership has been lost involuntarily, usually because some other widget or application volunteered to own it. This is a notification, not a request; the former owner has no choice in the matter.

The *widget* and *selection* arguments define which selection was lost; the XtLoseSelectionIncrProc is expected to provide any appropriate visual cue (removing highlighting, etc.) to indicate that ownership has been surrendered. Incremental transfers already in progress should be allowed to continue to completion, however.

The main difference between an XtLoseSelectionIncrProc and an XtLoseSelectionProc is that the incremental procedure receives a *client_data* argument which can be used to transfer data between the procedure and the rest of the application. The *client_data* is shared with the XtConvertSelectionIncr procedure and is often used to pass the request IDs of transfers in progress, and the address of buffers that may be freed by the XtLoseSelectionIncrProc.

XtLoseSelectionProc   **(R3)**

SYNOPSIS

```
typedef void (*XtLoseSelectionProc)( Widget, Atom* );
        Widget                          widget;
        Atom                            *selection;
```

ARGUMENTS

widget   in   Widget that just lost selection ownership.

selection   in   Pointer to an Atom specifying which selection was lost, e.g.
                            XA_PRIMARY.

DESCRIPTION

An XtLoseSelectionProc is an optional callback routine registered by a toolkit selection owner to be called if ownership of the selection is lost involuntarily. The procedure is expected to remove any highlighting that indicated that a selection had been made, and free any resources that had been allocated to a potential transfer.

USAGE

An XtLoseSelectionProc is an optional callback registered when a client volunteers to own the selection with XtOwnSelection. If the XtLoseSelectionProc is called it means that the selection ownership has been lost involuntarily, usually because some other widget or application volunteered to own it. This is a notification, not a request; the former owner has no choice in the matter.

The *widget* and *selection* arguments define which selection was lost; the XtLoseSelectionProc is expected to provide any required visual cues to the user to indicate that the selection ownership has been surrendered, and should free any storage allocated to an anticipated selection transfer.

An XtLoseSelectionProc receives no *client_data* argument, so any additional information required to deal with the lost selection is usually passed through global variables. This is a deficiency in the Intrinsics that must be worked around. Some toolkits (e.g. Motif, OLIT) provide for a "user data" resource that lets you attach arbitrary data to a widget instance. This can be retrieved with XtGetValues in routines that receive a widget ID but do not receive client data.

XtOrderProc   (R3)

SYNOPSIS

```
typedef Cardinal (*XtOrderProc)( Widget );
        Widget                          widget;
```

ARGUMENTS

widget   in   Widget ID of the new child.

DESCRIPTION

An XtOrderProc is called by the Intrinsics when a Composite widget is given a new child, and may specify the position of the new child in the manager's list of normal children.

USAGE

In some situations it is desirable to allow an application to control the order in which children of a manager widget appear in their parent's list of children. A menu, for example, often displays its children spatially in the order in which they are created. This order may need to be modified if a new child is to be added while enforcing alphabetical arrangement. The alternative - destroying and re-creating the children - would be very inefficient.

When a new child is created, the Intrinsics invoke the XtOrderProc specified by the parent's XtNinsertPosition resource. An XtOrderProc must return a value between 0 and the value of the parent's XtNnumChildren resource, inclusive. The returned value specifies the number of children which should precede the new child in the widget's list of children. A value of 0 indicates that the new child should appear before all others; a value equal to the value of XtNnumChildren indicates that it should be placed at the end of the list. The default XtOrderProc supplied by the Intrinsics always returns the value of XtNnumChildren.

An XtOrderProc is called only when a new child is created, and affects only the position of the new child. There is no generic way to reorder the list of children after this, but many manager widgets provide more useful ways to order their children using contraint resources.

XtResourceDefaultProc   **(R3)**

SYNOPSIS

```
typedef void (*XtResourceDefaultProc)( Widget, int, XrmValue* );
        Widget                    widget;
        int                       offset;
        XrmValue                  *value_return;
```

ARGUMENTS

widget	in	Widget for which a resource value is being calculated.
offset	in	Offset into widget data structure; describes location of resource field.
value_return	in/out	Pointer to a descriptor in which a pointer to the computed resource value is returned.

DESCRIPTION

An XtResourceDefaultProc is called to calculate a default resource value, when an entry in a resource list specifies its *default_type* as XtRCallProc.

USAGE

Every resource is described by an XtResource structure which, among other things, declares a default value for the resource. If the default value is such that it should be computed at run time, the *default_type* field may be specified as the symbolic value XtRCallProc. This asks the Intrinsics to interpret the *default_addr* field as a pointer to an XtResourceDefaultProc which is called to supply a value when the resource is initialized.

An XtResourceDefaultProc is always specific to a particular type of resource, and sometimes to a particular widget. The procedure should derive a default value appropriate to the resource and return a pointer to the computed value in *value_return->addr*. The storage pointed to by *value_return->addr* must not be a local variable, as this would be invalid when the procedure returns. The address of a static variable may be used, however. The Intrinsics automatically copy the data to new storage after the XtResourceDefaultProc returns.

The offset argument describes the location of the field in a widget data structure that will be set by the resource. The procedure should not set this field directly, but may use it to determine which field is being set, if the same resource default procedure is used to supply values for several resources.

XtSelectionCallbackProc (R3)

SYNOPSIS

```
typedef void (*XtSelectionCallbackProc)( Widget, XtPointer, Atom*, Atom*,
    XtPointer, unsigned long*, int* );
        Widget                          widget;
        XtPointer                       client_data;
        Atom                            *selection;
        Atom                            *type;
        XtPointer                       value;
        unsigned long                   *length;
        int                             *format;
```

ARGUMENTS

widget	in	Widget which is receiving the selection value(s).
client_data	in/out	Application-specific data supplied when selection was requested with `XtGetSelectionValue`.
selection	in	Pointer to an atom identifying which selection is available, e.g. `XA_PRIMARY`.
type	in	Pointer to an atom identifying the data type used to represent the selection value, e.g. `XA_STRING`.
value	in	Pointer to the selection value; this storage is owned by the selection requester, and may be freed with `XtFree` when it is no longer needed.
length	in	Pointer to a value specifying the number of data elements in *value*.
format	in	Pointer to a value specifying the size, in bits, of each data element in *value*; possible values: 8, 16, 32.

DESCRIPTION

An `XtSelectionCallbackProc` is registered by a client that requests the toolkit selection value, and is called by the Intrinsics when the selection has been retrieved and is ready to be picked up.

USAGE

An application requests a selection value by calling `XtGetSelectionValue` or one of its variants. The selection value is not returned immediately; instead, the Intrinsics fetch the selection from the current owner and call the `XtSelectionCallbackProc` registered by the requester when the selection value is ready.

An `XtSelectionCallbackProc` is called to receive both atomic and incremental selection transfers. If an incremental selection transfer is requested, the procedure is called repeatedly, each time receiving the next segment of the transfer. The final segment of a transfer is indicated by a non-NULL *value* (which must still be freed by the client) with *length* equal to zero.

The *type* argument indicates the data type used to represent the returned value. This is not necessarily the same as the requested target. It simply specifies the representation used to express the value - for example, the atom `XA_STRING` implies that the value is returned as a `String`.

If **type* is the value `XT_CONVERT_FAIL`, it indicates that an incremental transfer was disrupted. It is up to the requester to decide whether a partially-completed transfer is meaningful or not, and to free any storage associated with the partial transfer. If the procedure is called with *value* equal to NULL and **length* equal to zero, it means that that no owner could be found for the requested selection, or that the selection owner could not convert to the requested target.

The *format* argument indicates whether the received value should be treated as an array of 8, 16 or 32-bit elements. In C syntax, this corresponds to an array of char, short or long. This information is supplied by the selection owner and is used by the server to resolve byte-order differences between clients.

XtSelectionDoneIncrProc (R4)

SYNOPSIS

```
typedef void (*XtSelectionDoneIncrProc) (Widget, Atom*, Atom*,
    XtRequestId*, XtPointer );
        Widget                          widget;
        Atom                            *selection;
        Atom                            *target;
        XtRequestId                     *request_id;
        XtPointer                       client_data;
```

ARGUMENTS

widget	in	Widget that owns the selection.
selection	in	Pointer to an Atom identifying which selection was transferred, e.g. XA_PRIMARY.
target	in	Pointer to an Atom identifying the target to which the selection was converted, e.g. TEXT.
request_id	in	Pointer to a toolkit-assigned identifier for a particular incremental selection transfer.
client_data	in/out	Application-defined data registered when selection ownership was claimed with XtOwnSelectionIncremental.

DESCRIPTION

An XtSelectionDoneIncrProc is an optional procedure registered by a toolkit incremental selection owner to be called when an incremental selection transfer has been completed.

USAGE

An XtSelectionDoneIncrProc is optionally registered when a client volunteers to own the selection with XtOwnSelectionIncremental. The XtSelectionDoneIncrProc is called to notify the application that the selection has been successfully transferred; that is, the requester has received the final zero-length segment of an incremental transfer.

The sending application may consider the transfer complete, and the XtSelectionDoneIncrProc should free any resources that had been allocated to the transfer. If an XtSelectionDoneIncrProc is not registered, the Intrinsics automatically free memory associated with the final zero-length value returned by the XtConvertSelectionIncrProc. However, in no case does the Intrinsics free memory for intermediate segments of a transfer.

Since multiple transfers may be in progress simultaneously, *request_id* identifies the particular transfer which completed, and will match one previously seen by the XtConvertSelectionIncrProc.

The *client_data* argument can be used to transfer data between the procedure and the rest of the application. It is shared with the XtConvertSelectionIncr procedure and is often used to pass the request IDs of transfers currently in progress, and the address of buffers that may be freed by the XtSelectionDoneIncrProc.

XtSelectionDoneProc   (R3)

SYNOPSIS

```
typedef void (*XtSelectionDoneProc)( Widget, Atom*, Atom* );
        Widget                      widget;
        Atom                        *selection;
        Atom                        *target;
```

ARGUMENTS

widget	in	Widget which supplied the selection value.
selection	in	Pointer to an Atom identifying which selection was transferred, e.g. XA_PRIMARY.
target	in	Pointer to an Atom identifying the target to which the selection was converted, e.g. TEXT.

DESCRIPTION

An XtSelectionDoneProc is an optional procedure registered by a toolkit selection owner to be called when a selection transfer has been completed.

USAGE

An XtSelectionDoneProc is registered when a client volunteers to own the selection with XtOwnSelection. The XtSelectionDoneProc is called to notify the application that the selection has been successfully transferred.

The owner is expected to free any resources which had been allocated to the transfer, including any memory allocated by the XtConvertSelectionProc. If an XtSelectionDoneProc is not registered, the Intrinsics automatically call XtFree to free the storage allocated by the XtConvertSelectionProc for the selection value. In most cases, this is easier.

An XtSelectionDoneProc receives no *client_data* argument, so any additional information required to deal with the selection is often passed through global variables. This is a deficiency in the Intrinsics that must be worked around. Some toolkits (e.g. Motif, OLIT) provide for a "user data" resource that lets you attach arbitrary data to a widget instance. This can be retrieved with XtGetValues in routines that receive a widget ID but do not receive client data.

XtSignalCallbackProc   (R6)

SYNOPSIS

```
typedef void (*XtSignalCallbackProc)( XtPointer, XtSignalId* );
        XtPointer                    client_data;
        XtSignalId                   *signal_id;
```

ARGUMENTS

client_data	in/out	Application-defined data registered with XtAppAddSignal.
signal_id	in	Identifier of the signal callback/*client_data* combination.

DESCRIPTION

An XtSignalCallbackProc is called when a signal has been raised and noticed with XtNoticeSignal.

USAGE

Signal callbacks are used to respond to POSIX-style signals. An XtSignalCallbackProc is registered with XtAppAddSignal and is canceled with XtRemoveSignal. Any number of signal callbacks may be registered; each is identified by a unique ID.

A signal callback is invoked after XtNoticeSignal is called from within a signal handler established with signal(3). If XtNoticeSignal is called multiple times before the Intrinsics can invoke the signal callback, the signal callback is only called once. The signal callback must be prepared to handle the possibility that the signal was raised multiple times. If it cares how many times the signal was raised, the signal handler may keep count in a location that can be accessed by the signal callback. There is also a slight possibility that a signal could be raised immediately after the Intrinsics mark a signal as handled, but just before the signal callback gets control. In this case the signal callback will be called again even though all signals have been handled. A signal callback must also be prepared to handle this case.

An XtSignalCallbackProc may perform any appropriate computation, including calling toolkit functions, to respond to the signal. The *client_data* is sspecified when the signal callback is registered, and may be a single value or more commonly, a pointer to an application-specific data structure. It is used to transfer data between the callback and the rest of a program, and may be NULL if everything the signal callback needs to do its job can be derived from its other arguments. The *client_data* is cast to an XtPointer when registered and should be cast back to the appropriate type inside the signal callback.

Note that a signal callback does not receive the value of the signal that caused it to be called. The usual approach is to have a different signal callback for each signal that needs different treatment, and then call the appropriate one from within the signal handler. Another alternative is to have the signal handler pass the signal value through the *client_data*.

Signal callbacks must not be used in threaded applications, as POSIX does not define the behavior of signals in a multi-threaded environment.

XtTimerCallbackProc (R3)

SYNOPSIS

```
typedef void (*XtTimerCallbackProc)( XtPointer, XtIntervalId* );
        XtPointer                client_data;
        XtIntervalId             *timer_id;
```

ARGUMENTS

client_data	in/out	Application-defined data specified when the timer callback was registered with XtAppAddTimeOut.
timer_id	in	Identifier of the timeout.

DESCRIPTION

An XtTimerCallbackProc is called by the Intrinsics after a specified interval of time has passed.

USAGE

Timer callbacks are used to implement alarms, timeouts, blinking, and other features that must be invoked when a specified period of time has passed. An XtTimerCallbackProc is registered with XtAppAddTimeOut or XtAddTimeOut (obsolete) and is canceled with XtRemoveTimeOut. When the specified interval has expired, the timer callback is invoked once and is then removed from the timer queue. A timer callback that wishes to be called repeatedly may re-register itself each time it is called.

Any number of timers may be active simultaneously; if a particular timer callback is registered more than once, *timer_id* may be used to distinguish which instance of the timeout has expired.

The *client_data* is specified when a timeout is registered, and may be a single value or more commonly, a pointer to an application-specific data structure. It is used to transfer data between the callback procedure and the rest of a program. The *client_data* is cast to an XtPointer when registered and should be cast back to the appropriate type inside the callback.

An XtTimerCallbackProc may perform any appropriate computational, graphics or toolkit function, but must return quickly.

XtTypeConverter   (R4)

SYNOPSIS

```
typedef Boolean (*XtTypeConverter)( Display*, XrmValue*, Cardinal*,
    XrmValue*, XrmValue*, XtPointer* );
        Display                         *display ;
        XrmValue                        *args;
        Cardinal                        *num_args;
        XrmValue                        *from;
        XrmValue                        *to_return;
        XtPointer                       *convert_data_return;
```

display	in	Identifies the display with which the conversion is associated.
args	in	Pointer to a list of additional arguments required to perform the conversion. These are supplied by the Intrinsics when the converter is called, and are derived from the *convert_args* supplied when the converter is registered. (See XtAppSetTypeConverter).
num_args	in	Pointer to a value specifying the number of arguments in *args*.
from	in	Pointer to a descriptor specifying the input value in the source data type.
to_return	in/out	Pointer to a descriptor to receive the converted value in the destination data type.
convert_data_return	in/out	Pointer to storage where the converter may place conversion-specific data, if any, needed by the destructor to free the conversion resources.

DESCRIPTION

An XtTypeConverter is a more robust form of resource type converter defined by the R4 Intrinsics to replace the XtConverter procedure type defined in earlier releases. An XtTypeConverter is responsible for converting a value expressed in one data type (usually a String) to a new value expressed in a different data type. The main distinctions of new-format converters are that they return a value to indicate the success of the conversion, they receive a display pointer argument, and they may save information to support resource caching.

A converter is specific to a single source/destination type conversion, and is called automatically when the Intrinsics fetch resource values of the destination type from resource files. New-format converters may also be invoked explicitly with the routines XtConvertAndStore, XtCallConverter, or XtConvert (obsolete).

USAGE

The main job of resource converters is helping the toolkit interpret resource values declared in resource files. Resource files contain character strings, but there are very few resources that can use such a representation internally. Most resource values are expressed in language-specific or toolkit-specific data types such as int, Pixel, XFontStruct*, XmString, Widget, Pixmap, etc. When the toolkit attempts to initialize a new widget, or when application resource are fetched with XtGetApplicationResources, converters are called to read the strings and produce valid resource values of the proper type. The toolkit knows which data type is required - it is documented in the resource list - and uses this information to look up the appropriate converter.

An XtTypeConverter is registered with XtSetTypeConverter or XtAppSetTypeConverter for a specific source/destination type conversion. When the toolkit is initialized, the Intrinsics automatically register built-in converters that accept strings and convert them to the major toolkit resource types. Converters for other source/destination combinations may be supplied by widgets or applications. Widgets register type converters for class-specific types when the first widget of a particular class is created, or when the class is initialized with XtInitializeWidgetClass.

The existing converters are adequate for most putposes. You will need to register additional converters only if you define new data types for application resources, or if you don't like how an existing converter does its job and want to replace it. Converters are replaced by registering a new one for the same source/destination combination. You can't exactly unregister a type converter, but you can register a NULL converter to replace it.

The value to be converted is pointed to by *from->addr*. A converter is registered only for a single source/destination type pair, so it must assume that the *from* data is of the appropriate type. The *args* argument supplies any additional data required by the converter - a converter that produces Pixel values, for example, might require the colormap of the widget for which the conversion is being undertaken. Values supplied in *args* are computed by the Intrinsics when the converter is called, based on the *convert_args* specified to XtSetTypeConverter when the converter was registered. A converter should always check *num_args* to be sure that the appropriate number of arguments are present before attempting the conversion.

The *display* argument may be used if server resources must be allocated to satisfy the conversion. It can also used with XtDisplayToApplicationContext to derive the application context, which is required if XtAppWarningMsg is called to report a conversion error.

If a converter is registered in such a way that the toolkit caches conversion values, a procedure of type XtDestructor will be called to free the conversion value when it is no longer needed. *Convert_args_return* is used to store any special data that will be required by the destructor. Data returned through *convert_args_return*, if any, is saved by the toolkit and reported to the destructor when it is called. If more than a single value must be passed, *convert_args_return* may be used to pass a pointer to allocated storage, which must be freed by the destructor.

If the conversion is successful, a converter should return True, and pass the converted value through the *to_return* argument. The conventions for returning the converted value are somewhat complex. If *to_return->addr* is not NULL, it specifies an address into which the converted value is returned. The converter must check *to_return->size* to make sure there is room for the converted value. If *to_return->size* indicates there is insufficient storage, the converter should return False (the conversion fails) and place the required size in *to_return->size*.

If *to_return->addr* is NULL, the converter is expected to allocating storage for the converted value, and return a pointer to this storage in *to_return->addr*. The address written to *to_return->addr* cannot be a pointer to a local variable, as this would be invalid after the converter returns; however, a pointer to static storage is acceptable. The caller in this case is expected to copy the data to its own storage.

If a conversion fails, a converter should issue a warning message with XtAppWarningMsg or XtDisplayStringConversionWarning and return False.

XtWorkProc (R3)

SYNOPSIS

```
typedef Boolean (*XtWorkProc)( XtPointer );
      XtPointer                   client_data;
```

ARGUMENTS

client_data   in/out   Application-defined data specified when the work procedure is registered with XtAppAddWorkProc.

DESCRIPTION

An XtWorkProc is called when XtAppNextEvent finds no other conditions to process and would ordinarily block, waiting for input.

USAGE

A queue of work procedures is maintained by the application context. When XtAppNextEvent finds nothing else to do, it calls the work procedure at the head of the queue. Work procedures are used to implement a crude form of "background" processing which allows potentially compute-intensive tasks to be accomplished without impacting the responsiveness of the user interface. An XtWorkProc is registered with XtAppAddWorkProc or XtAddWorkProc (obsolete) and is canceled with XtRemoveWorkProc.

A work procedure should accomplish a small amount of work, save any data that it may need later, and return. Work procedures are executed in the application thread of control, and are not forked off as separate processes. Therefore, the criteria used to determine when a work procedure has computed "enough" should be chosen carefully so that it returns quickly.

An XtWorkProc is one of the few callback types that returns a value. When a work procedure has completed its task, it should return True, whereupon it is removed from the execution queue. The next work procedure in the queue is then available for processing. If a work procedure returns False, it is placed back at the head of the queue, and is executed repeatedly whenever the main loop waits for input. The last-registered work procedure has the highest priority, and is executed repeatedly until it returns True. If a work procedure registers another work procedure, the second work procedure is queued at a lower priority.

The *client_data* is supplied when the callback is registered, and may be a single value or more commonly, a pointer to an application-specific data structure. The *client_data* argument is used to convey information between the work procedure and the rest of a program; it is cast to an XtPointer when registered and should be cast back to the appropriate type inside the callback.

A work procedure may perform any appropriate computational, Xlib or toolkit operation, but must return quickly. The Intrinsics do not provide any notification when a work procedure has completed its work, nor are there any toolkit methods to determine if a work procedure is still active, or to interrupt a work procedure. Synchronization between work procedures and the rest of a program must be carried out through global variables or the *client_data* argument.

Work procedures lend themselves to tasks that can be broken down into small discrete chunks. A common use of work procedures is to create parts of the user interface while the user is admiring the initial screen. Each time the work procedure is called back, it creates another widget. For more robust background processing it is preferable to fork a separate process.

Appendix C

X TOOLKIT INTRINSICS REFERENCE MANUAL

This is an alphabetical reference to the X Toolkit Intrinsic routines, intended primarily for application programmers who are using an existing toolkit. Routine descriptions follow the format below:

RoutineName   **(Version)**

The name of the Intrinsics routine and the Intrinsics Versions in which it is available. As of R6, all routines listed as obsolete are still supported for backwards compatibility:

(RN)	Routine first supported in Release N of the Intrinsics
(RNO)	Release N routine that is obsolete as of R6
(O)	Obsolete routine provided for compatibility with pre-R3 Intrinsics

SYNOPSIS

Summary of the routine's "C" language binding, arguments and return value.

ARGUMENTS

Description of input and return arguments to the routine. Arguments defined as in/out represent values returned by side-effect. Because the C language binding passes arguments by value, these arguments must be pointers to application variables that receive the returned values. In these cases, you are responsible for allocating the memory into which to return the value.

DESCRIPTION

Description of the routine's actions and effects.

USAGE

Discussion of the routine's purpose, and appropriate ways and situations in which to use it.

CAUTION

Discussion of potentially undesirable side effects and improper usage.

SEE ALSO

List of related routines.

XtAddActions (O)

Registers application-defined action procedures

SYNOPSIS

```
void XtAddActions( actions, num_actions )
        XtActionList                    actions;
        Cardinal                        num_actions;
```

ARGUMENTS

actions	in	Pointer to a list of action name/action procedure pairs.
num_actions	in	Number of name/action pairs in *actions*.

DESCRIPTION

XtAddActions registers a new action table within the default application context created by XtInitialize. The action table associates action names (e.g. "SelectLine") with application procedures (e.g. SelectLine()), and is used to resolve application-defined translations.

USAGE

See XtAppAddActions.

CAUTION

XtAddActions is an obsolete routine supplied for backwards compatibility with earlier versions of the Intrinsics, and is superseded by XtAppAddActions in the Release 3 and later Intrinsics. XtAddActions uses the default application context established by XtInitialize, which must be called first.

SEE ALSO

Routines: XtAppAddActions, XtInitialize

XtAddCallback   **(R3)**

Adds a callback routine to a widget's callback list

SYNOPSIS

```
void XtAddCallback( w, callback_name, callback_proc, client_data )
        Widget                  w;
        String                  callback_name;
        XtCallbackProc          callback_proc;
        XtPointer               client_data;
```

ARGUMENTS

w	in	The widget to which callbacks are added.
callback_name	in	Resource name of the callback list to which callbacks are added.
callback_proc	in	Callback procedure to add to list.
client_data	in	Application-defined data to be passed as second argument to the callback procedure when it is executed, or NULL if none is required.

DESCRIPTION

XtAddCallback adds a callback procedure and associated client data to a widget's callback list. A callback routine may be added to a callback list repeatedly and is called as many times as it is found in the list. If a callback list of the specified name is not found, XtAddCallback issues a warning and returns.

USAGE

The callback lists maintained by a widget are determined by its class. Each is associated with a separate condition that the widget wants to report. When a widget detects an internal change in state associated with one of its callback lists, it calls each routine on the list. Callback routines, then, represent the most common and important way to respond to user input and other conditions.

Use XtAddCallback routine to bind a callback to a widget's callback list. The *callback_name* is usually a resource name of the form "*something*Callback" or the corresponding symbolic constant XtN*something*Callback. To add multiple callback routines in a single call, use XtAddCallbacks. A callback routine may be removed from a callback list with XtRemoveCallback.

Widget callback routines must be of type XtCallbackProc (see Appendix B). The specified *client_data* is stored in the callback list, and is passed as the second argument to the callback routine. It is used to pass application data needed by the callback routine, and may be any longword value or (more commonly) a pointer to an application-defined data structure. To avoid compiler warnings, *client_data* is cast as type XtPointer when registered and is then cast again inside the callback routine to examine any type-specific fields.

CAUTION

The order in which callback routines are executed is undefined because successive calls to XtAddCallback(s) and XtRemoveCallback(s) may reorder the callback list in unpredictable ways. Also, cooperating widgets in a particular toolkit may add and remove callback routines from each others' callback lists without the knowledge of the application programmer. Callback procedures must return quickly so that events from the server or other sources can be handled promptly.

SEE ALSO

Routines: XtAddCallbacks, XtCallCallbackList, XtCallCallbacks,
            XtHasCallbacks, XtRemoveAllCallbacks, XtRemoveCallback,
            XtRemoveCallbacks

XtAddCallbacks

(R3)

Adds a list of callback routines to a widget's callback list

SYNOPSIS
```
void XtAddCallbacks( w, callback_name, callbacks )
        Widget                        w;
        String                        callback_name;
        XtCallbackList                callbacks;
```

ARGUMENTS

w	in	The widget to which callbacks are to be added.
callback_name	in	Resource name of the callback list to which callbacks should be added.
callbacks	in	Pointer to a NULL-terminated array of procedure/client_data pairs.

DESCRIPTION

XtAddCallbacks adds a NULL-terminated list of callback procedure/client data pairs to the specified callback list. A callback routine may be added to a callback list repeatedly and is called as many times as it occurs in the list. If a callback list of the specified name is not found, XtAddCallbacks issues a warning.

USAGE

Use this routine to bind multiple callback routines to a widget in a single call. The callback list is usually referenced by a resource name of the form "*something*Callback" or the corresponding symbolic constant XtN*something*Callback.

The *callbacks* argument is usually declared as a static array of type XtCallbackRec (see Appendix A). The *closure* specified with each callback routine is stored in the callback list and passed as the second argument to that callback routine. It used to pass application data required by the callback routine, and may be a longword value or (more commonly) a pointer to an application-defined data structure. To avoid compiler warnings, each client data value is cast as type XtPointer and is then cast again inside the callback routine to examine any type-specific fields.

The routine XtAddCallback may be used instead if only a single callback is to be added to the callback list. Callbacks registered with XtAddCallbacks may be removed from the callback list with XtRemoveCallback or XtRemoveCallbacks.

CAUTION

The list of *callbacks* must be NULL-terminated or a system error will occur. The order in which callback routines are executed is undefined because successive calls to XtAddCallback(s) and XtRemoveCallback(s) may reorder the callback list in unpredictable ways. Also, cooperating widgets in a particular toolkit may add and remove callbacks from a widget's callback lists without the knowledge of the programmer. Callback procedures must return quickly so that events from the server or other sources may be handled.

SEE ALSO

Routines: XtAddCallback, XtCallCallbackList, XtCallCallbacks, XtHasCallbacks, XtRemoveAllCallbacks, XtRemoveCallback, XtRemoveCallbacks

XtAddConverter   (O)

Registers an old-format resource type converter

SYNOPSIS

```
void XtAddConverter( from_type, to_type, converter, convert_args,
    num_args )
        String                          from_type;
        String                          to_type;
        XtConverter                     converter;
        XtConvertArgList                convert_args;
        Cardinal                        num_args;
```

ARGUMENTS

from_type	in	String identifying the source data type for the conversion, e.g. "String", or symbolic constant XtRString.
to_type	in	String identifying the destination data type for the conversion, e.g. "Int", or symbolic constant XtRInt.
converter	in	Converter to be registered, specific to the from/to combination.
convert_args	in	Argument specifying how to compute additional arguments to be supplied to converter, or NULL if none are required.
num_args	in	Number of additional arguments described by *convert_args*, or zero.

DESCRIPTION

XtAddConverter registers an old-format resource type converter within all application contexts. This routine is superseded in the R4 and later Intrinsics by the routine XtSetTypeConverter. XtAddConverter is equivalent to calling XtSetTypeConverter with *cache_type* equal to XtCacheAll.

USAGE

XtAddConverter is most often called by old widget implementation code. For more information on resource converters, see the discussion under XtSetTypeConverter, and the descriptions of XtConverter and XtTypeConverter in Appendix B.

CAUTION

XtAddConverter is an obsolete routine supplied for backwards compatibility with Release 3 of the Intrinsics, and is superseded by XtSetTypeConverter in the R4 and later Intrinsics. XtAddConverter can only be used to register old-format type converters of type XtConverter.

SEE ALSO

Routines: XtAppAddConverter, XtAppSetTypeConverter, XtCallConverter,
            XtConvert, XtConvertAndStore, XtDirectConvert, XtSetTypeConverter

XtAddEventHandler

(R3)

Adds an event handler to a widget

SYNOPSIS

```
void XtAddEventHandler(w, event_mask, nonmaskable, event_handler,
        client_data )
        Widget                          w;
        EventMask                       event_mask;
        Boolean                         nonmaskable;
        XtEventHandler                  event_handler;
        XtPointer                       client_data;
```

ARGUMENTS

w	in	The widget to which the event handler is to be added; must be of class Core or any subclass thereof.
event_mask	in	Mask specifying which X event types the handler should be called for.
nonmaskable	in	True if event handler should be called when nonmaskable events (GraphicsExpose, NoExpose, SelectionClear, SelectionRequest, SelectionNotify, ClientMessage, MappingNotify) are received.
event_handler	in	The event handler to be registered.
client_data	in	Application-defined data to be passed to event handler when it is called.

DESCRIPTION

XtAddEventHandler registers an event handler to be called whenever a single XEvent of the type or types selected by *event_mask* is received by widget *w*. The *event_mask* is a bitwise OR of any of the mask bits listed in Table 9-2. If *nonmaskable* is True, the handler is also called when any nonmaskable events are detected. The specified *client_data* is passed as the second argument to the event handler and may be any longword value or (more commonly) a pointer to an application-defined data structure.

A given *event_handler/client_data* pair occurs exactly once in the widget's list of event handlers. If an event handler is registered twice for the same event type, but with different *client_data*, it is called twice when a specified event is received. If an event handler is registered twice with the same *client_data* but for different event types, the mask associated with that event handler/client_data pair is simply augmented. The handler would be called once when an event of any selected type is detected.

If the event mask specifies a type of event that had not been previously selected, XSelectInput is called automatically to enable the widget's window to receive the events.

USAGE

Event handlers are useful when you want to examine events individually and with a minimum of overhead. A common use is handling MotionNotify events to move a software cursor or do rubberbanding. Generally, they should be used sparingly, since they are a much less robust mechanism than translation management. Event handlers can only be registered by a programmer and cannot be modified by the user to respond to different events, like translations and action procedures can. But, they can be useful when you do not want the user to be able to modify the events that trigger a function; for this reason, event handlers are often used to detect ButtonPress events that control pop-up menus.

Event handlers must be of type XtEventHandler (see Appendix B). The specified *client_data* is used to pass application data needed by the handler. To avoid compiler warnings, *client_data* is cast as type XtPointer when registered and is then cast again inside the event handler to examine any type-specific fields.

An event handler registered with XtAddEventHandler may be unregistered with XtRemoveEventHandler. If an event handler should be registered without modifying the window's event mask (rarely done), use XtAddRawEventHandler. To register a handler that responds to extension events, call XtInsertEventTypeHandler.

CAUTION

Event handlers respond to single X events and only distinguish events at the granularity of an event mask. A handler registered with the StructureNotifyMask, for example, will receive several different types of event (see Table 9-2). Any important event details must be examined inside the event handler. For these reasons, you should usually use translation management as the "proper" way to tell a widget to trap a specific event or sequence of events (See Chapter 9 and Appendix D).

If several handlers are registered to respond to the same event type, the toolkit does not guarantee the order in which they are called. The routine XtInsertEventHandler may be used to register event handlers that are called before or after all previously-registered handlers, but succeeding calls to XtAddEventHandler could still reorder the list.

SEE ALSO

Routines: XtAddRawEventHandler, XtBuildEventMask, XtDispatchEvent,
             XtInsertEventHandler, XtInsertRawEventHandler,
             XtInsertEventTypeHandler, XtRemoveEventHandler,
             XtRemoveRawEventHandler

XtAddExposureToRegion **(R3)**

Merges information from an Expose event into a Region

SYNOPSIS

```
void XtAddExposureToRegion( event, region )
        XEvent                   *event;
        Region                   region;
```

ARGUMENTS

event   in   Pointer to an Expose event to be added to the specified region.

region   in/out   Region to which the exposure should be added.

DESCRIPTION

If *event* is of type `Expose` or `GraphicsExpose`, `XtAddExposureToRegion` merges the exposed rectangle described in the event structure into the specified region.

USAGE

`XtAddExposureToRegion` is used internally by the Intrinsics to merge the refresh area from a contiguous series of Expose events into a single region, which may be refreshed later as a single operation. This may be more economical for a refresh algorithm to handle than a series of individual rectangles, and may also be used as a clipping area for drawing operations to yield a more attractive redisplay. `XtAddExposureToRegion` is called automatically by the toolkit Intrinsics during an event dispatch, if a widget class has requested exposure compression. It can also be used by application programmers to compress exposures received in a drawing area widget (see Chapter 12).

CAUTION

The region must already exist, and should be created by the caller with `XCreateRegion`; the caller is also responsible for freeing it with `XDestroyRegion` when it is no longer required. The region should be reset to the empty region after each series of Expose events is handled.

SEE ALSO

Routines: `XtDispatchEvent`

XtAddGrab (R3)

Adds a widget to the grab list

SYNOPSIS

```
void XtAddGrab( w, exclusive, spring_loaded )
        Widget                        w;
        Boolean                       exclusive;
        Boolean                       spring_loaded;
```

ARGUMENTS

w	in	Widget to be added to the modal cascade; must be of class Core or any subclass thereof.
exclusive	in	True if user events should be dispatched only as far as this widget.
spring_loaded	in	True if widget should receive all events directed to its descendants as well as its own.

DESCRIPTION

XtAddGrab adds a widget and all its normal (non pop-up) descendants to the grab list associated with the specified widget's application context. If *spring_loaded* is True, *exclusive* must also be True, or XtAddGrab issues a warning and sets *exclusive* to True. When at least one widget is found in the grab list, events are handled as discussed below.

USAGE

The grab list is attached to the application context, and manages a list of widgets called the "modal cascade". Widgets on the grab list "grab" user input that would normally go to other widgets. This is mainly used to support pop-up dialog boxes or menus that need to freeze input to the rest of the user interface while they do their work. No server-side grab is involved; the toolkit simply remaps events after they are received.

A widget is added to the grab list with XtAddGrab and is removed with XtRemoveGrab. These are automatically called by XtPopup and XtPopdown, respectively. Since the most common use of toolkit grabs is to implement modal pop-ups, you'll usually call XtPopup specifying an appropriate *grab_kind*, rather than calling XtAddGrab explicitly. In very rare cases it may be appropriate to add a normal widget to the grab list - for example, to prevent a user from reassigning focus from a password entry field.

Widgets are added to or deleted from the grab list in chronological order, and may be registered with *nonexclusive* or *exclusive* grab. If a manager widget is added, all of its normal managed descendants are implicitly added, too. The *active set* consists of all widgets on the grab list back to and including the most recent widget with exclusive grab. A widget with exclusive grab, then, establishes a new active set, while a widget with nonexclusive grab simply becomes part of the current active set. An example: if a dialog box is added to the grab list with exclusive grab, only the controls inside that dialog box are active. If that dialog box in turn pops up another with nonexclusive grab, then both dialog boxes are active, but the rest of the application is not. If the second dialog box were popped up with exclusive grab, though, it and its descendants would become the new active set, and only the new dialog box would accept input.

A widget with exclusive grab may also be designated as spring-loaded. This is exclusively reserved for pop-up menus. The toolkit makes sure that a spring-loaded widget gets all user input directed to the application; if an event arrives for a descendant of the spring-loaded widget, both widgets receive the event. This is useful when a button widget in a menu is activated by a ButtonRelease, but the surrounding menu widget must also see the event (so that it knows to pop itself down). This is, in fact, the origin of the term "spring-loaded". A spring-loaded widget is supposed to be popped up on a ButtonPress event, and pops back down on the ButtonRelease event, as though it were on a spring. Spring-loaded widgets are always popped up with XtPopupSpringLoaded; you'll never call XtAddGrab to specify a spring-loaded widget directly.

Toolkit grabs only affect user input events: KeyPress, KeyRelease, ButtonPress, ButtonRelease, MotionNotify, EnterNotify and LeaveNotify. Other events are delivered normally, so that non-grabbing widgets can refresh their graphics and maintain their internal state. Here is how user events are handled if there are widgets on the grab list:

- Widgets in the active set receive all their own events normally.

- If there is a spring-loaded widget in the active set, any user events occurring in the active set are first sent to their respective widgets, and are then remapped to the most recently added spring-loaded widget, too. Both widgets receive the event.

- A KeyPress, KeyRelease, ButtonPress or ButtonRelease event in a widget outside the active set is not delivered to its own widget, but is remapped to the most recent widget with exclusive grab (which might be spring-loaded as well).

- EnterNotify and MotionNotify events in widgets outside the active set are discarded.

- All other events are delivered normally.

CAUTION

The grab list is a client-side mechanism which remaps events within a widget tree, and is not the same as grabs implemented by the server. However, the grab list does interact with keyboard and pointer grabs established with XtGrabButton, XtGrabKey, XtGrabKeyboard and XtGrabPointer, and with keyboard forwarding set with XtSetKeyboardFocus. See the descriptions of these routines for more detail.

SEE ALSO

Routines: XtDispatchEvent, XtRemoveGrab, XtPopup, XtPopupSpringLoaded, XtPopdown

XtAddInput (O)

Registers a callback to handle a file input source

SYNOPSIS

```
XtInputId XtAddInput( source, condition, input_proc, client_data )
        int                         source;
        unsigned long               condition;
        XtInputCallbackProc         input_proc;
        XtPointer                   client_data;
```

ARGUMENTS

source	in	File descriptor of input source or sink.
condition	in	Mask specifying condition on which callback procedure should be called. This argument is operating-system dependent, but on POSIX-based systems is some union of `XtInputReadMask`, `XtInputWriteMask`, and/or `XtInputExceptMask`.
input_proc	in	Procedure to be called when specified condition is detected on the input source.
client_data	in	Application-specified data to be passed to callback procedure when it is executed.

DESCRIPTION

XtAddInput registers a file descriptor within the default application context established by XtInitialize, and returns a unique identifier for the callback/condition/client_data combination. Depending on the supplied *condition* mask, a read, write, exception or operating-system dependent condition on the specified file causes *input_proc* to be executed. The specified *client_data* is delivered as the first argument to the callback procedure when it is executed, and may be a single longword value or, more commonly, a pointer to an application-defined data structure.

USAGE

See XtAppAddInput.

CAUTION

XtAddInput is an obsolete routine supplied for backwards compatibility with earlier versions of the Intrinsics, and is superseded by XtAppAddInput in the Release 3 and later Intrinsics. XtAddInput uses the default application context established by XtInitialize, which must be called first.

SEE ALSO

Routines: XtAppAddInput, XtInitialize, XtMainLoop, XtNextEvent, XtProcessEvent, XtRemoveInput

XtAddRawEventHandler   (R3)

Adds an event handler to a widget without updating its event mask

SYNOPSIS

```
void XtAddRawEventHandler( w, event_mask, nonmaskable, event_handler,
   client_data )
        Widget                          w;
        EventMask                       event_mask;
        Boolean                         nonmaskable;
        XtEventHandler                  event_handler;
        XtPointer                       client_data;
```

ARGUMENTS

w	in	The widget to which the event handler is to be added; must be of class Core or any subclass thereof.
event_mask	in	Mask specifying which X event types the handler should be called for.
nonmaskable	in	True if event handler should be called when nonmaskable events (GraphicsExpose, NoExpose, SelectionClear, SelectionRequest, SelectionNotify, ClientMessage, MappingNotify) are received.
event_handler	in	The event handler to be registered.
client_data	in	Application-defined data to be passed to event handler when it is called.

DESCRIPTION

XtAddRawEventHandler is identical to XtAddEventHandler, but does not issue an XSelectInput call on the widget's window. This means that the widget is ready to handle the specified events, but its own window might not deliver them.

USAGE

Raw event handlers are used to allow a widget to deal with events that don't really come from its window. Examples would include events delivered because of a remapping or grab, or synthetic events dispatched with XtDispatchEventToWidget to simulate input. In these cases, the widget's window need not have its event mask set, since the events are actually detected elsewhere. Such cases are very rare. An event handler registered with XtAddRawEventHandler may be unregistered with XtRemoveRawEventHandler.

CAUTION

See XtAddEventHandler.

SEE ALSO

Routines: XtAddEventHandler, XtInsertRawEventHandler, XtRemoveEventHandler,
       XtRemoveRawEventHandler

XtAddTimeOut (O)

Registers a callback to respond to a timeout

SYNOPSIS

```
XtIntervalId XtAddTimeOut( interval, timer_proc, client_data )
            unsigned long              interval;
            XtTimerCallbackProc        timer_proc;
            XtPointer                  client_data;
```

ARGUMENTS

interval	in	Interval, expressed in milliseconds, after which the timeout expires.
timer_proc	in	Procedure to be called when the timer expires.
client_data	in	Application-defined data to be passed to the callback procedure.

DESCRIPTION

XtAddTimeOut registers a timeout within the default application context, and returns a unique identifier for the interval/timer_proc/client_data triplet. The specified XtTimerCallbackProc *timer_proc* is called when the timeout expires, and is passed the specified *client_data* as its first argument. After the callback procedure is invoked, the timeout is automatically canceled and will not be called again.

USAGE

See XtAppAddTimeOut.

CAUTION

XtAddTimeOut is an obsolete routine supplied for backwards compatibility with earlier versions of the Intrinsics, and is superseded by XtAppAddTimeOut in the Release 3 and later Intrinsics. XtAddTimeOut uses the default application context established by XtInitialize, which must be called first.

SEE ALSO

Routines: XtAppAddTimeOut, XtMainLoop, XtNextEvent, XtProcessEvent,
           XtRemoveTimeOut

XtAddWorkProc   **(O)**

Registers a callback to be invoked when the toolkit has nothing more important to do

SYNOPSIS

```
XtWorkProcId XtAddWorkProc( work_proc, client_data )
        XtWorkProc                   work_proc;
        XtPointer                    client_data;
```

ARGUMENTS

work_proc   in   A work procedure to be executed when XtNextEvent is waiting for
                        events.

client_data   in   Application-defined data to be passed to the work procedure when it is
                        executed.

DESCRIPTION

XtAddWorkProc registers a work procedure within the default application context, and returns a unique
identifier for the work_proc/client_data pair. The specified procedure is placed at the head of the queue of
work procedures, and is called whenever XtNextEvent finds no events to process. The work procedure at
the head of the execution queue is called repeatedly as long as it returns False. When the work procedure
returns True, it is removed from the execution queue. The specified *client_data* is delivered as the first
argument to the work procedure when it is executed, and may be a single longword value or, more
commonly, a pointer to an application-defined data structure.

USAGE

See XtAppAddWorkProc.

CAUTION

XtAddWorkProc is an obsolete routine supplied for backwards compatibility with earlier versions of the
Intrinsics, and is superseded by XtAppAddWorkProc in the Release 3 and later Intrinsics.
XtAddWorkProc uses the default application context established by XtInitialize, which must be
called first.

SEE ALSO

Routines: XtAppAddWorkProc, XtMainLoop, XtNextEvent, XtProcessEvent,
           XtRemoveWorkProc

XtAllocateGC   (R5)

Allocates a shared modifiable GC

SYNOPSIS

```
GC XtAllocateGC( w, value_mask, values, dynamic_mask, unused_mask )
        Widget                    w;
        Cardinal                  depth;
        XtGCMask                  value_mask;
        XGCValues                 *values;
        XtGCMask                  dynamic_mask;
        XtGCMask                  unused_mask;
```

ARGUMENTS

w	in	Widget from which screen and depth of GC are derived; must be of class Object or any subclass thereof.
depth	in	Specifies depth for which GC is valid; if 0, depth is derived from *w*.
value_mask	in	Mask specifying which initial fields are set in *values*.
values	in	Pointer to XGCValues data structure defining initial GC values.
dynamic_mask	in	Mask specifying which GC attributes may be changed by caller.
unused_mask	in	Mask specifying which GC attributes are unused by caller.

DESCRIPTION

XtAllocateGC returns a shared modifiable GC with the specified initial values. The caller must update any fields in the *dynamic_mask* prior to each use of the GC. The caller cannot know, and should not care, what values are in the fields specified by *unused_mask*. If a previously-allocated GC can be modified to satisfy the caller without disturbing previous users, the Intrinsics return the ID of the previously-allocated GC, and increment its reference count by one. Otherwise, a new GC is created.

USAGE

Graphics Contexts (GCs) are server objects that control the attributes of drawing primitives. Shared GCs are a toolkit client-side optimization which decreases server resource utilization when many widgets use the same graphic rendition, and could therefore use the same GC. Shared GCs are mainly used in widget implementation code, when it is likely that many widgets in a toolkit will use the same colors, fonts and patterns to draw their graphics. Shared GCs may also be used by application programmers in an effort to decrease the number of server resources required by application graphics code.

You may reserve a shared modifiable GC with XtAllocateGC. The *value_mask* and values define the initial state of the GCs fields. The *dynamic_mask* indicates to the toolkit which fields you intend to modify. You must set these fields with XChangeGC or Xlib convenience routines prior to each use of the GC. The *unused_mask* tells the toolkit that you do not care what is in those fields. Any fields not in *dynamic_mask* or *unused_mask*, and not set by *value_mask* and *values*, can be assumed to have their default values.

When XtAllocateGC is called, the toolkit tries to find an existing shared GC that could satisfy the caller's needs. In particular, if the fields that one caller wants to set are those that a previous caller "didn't care" about, the toolkit figures that the same GC could be used for both callers, since they won't step on each other's toes. Note that if XtAllocateGC is called with a zero *unused_mask*, it says that the caller cares about *all* the fields in the GC, making it pretty hard to share.

If a GC created by an earlier call to XtAllocateGC can be modified to satisfy the new caller without disturbing the old, the Intrinsics return the ID of the previously-allocated GC, and increment its reference count. If incompatible GC values are specified, the server is asked to create a new GC, and the GC is cached for later reference. XtReleaseGC releases a reference to a shared GC when it is no longer needed. When the last reference to a shared GC is released, the GC is destroyed.

CAUTION

"Shared" GCs are implemented strictly within a single client; neither the Intrinsics nor Xlib provide mechanisms for sharing GCs between clients.

SEE ALSO

Routines: XtGetGC, XtDestroyGC, XtReleaseGC

XtAppAddActionHook (R4)

Registers an action hook procedure

SYNOPSIS

```
XtActionHookId XtAppAddActionHook( app_context, action_hook_proc,
    client_data )
            XtAppContext                app_context;
            XtActionHookProc            action_hook_proc;
            XtPointer                   client_data;
```

ARGUMENTS

app_context	in	The application context in which the action hook procedure applies.
action_hook_proc	in	Procedure to be called immediately before any toolkit named action.
client_data	in	Application-defined data to be passed to *action_hook_proc* when it is called.

DESCRIPTION

XtAppAddActionHook adds a procedure to the list of action hooks maintained within the specified application context, and returns a unique identifier for procedure/client_data pair.

All registered action hook procedures are called in descending order from last-registered to first-registered immediately before any action routine is invoked. The action procedure may be supplied by a widget or may have been registered by an application with XtAddActions or XtAppAddActions. Action hooks are executed whether the action routine is invoked by widget internal translation management, or explicitly with XtCallActionProc.

The specified *client_data* is passed as the second argument to the action hook procedure when it is called. The action hook procedure also receives information about the action about to be dispatched and its arguments.

USAGE

An action hook procedure may be used as a debugging aid, to log or report on which action procedures are executed, or to record actions and their parameters for later playback with XtCallActionProc. This could be used to journal user input, implement "teach" or "demo" modes in an application, or build a macro record and playback facility. Operations processed by event handlers do not invoke action hook procs, and cannot be journaled in this way.

An action hook procedure must be of type XtActionHookProc (see Appendix B). An action hook registered with XtAppAddActionHook may be unregistered with XtRemoveActionHook. The list of action hook procedures is automatically destroyed when the associated application context is destroyed.

CAUTION

An action hook procedure must not modify any of the data pointed to by its arguments, other than the *client_data* registered by the application.

SEE ALSO

Routines: XtAppAddActions, XtCallActionProc, XtRemoveActionHook

XtAppAddActions   **(R3)**

Registers application-defined action procedures

SYNOPSIS

```
void XtAppAddActions( app_context, actions, num_actions )
        XtAppContext                    app_context;
        XtActionList                    actions;
        Cardinal                        num_actions;
```

ARGUMENTS

app_context	in	The application context to which actions are added.
actions	in	Pointer to list of action name/procedure pairs.
num_actions	in	Number of action name/procedure pairs in action table.

DESCRIPTION

XtAppAddActions registers a list of action procedures within the specified application context. The action table associates the names (e.g. "SelectLine") by which action procedures (e.g. SelectLine()) are referenced in translation tables.

USAGE

XtAppAddActions lets you register your own procedures to be called in response to an event or sequence of events detected by a widget. You first write an XtActionProc (see Appendix B), and then register it with an action name, using XtAppAddActions. The argument *actions* is usually a statically-declared array of XtActionsRecs. By convention, the action name is identical to the procedure name.

To get a widget to use your action, you must supply a translation table defining the event or event sequence that is to trigger it. You can do this by defining the XtNtranslations resource of a widget when it is created, or by calling XtOverrideTranslations or XtAugmentTranslations.

When resolving a reference to an action, the Intrinsics first search actions registered by widgets, their ancestors and superclasses. Action tables registered with XtAppAddActions or XtAddActions are searched last. If more than one action with the same name is registered in separate calls to XtAppAddActions, the Intrinsics use the most recently registered one. If two actions in a single action table have the same name, the Intrinsics use the first one found.

There is no way to unregister an action procedure registered with XtAppAddActions; instead, a dummy action procedure that simply returns should be registered with the same name.

CAUTION

If an action is referenced by a translation table defined in a resource file, it must be registered before the widget that needs it is realized. Since application-supplied action tables are searched last when the Intrinsics resolve translations, you should choose action names that are not already used by a toolkit, or there is a good chance that your action will never be found. Many toolkits document action names in the manpage of the widget that supplies them. The Intrinsics reserve all action names and parameters starting with "Xt".

SEE ALSO

Routines: XtAppAddActionHook, XtAugmentTranslations, XtCallActionProc,
           XtOverrideTranslations, XtParseTranslationTable, XtRealizeWidget

XtAppAddBlockHook (R6)

Register a procedure to be called just before the toolkit waits for something

SYNOPSIS

```
XtBlockHookId XtAppAddBlockHook( app_context, block_hook_proc,
    client_data )
        XtAppContext                      app_context;
        XtBlockHookProc                   block_hook_proc;
        XtPointer                         client_data;
```

ARGUMENTS

app_context	in	The application context in which the block hook procedure applies.
block_hook_proc	in	Procedure to be called immediately before toolkit waits for something.
client_data	in	Application-defined data to be passed to *block_hook_proc* when it is called.

DESCRIPTION

`XtAppAddBlockHook` registers a routine to be called just before the toolkit enters an implementation-dependent blocking wait for input. Any number of block hook procedures may be registered, and are called in order from last-to-first registered. The specified *client_data* is passed as the single argument to the block hook procedure when it is called. `XtAppAddBlockHook` returns a unique identifier for a particular procedure/*client_data* pair, so a block hook procedure may be registered more than once with different *client_data*.

USAGE

Just before performing an implementation-dependent wait for something, the Intrinsics call the list of block hook procedures registered with `XtAppAddBlockHook`. A block hook must be of type `XtBlockHookProc` (see Appendix B), and differs from a work proc in that all block hooks are called when the toolkit prepares to wait, whereas only a single work procedure at the head of the work proc queue is executed.

A block hook procedure registered with `XtAppAddBlockHook` may be unregistered at any time with `XtRemoveBlockHook`, after which it will no longer be called. The list of block hook procedures is automatically destroyed when its associated application context is destroyed.

CAUTION

None

SEE ALSO

Routines: `XtRemoveBlockHook, XtAppNextEvent`

XtAppAddConverter (R3O)

Registers an old-format type converter

SYNOPSIS

```
void XtAppAddConverter( app_context, from_type, to_type, converter,
    convert_args, num_args )
        XtAppContext            app_context;
        String                  from_type;
        String                  to_type;
        XtConverter             converter;
        XtConvertArgList        convert_args;
        Cardinal                num_args;
```

ARGUMENTS

app_context	in	Application context within which to register converter.
from_type	in	String identifying the source data type for the conversion, e.g. "String", or symbolic constant XtRString.
to_type	in	String identifying the destination data type for the conversion, e.g. "Int", or symbolic constant XtRInt.
converter	in	Old-format converter to be registered, specific to from/to combination.
convert_args	in	Argument specifying how to compute additional arguments to· be supplied to converter, or NULL if none are required.
num_args	in	Number of additional arguments supplied to the converter, or zero if none.

DESCRIPTION

XtAppAddConverter registers an old-format resource type converter within the specified application context. XtAppAddConverter is equivalent to calling XtAppSetTypeConverter with *cache_type* equal to XtCacheAll.

USAGE

XtAppAddConverter is most often called by older widget implementation code. This routine is superseded in the R4 and later Intrinsics by the routine XtAppSetTypeConverter. For more information on resource converters, see the discussion under XtAppSetTypeConverter, and the descriptions of XtConverter and XtTypeConverter in Appendix B.

CAUTION

XtAppAddConverter is an obsolete routine supplied for backwards compatibility with Release 3 of the Intrinsics, and is superseded by XtAppSetTypeConverter in the R4 and later Intrinsics. XtAppAddConverter can only be used to register old-format type converters of type XtConverter.

SEE ALSO

Routines: XtAddConverter, XtAppSetTypeConverter, XtCallConverter, XtConvert, XtConvertAndStore, XtDirectConvert, XtSetTypeConverter

XtAppAddInput   (R3)

Registers a callback to handle a file input source

SYNOPSIS

```
XtInputId XtAppAddInput( app_context, source, condition, input_proc,
    client_data )
        XtAppContext                    app_context;
        int                             source;
        unsigned long                   condition;
        XtInputCallbackProc             input_proc;
        XtPointer                       client_data;
```

ARGUMENTS

app_context	in	Application context in which input source is to be registered.
source	in	File descriptor identifying the input source.
condition	in	Mask specifying condition on which input procedure should be called; on POSIX-based systems this is some union of XtInputReadMask, XtInputWriteMask and/or XtInputExceptMask.
input_proc	in	Procedure to be called when *condition* is detected on *source*.
client_data	in	Application-specified data to be passed to *input_proc*.

DESCRIPTION

XtAppAddInput registers a file descriptor within the specified application context and returns a unique identifier for the combination of input source, condition, callback and client_data. Depending on the *condition* mask, the callback will be invoked when the specified file descriptor becomes available for reading or writing, or when an exception condition is detected. The specified *client_data* is delivered as the first argument to the callback procedure when it is executed, and may be a single longword value or, more commonly, a pointer to an application-defined data structure, cast as type XtPointer. If the *condition* mask is not valid, XtAppAddInput issues a fatal error.

USAGE

Applications often need to handle other input or output sources in addition to the X server. These might include data files, sockets or pipes used to communicate with other processes, terminal lines, and other I/O channels. After a file descriptor has been established for an input source, it may be registered with the Intrinsics by calling XtAppAddInput. An input callback procedure will be invoked any time the specified condition is detected on the file. A well-behaved input callback procedure reads or writes a small amount on its file and then returns, waiting to be called again. It will be called repeatedly as long as the specified condition remains true.

The *input_proc* must be of type XtInputCallbackProc (see Appendix B). Since an input callback is not notified of the condition that triggered it, you usually register a separate callback for each condition that you want to detect. An input callback can be unregistered at any time with XtRemoveInput.

Input callbacks are processed automatically by XtAppMainLoop. If you supply your own main loop, you must call XtAppNextEvent or XtAppProcessEvent to properly dispatch alternate input events.

CAUTION

The value of *source* is implementation-dependent; on POSIX-based systems it is a file descriptor assigned with `open()`, `socket()`, `pipe()` or `accept()` - but on OpenVMS, for example, it is an event flag. Under no circumstances should blocking reads be attempted in input callbacks.

SEE ALSO

Routines: `XtAppMainLoop, XtAppNextEvent, XtAppPending, XtAppProcessEvent,`
`XtRemoveInput`

XtAppAddSignal (R6)

Registers a callback to handle POSIX signals

SYNOPSIS

```
XtSignalId XtAppAddSignal( app_context, signal_proc, client_data )
        XtAppContext                    app_context;
        XtSignalCallbackProc            signal_proc;
        XtPointer                       client_data;
```

ARGUMENTS

app_context   in   Application context in which callback is registered.

signal_proc   in   Procedure to be called when signal is raised.

client_data   in   Application-specified data to be passed to signal callback .

DESCRIPTION

XtAppAddSignal registers a signal callback within the specified application context and returns a unique identifier for the signal callback/client_data combination. The callback will be invoked after XtNoticeSignal is called from within a signal handler. The specified *client_data* is delivered as the first argument to the callback, and may be a single longword value or, more commonly, a pointer to an application-defined data structure, cast as type XtPointer.

USAGE

Signal callbacks are used to respond to POSIX-style signals. The Intrinsics cannot invoke a signal callback immediately when a signal is raised, since the signal could interrupt in the middle of any routine. Instead, a signal callback is invoked when it is safe to do so - that is, when any event dispatch in progress has returned to the main loop.

To implement signal handling, first register a signal callback of type XtSignalCallbackProc (see Appendix B) with XtAppAddSignal. Then, establish a signal handler with signal(3). The signal handler should in turn call XtNoticeSignal when the signal is raised, referencing the identifier returned by XtAppAddSignal. This causes the Intrinsics to call the signal callback as soon as it is safe to do so.

Although a signal *handler* is specific to a particular signal or signals, a signal *callback* is not. The signal callback does not see the signal directly; to help it distinguish between different signals, you could register a separate callback routine for each signal to be handled, or use the *client_data* to send the signal to the callback. A signal callback is canceled with XtRemoveSignal.

To support backwards compatibility for applications that still call XtInitialize, the R6 sources include the undocumented routine XtAddSignal, which registers a signal callback in the default application context established by XtInitialize.

CAUTION

Signal callbacks must not be used in multi-threaded applications, since POSIX does not define the behavior of a signal in a threaded environment. If a signal handler is active, only a single thread can be running.

SEE ALSO

Routines: XtAppMainLoop, XtAppNextEvent, XtAppPending, XtAppProcessEvent,
        XtNoticeSignal, XtRemoveSignal

XtAppAddTimeOut   (R3)

Registers a callback to respond to a timeout

SYNOPSIS

```
XtIntervalId XtAppAddTimeOut( app_context, interval, timer_proc,
    client_data )
            XtAppContext                    app_context;
            XtPointer                       interval;
            XtTimerCallbackProc             timer_proc;
            XtPointer                       client_data;
```

ARGUMENTS

app_context	in	Application context in which timeout is to be registered.
interval	in	Interval, expressed in milliseconds, after which timeout expires.
timer_proc	in	Procedure to be called when timeout expires.
client_data	in	Application-specified data to be passed to the callback procedure .

DESCRIPTION

XtAppAddTimeOut registers a timeout within the specified application context, and returns a unique identifier for the timer_proc/interval/client_data combination. The *timer_proc* is called once when the specified interval has passed. The *client_data* is delivered as the first argument to the callback procedure, and may be a single longword value or, more commonly, a pointer to an application-defined data structure, cast as type XtPointer.

USAGE

Timeouts are used anywhere you need to receive notification after a specified interval has passed. Any number of timeouts may be registered simultaneously; common uses include blinking objects, repeating actions (as in "press-and-hold" buttons), timing out user input or communication with other processes, etc. Timer callbacks are of type XtTimerCallbackProc (see Appendix B), and are called once when their timeout expires. A timer callback may register itself to be called again if it needs to be called repeatedly.

Timer callbacks are processed automatically by XtAppMainLoop. If you write your own main loop, you should use XtAppNextEvent or XtProcessEvent to properly dispatch timeouts. A timeout is automatically canceled after invoking its callback, but can be canceled before it expires with XtRemoveTimeOut.

CAUTION

The Intrinsics check for expired timeouts synchronously each time through the main loop. Timeouts do not signal asynchronously, so there is no guarantee that a timer callback is invoked "immediately" when the specified interval has passed. Applications that plan to cancel timeouts explicitly should keep a list of active timeouts, as it is an error to attempt to cancel a timeout after it has expired.

SEE ALSO

Routines: XtAppMainLoop, XtAppNextEvent, XtAppPending, XtAppProcessEvent,
            XtRemoveTimeOut

XtAppAddWorkProc (R3)

Registers a callback to be invoked when the toolkit has nothing more important to do

SYNOPSIS

```
XtWorkProcId XtAppAddWorkProc(app_context, work_proc, client_data)
        XtAppContext                    app_context;
        XtWorkProc                      work_proc;
        XtPointer                       client_data;
```

ARGUMENTS

app_context	in	Application context within which work procedure is registered.
work_proc	in	Work procedure to be called while XtAppNextEvent is waiting for events.
client_data	in	Application-defined data to be passed to work procedure when it is executed.

DESCRIPTION

XtAppAddWorkProc registers a work procedure within the specified application context, and returns a unique identifier for the work proc/client_data pair. The specified procedure is placed at the head of the application queue of work procedures, and is called whenever XtAppNextEvent finds no X events, timeouts or alternate input to process. If the work procedure returns False, it is placed back at the head of the queue for re-execution, and is called repeatedly as long as XtAppNextEvent is waiting for other input. When it returns True, it is removed from the execution queue. The specified *client_data* is passed as the first argument to the work procedure each time it is called, and may be a single longword value or, more commonly, a pointer to an application-defined data structure, cast as type XtPointer.

USAGE

Work procedures are used to do some computing without impacting the user interface. Though a work proc could perform a purely computational task, a more common use is creating parts of a user interface that do not need to be immediately visible at application startup. This decreases apparent application startup time.

Work procedures execute in the application thread of execution; they are *not* forked off as child processes. A work procedure should compute a bit, save its state and return False, waiting to be called again. When called again, it should resume at the point at which it left off, and compute a bit more. When a work procedure is finished computing it should return True.

A work procedure is of type XtWorkProc (see Appendix B). A work procedure can register another work procedure, but the new work procedure will be at a lower priority in the execution queue. Work procedures registered with XtAppAddWorkProc can be explicitly canceled with XtRemoveWorkProc. A work procedure should return True to cancel itself.

CAUTION

Work procedures are not time-sliced or executed in round-robin order; the procedure at the head of the queue is executed repeatedly until it returns True or is removed explicitly. The Intrinsics do not provide any notification when a work proc has finished, nor is there any way to query how many work procs are queued. You are responsible for providing any synchronization between the results of a work procedure and other elements in a user interface, including other work procedures. Any state that must be saved between successive calls to a work proc must be passed through the *client_data* or global variables.

Work procedures must return quickly (on the order of 100 milliseconds, say), or the user interface may not be able to keep up with arriving X events and other input sources. There is no safe way to interrupt a work procedure while it is executing, so you must carefully choose the criteria that it uses to decide when it has computed "enough". Work procedures lend themselves mainly to tasks that can be divided into small, discrete chunks.

Because of these issues, work procedures are not a good substitute for multi-tasking or threads. Long computational jobs should generally be forked as child processes, and should communicate with the parent through pipes or sockets registered as input sources.

SEE ALSO

Routines: `XtAppMainLoop, XtAppNextEvent, XtAppProcessEvent, XtRemoveWorkProc`

XtAppCreateShell (R3)

Creates a parentless shell to root an application widget tree

SYNOPSIS

```
Widget XtAppCreateShell( app_name, app_class, widget_class, display,
    args, num_args )
            String                      app_name;
            String                      app_class;
            WidgetClass                 widget_class;
            Display                     *display;
            ArgList                     args;
            Cardinal                    num_args;
```

ARGUMENTS

app_name	in	Resource name of the application instance to be rooted by the new shell, e.g. "myApp".
app_class	in	Resource class of the application instance to be rooted by the new shell, e.g. "MyApp".
widget_class	in	Class pointer specifying type of widget to create. Must specify a subclass of Shell (usually applicationShellWidgetClass).
display	in	Specifies display on which shell is to be created.
args	in	An array of Args specifying resources to override declarations in resource files or the command line.
num_args	in	Number of name/value pairs in *args*.

DESCRIPTION

XtAppCreateShell creates a shell of the specified class on the specified display, and returns its widget ID. The shell has a NULL parent and is used to root an application's widget instance tree. Resources supplied in *args* set the initial state of the shell, and override values declared in resource files or command-line arguments. If *widget_class* is NULL, or is not a subclass of Shell, XtAppCreateShell issues a fatal error.

USAGE

XtAppCreateShell is used to create the first widget in an application widget tree. The *widget_class* argument is usually applicationShellWidgetClass in R4 and R5 applications, or sessionShellWidgetClass in R6 applications that wish to use session manager protocols.

The *app_name* and *app_class* arguments specify the name and class by which the shell will be known, and provide a root for all resource names in the application. By convention, these should be the same *app_name* and *app_class* specified in a previous call to XtOpenDisplay or XtDisplayInitialize. By convention, the application name starts with a lower-case letter and is the same as the program binary. The application class starts with an uppercase letter and is usually a permutation of the application name. Application resources to be fetched with XtGetApplicationResources and resources that apply to the shell itself should be specified in a resource file as follows:

> *app_name*.resource: **string**   or
> *app_class*.resource: **string**

Resources to apply to all widgets in the application may be specified as shown below:

> *app_name**resource: **string**   or
> *app_class**resource: **string**

Only one application shell should be created for each application instance on the display. If you require multiple "main" windows, or several secondary windows, they may be created with XtCreatePopupShell.

XtVaAppCreateShell is the varargs variant of this routine. XtAppCreateShell replaces the routine XtCreateApplicationShell used in earlier releases of the Intrinsics.

CAUTION

The *app_name* and *app_class* arguments should be the same as those specified in a previous call to XtOpenDisplay or XtDisplayInitialize.

SEE ALSO

Routines: XtAppInitialize, XtCreatePopupShell, XtDisplayInitialize,
            XtOpenDisplay, XtVaAppCreateShell

XtAppError (R3)

Calls the toolkit low-level error handler

SYNOPSIS

```
void XtAppError( app_context, message )
        XtAppContext                    app_context;
        String                          message;
```

ARGUMENTS

app_context	in	Application context within which error handler is registered.
message	in	NULL-terminated string specifying an error message to be displayed or logged.

DESCRIPTION

XtAppError calls the error handler currently registered by XtAppSetErrorHandler in the specified application context, or the default error handler if none has been registered. The error handler displays the specified message and then exits.

USAGE

The Intrinsics call XtAppError to report severe errors, and applications may do so also. Error handlers are of type XtErrorHandler (see Appendix B). A default error handler is automatically registered which logs the supplied message to stderr and calls exit(). If you need to perform other actions, such as neatly closing files or terminating network connections, you may register application-specific error handlers with XtAppSetErrorHandler.

XtAppError is useful for debugging, but the final version of an application should generally use XtAppErrorMsg instead, as it provides for user-customized messages.

CAUTION

XtAppError should be used sparingly, as it assumes by default that the user has a console connected to stderr. It is usually reserved for conditions that cannot be reported reliably through an application's normal user interface. Ordinary warnings regarding data entry errors, etc. should be presented in the user interface proper, perhaps in a long-term message area of the main window. An error handler is expected to call exit(), so a call to XtAppError will not return.

SEE ALSO

Routines: XtAppErrorMsg, XtAppSetErrorHandler, XtAppSetErrorMsgHandler

XtAppErrorMsg   (R3)

Calls the toolkit high-level error message handler

SYNOPSIS

```
void XtAppErrorMsg( app_context, name, type, class, default, params,
    num_params )
        XtAppContext              app_context;
        String                    name;
        String                    type;
        String                    class
        String                    default;
        String                    *params;
        Cardinal                  *num_params;
```

ARGUMENTS

app_context	in	Application context in which error message handler is established.
name	in	Resource name of message, e.g. "invalidClass".
type	in	Secondary resource name of message, e.g. "xtPopup".
class	in	Resource class of message, e.g. "XtToolkitError".
default	in	Default message to display if no match is found.
params	in	Pointer to a list of string values to be substituted in the error message when it is output.
num_params	in	Pointer to variable specifying number of string values in *params* list.

DESCRIPTION

XtAppErrorMsg calls the error message handler currently registered by XtAppSetErrorMsgHandler in the specified application context, or the default error message handler if none has been registered. The error message handler displays a message generated from the arguments, and then exits.

The *name*, *type* and *class* identify the message to be displayed, while *params* supplies details to be substituted in the error message text. All toolkit errors have the class "XtToolkitError". If a message is not found to match the specified *name* and *type*, the *default* argument message text is used.

Parameters specified in *params* are substituted into the error message using printf() formatting conventions. For example, if the entry in the error database resource file is:

name.type: Error message with one "%s" string substitution

the first string in *params* would be substituted for the "%s" in the message.

USAGE

An error message handler provides a more robust interface for error reporting than a simple error handler. Whereas an error handler simply logs the message that it is given, an error message handler accesses a resource database, looks up the appropriate message for the specified condition, and edits it to include specific details. This approach provides for more robust internationalization and customization of error messages.

Error message handler procedures are of type XtErrorMsgHandler (see Appendix B). The Intrinsics automatically register a default error message handler which looks up an error message with XtAppGetErrorDatabaseText, performs any required parameter substitution, and then calls XtAppError, passing the constructed message. If you need to perform other actions you may register an application-specific error message handler with XtAppSetErrorMsgHandler.

CAUTION

XtAppErrorMsg should be used sparingly, as it assumes by default that the user has a console connected to stderr. It is usually reserved for conditions that cannot be reported reliably through an application's normal user interface. Ordinary warnings regarding data entry errors, etc. should be presented in the user interface proper, perhaps in a long-term message area of the main window. An error message handler is expected to call exit(), so a call to XtAppErrorMsg will not return.

SEE ALSO

Routines: XtAppError, XtAppGetErrorDatabase, XtAppGetErrorDatabaseText,
           XtAppSetErrorMsgHandler

XtAppGetErrorDatabase   **(R3)**

Returns the error message database

SYNOPSIS

```
XrmDatabase *XtAppGetErrorDatabase( app_context )
        XtAppContext                 app_context;
```

ARGUMENTS

app_context   in   Application context in which database is registered.

DESCRIPTION

XtAppGetErrorDatabase returns a pointer to the resource database from which toolkit error and warning messages are extracted. This resource database is merged on POSIX-based systems from the resource file /usr/lib/X11/XtErrorDB.

USAGE

Toolkit error message handlers retrieve the text for error and warning messages from a resource database using the routine XtAppGetErrorDatabaseText. The routine XtAppGetErrorDatabase is provided so that you can directly retrieve messages from the database using Xlib "Xrm" routines, or merge it with other databases created by your application.

CAUTION

Note that this routine, unlike XtDatabase or XtScreenDatabase, returns the *address* of an XrmDatabase. The error database is not actually merged from the source resource file until the first call to XtAppGetErrorDatabaseText. Prior to this, the contents of the database are undefined.

SEE ALSO

Routines: XtAppErrorMsg, XtAppGetErrorDatabaseText, XtAppSetErrorMsgHandler, XtAppSetWarningMsgHandler, XtAppWarningMsg

XtAppGetErrorDatabaseText (R3)

Fetches an error message from the message database

SYNOPSIS

```
void XtAppGetErrorDatabaseText( app_context, name, type, class, default,
    buffer_return, buffer_size, database )
        XtAppContext                    app_context;
        String                          name;
        String                          type;
        String                          class;
        String                          default;
        char                            *buffer_return;
        int                             buffer_size;
        XrmDatabase                     database;
```

ARGUMENTS

app_context	in	Application context in which error database is found.
name	in	Resource name of message, e.g. "invalidClass".
type	in	Secondary resource name of message, e.g. "xtPopup".
class	in	Resource class of message, e.g. "XtToolkitError".
default	in	A default message to be returned if the requested message is not found.
buffer_return	in/out	Address of a buffer to hold the returned message string.
buffer_size	in	Size of *buffer_return*, in bytes.
database	in	Application private resource database to query, or NULL if the default error database should be used.

DESCRIPTION

XtAppGetErrorDatabaseText retrieves the message specified by *name*, *type* and *class* from the specified XrmDatabase, or from the default error database if *database* is not specified. On POSIX-based systems, the default database is merged from the file /usr/lib/X11/XtErrorDB on the first call to XtAppGetErrorDatabaseText.

The resource name for a message is generated by concatenating *name* and *type*, in that order, separated by a period ("."). When used to retrieve error messages, *name* usually specifies a general error, and *type* specifies more particular information, often the name of the routine that generated the error. The resource class for all toolkit error messages is "XtToolkitError".

USAGE

XtAppGetErrorDatabaseText is used in warning and error message handlers to retrieve a message from a resource file. This makes it possible for the user to customize messages by rewriting the resource file, rather than recompiling the source code. Entries in an error message resource file are of the form:

```
name.type:  Error message with one "%s" string substitution
```

The substitution of any application-specific values for the "%s" is the responsibility of the caller. This is usually done by using the message string as the format for a call to printf() or sprintf().

To provide a private error database, use the Xlib routine `XrmReadFileDatabase` to read an application-specific resource file and merge it into an `XrmDatabase`. This can then be passed as the *database* argument to `XtAppGetErrorDatabaseText`.

If *database* is not specified, `XtAppGetErrorDatabaseText` searches the default error message database, so as an alternative, you could add entries to `/usr/lib/X11/XtErrorDB`. This may be risky since this file is liable to be modified during operating system or window system software upgrades.

You can register application-specific warning and error message handlers with `XtAppSetWarningMsgHandler` and `XtAppSetErrorMsgHandler`, respectively. The currently-registered warning or error message handler is invoked when `XtAppWarningMsg` or `XtAppErrorMsg` is called.

CAUTION

You must provide a large enough return buffer for the returned message. If the return buffer is too small the message will be truncated.

SEE ALSO

Routines: `XtAppErrorMsg, XtAppGetErrorDatabase, XtAppSetErrorMsgHandler, XtAppSetWarningMsgHandler, XtAppWarningMsg`

XtAppGetExitFlag (R6)

See if any thread has set the exit flag for XtAppMainLoop

SYNOPSIS

```
Boolean XtAppGetExitFlag( app_context )
        XtAppContext                    app_context;
```

ARGUMENTS

app_context   in   Application context in which main loop is running.

DESCRIPTION

XtAppGetExitFlag returns True if any thread (including the calling thread) has requested that XtAppMainLoop stop and return.

USAGE

In the pre-R6 Intrinsics, XtAppMainLoop would loop forever. This was a problem for applications that wanted to perform rundown functions before an exit, and did not wish to simply call exit() from within a callback routine. XtAppSetExitFlag sets a flag that is checked after each event dispatch. If the exit flag is True, XtAppMainLoop returns.

In the pre-R6 Intrinsics, XtAppMainLoop would loop forever. If you write your own variant of a main loop using the R6 Intrinsics, you should check the exit flag periodically with XtAppGetExitFlag and return if it has been set True.

In threaded applications, a thread that wishes to know whether another thread has expressed a desire to exit can call XtAppGetExitFlag to see if the exit flag has been set. By checking the exit flag, a thread can avoid performing a time-consuming operation that would be superfluous in the face of an impending exit.

CAUTION

None

SEE ALSO

Routines: XtAppSetExitFlag, XtAppMainLoop

XtAppGetSelectionTimeout   (R3)

Returns the selection timeout value, in milliseconds

SYNOPSIS

```
unsigned long XtAppGetSelectionTimeout( app_context )
        XtAppContext                    app_context;
```

ARGUMENTS

app_context   in   The application context within which the timeout applies.

DESCRIPTION

XtAppGetSelectionTimeout retrieves the current value of the selection timeout, expressed in milliseconds. The selection timeout is the interval within which two applications must respond to one another when using the toolkit selection mechanism. If a request for the selection is not honored within the selection timeout, the Intrinsics cancel the request. The initial timeout value is set by the "selectionTimeout" application resource, and defaults to five seconds if not otherwise specified.

USAGE

XtAppGetSelectionTimeout may be used to query the current value of the selection timeout. This may be useful for rejecting inappropriately large or small values specified as an application resource. The selection timeout value may be set with XtAppSetSelectionTimeout.

CAUTION

Setting the selection timeout value too high can adversely impact an application if selection cannot be accomplished for reasons other than an overloaded system. Setting the timeout value too low may render an application incapable of receiving the selection from other applications.

SEE ALSO

Routines: XtAppSetSelectionTimeout.

XtAppInitialize　　　　　　　　　　　　　　　　　**(R4O)**

Initializes the toolkit, opens a display and creates an application shell

SYNOPSIS

```
Widget XtAppInitialize( app_context, app_class, options, num_options,
    argc, argv, fallback_resources, args, num_args )
        XtAppContext          *app_context;
        String                app_class;
        XrmOptionDescList     options;
        Cardinal              num_options;
        int                   *argc;
        String                *argv;
        String                *fallback_resources;
        ArgList               args;
        Cardinal              num_args;
```

ARGUMENTS

app_context	in/out	Pointer to a variable to receive the new application context.
app_class	in	Resource class of the application.
options	in	Pointer to a list of option description records specifying command-line arguments that set resource values.
num_options	in	Number of option descriptors in the list.
argc	in/out	Pointer to a variable specifying the argument count provided to main() at image activation; returns the number of unparsed arguments remaining after XtAppInitialize has parsed *argv*.
argv	in/out	Argument vector provided to main() at image activation; returns all unparsed arguments.
fallback_resources	in	Resource values to be used if the application class resource file cannot be found or opened, expressed as a NULL-terminated list of strings in resource file format. NULL if no fallback resources are to be specified.
args	in	An array of Args that are to override any other resource specifications for the created Shell.
num_args	in	Number of resource name/value pairs in *args*.

DESCRIPTION

XtAppInitialize is a convenience routine that calls XtToolkitInitialize, XtCreateApplicationContext, XtAppSetFallbackResources, XtOpenDisplay and XtAppCreateShell in turn, and returns the widget ID of a new application shell. Arguments are used as they are in the separate routines which XtAppInitialize replaces. The new application context is returned by side-effect in the *app_context* argument. The display pointer is not returned directly, but may be found by calling XtDisplay and passing the widget ID of the new shell. XtAppInitialize merges the per-display and per-screen resource databases; for more information on how this is performed, see XtDisplayInitialize. If the display cannot be opened, XtAppInitialize issues a fatal error.

USAGE

The shell returned by XtAppInitialize is used as the root for an application's widget tree. XtAppInitialize is used as a single, blanket initialization routine by R4 and R5 applications that require a single application context, display and application shell.

XtAppInitialize replaces the convenience routine XtInitialize used in earlier releases of the Intrinsics. XtVaAppInitialize is the varargs variant of this routine. As of R6, XtAppInitialize is itself superseded by XtOpenApplication.

CAUTION

XtAppInitialize calls XtToolkitInitialize, and therefore may only be called once. XtAppInitialize assumes that the application name is *argv[0]*, the name of the program itself. This is overridden by the value of the environment variable RESOURCE_NAME, if it is defined, or the name specified by the -name command-line option. XtAppInitialize assumes that the class of the new shell should be applicationShellWidgetClass.

SEE ALSO

Routines: XtAppCreateShell, XtAppSetFallbackResources, XtCreateApplicationContext, XtDisplayInitialize, XtInitialize, XtOpenDisplay, XtToolkitInitialize, XtVaAppInitialize, XtOpenApplication

XtAppLock (R6)

Locks thread access to an application context and all related displays and widgets

SYNOPSIS

```
void XtAppLock( app_context )
        XtAppContext                            app_context;
```

ARGUMENTS

app_context   in   The application context to be locked.

DESCRIPTION

XtAppLock locks access to the specified application context, including all of its displays and widgets. XtAppLock blocks until it acquires the lock. A thread may assert a lock more than once, and the locks are cumulative. A thread must release the lock as many times as it has acquired it before the lock becomes accessible to other threads.

USAGE

XtAppLock and XtAppUnlock may be used to construct thread-safe toolkit programs. Before taking any action that would affect the application context, a display or a widget, a thread is expected to call XtAppLock. If another thread attempts to acquire the lock, that thread will block until the lock has been released. After a successful completion of the change, the thread must call XtAppUnlock.

This is done internally by the Intrinsics routines that access such structures, so there is usually no need for you to call XtAppLock. The exceptions are applications that call resource converters directly, and those cases in which it is desirable to have a series of Intrinsics routines act as an atomic operation. Special widget access functions that do not use the normal Intrinsics methods, but go straight to widget data structures, must be sure to acquire the lock before doing so.

CAUTION

Locking is enforced only if participating threads follow the convention of acquiring the lock with XtAppLock before accessing the locked data structures. There is really nothing to stop a thread from accessing a locked structure if it ignores the convention and accesses it directly. Threads that access locked structures through the normal Intrinsics routines (XtManageChild, XtSetValues, etc.) do not have to worry about this, because the Intrinsics routines themselves enforce the convention. Threaded applications must call XtToolkitThreadInitialize to initialize thread support before calling XtAppLock or XtAppUnlock.

SEE ALSO

Routines: XtToolkitThreadInitialize, XtAppUnlock, XtProcessLock, XtProcessUnlock

XtAppMainLoop   **(R3)**

Starts the main event processing loop

SYNOPSIS

```
void XtAppMainLoop( app_context )
        XtAppContext                    app_context;
```

ARGUMENTS

app_context   in   Application context from which to retrieve and dispatch events.

DESCRIPTION

XtAppMainLoop starts the widget event parsing loop within the specified application context. XtAppMainLoop does not return, being simply an endless loop of XtAppNextEvent and XtDispatchEvent. X events are processed in the order in which they are received from displays within the application context. Timeouts, signal sources (R6) and input sources are checked each time through the loop. Work procedures are executed whenever there are no other events to process.

USAGE

XtAppMainLoop is the only event processing routine required by most applications. You should call XtAppMainLoop after the initial widget tree has been created, managed and realized. In versions of the Intrinsics prior to R6, XtAppMainLoop does not return, so application code following XtAppMainLoop will never be reached. In R6, you can call XtAppSetExitFlag, causing XtAppMainLoop to exit as soon as it is safe to do so.

If you must check execution flags or poll other devices you may feel free to implement your own version of MainLoop using XtAppNextEvent, XtAppPending, XtAppProcessEvent, XtAppPeekEvent and XtDispatchEvent.

CAUTION

If all of the widgets associated with a given application context are destroyed or unrealized, but XtAppMainLoop has not exited, your application can be left in a state in which it waits for events but has no windows to deliver them nor widgets to process them. This can also happen if XtAppMainLoop is entered prematurely - that is, before any widgets have been realized.

Applications which employ more than one application context must of necessity supply their own implementation of MainLoop, since XtAppMainLoop only handles events in a single application context.

SEE ALSO

Routines: XtAppAddInput, XtAppAddTimeOut, XtAppAddWorkProc, XtAppNextEvent,
            XtAppPeekEvent, XtAppPending, XtAppProcessEvent, XtDispatchEvent,
            XtAppSetExitFlag, XtAppGetExitFlag

XtAppNextEvent   (R3)

Returns the next X event and removes it from the input queue

SYNOPSIS

```
void XtAppNextEvent( app_context, event )
        XtAppContext                    app_context;
        XEvent                          *event;
```

ARGUMENTS

app_context	in	Application context specifying display(s) from which events are to be delivered.
event	in/out	Pointer to an XEvent structure to receive the returned event.

DESCRIPTION

XtAppNextEvent examines the input queues associated with the specified application context, and copies the next X event into *event*, removing it from the head of the input queue. If no X events are found, XtAppNextEvent flushes the output buffer for each display in the application context, and waits for the next event.

While waiting, XtAppNextEvent executes the latest work procedure, if any, registered with XtAppAddWorkProc. If any alternate input sources registered with XtAppAddInput are waiting, or timeouts registered with XtAppAddTimeOut have expired, or signal callbacks registered with XtAppAddSignal have been noticed, their associated callback procedures are invoked.

XtAppNextEvent can handle multiple displays if they are registered in the same application context. The order in which displays are handled is undefined; however, the Intrinsics guarantee that no one display will be able to saturate the input stream to the exclusion of another.

USAGE

XtAppMainLoop calls XtAppNextEvent and XtDispatchEvent in an endless loop. You may call XtAppNextEvent explicitly if you provide your own version of main loop. X events returned by XtAppNextEvent are usually dispatched with XtDispatchEvent.

CAUTION

The caller is responsible for allocating storage for the return XEvent structure.

SEE ALSO

Routines: XtAppAddInput, XtAppAddTimeOut, XtAppAddWorkProc, XtAppMainLoop, XtAppPeekEvent, XtAppPending, XtAppProcessEvent, XtDispatchEvent

XtAppPeekEvent

(R3)

Returns the next X event without removing it from the input queue

SYNOPSIS

```
Boolean XtAppPeekEvent( app_context, event )
        XtAppContext              app_context;
        XEvent                    *event;
```

ARGUMENTS

app_context	in	Application context specifying display(s) from which X events are to be delivered.
event	in/out	Pointer to XEvent structure to receive returned event.

DESCRIPTION

If an X event is found at the head of the input queue, XtAppPeekEvent copies it into *event* and returns True. The event is not removed from the input queue. If no events are found, XtAppPeekEvent flushes the output buffer for each display in the application context, and waits for the next input from any source.

If the next event received is an X event, XtAppPeekEvent copies it into *event* without removing it from the input queue, and returns True. Otherwise, it is some other kind of input, and XtAppPeekEvent returns False.

USAGE

XtAppPeekEvent could be used to implement application-specific main loops; however, this is rare. usually you'll want to get the event off the queue and will find XtAppNextEvent or XtAppProcessEvent more useful.

CAUTION

You are responsible for allocating storage for the return XEvent structure.

SEE ALSO

Routines: XtAppAddInput, XtAppAddTimeOut, XtAppMainLoop, XtAppNextEvent, XtAppPending, XtDispatchEvent, XtAppProcessEvent

XtAppPending (R3)

Reports which X events, timeouts, signals or other input sources are waiting

SYNOPSIS

```
XtInputMask XtAppPending( app_context )
        XtAppContext                    app_context;
```

ARGUMENTS

app_context   in   Application context to be checked for pending events.

DESCRIPTION

XtAppPending returns non-zero if there are any X events, alternate input events, signals (R6), or expired timeout events waiting in any input queue(s) associated with the specified application context. The value returned is a mask which is the bitwise inclusive OR of XtIMXEvent, XtIMTimer, XtIMAlternateInput, and XtIMSignal (R6), depending on what type(s) of input are waiting. If there are no events waiting, XtAppPending flushes the output buffer for each display in the application context and returns zero.

USAGE

This routine can be used as a filter to control whether an application-supplied main loop executes. This can be used to build non-blocking variants of main loop that work with multiple application contexts, or need to be temporarily executed within a callback routine (see Chapter 9). Example:

```
XtInputMask mask;
while (mask = XtAppPending(app_context)) {
    XtAppProcessEvent(app_context, mask);
}
```

CAUTION

Mini-main loops inside callback routines should be used with great caution, if at all, to avoid the possibility of arbitrarily deep recursive calls to XtDispatchEvent. They are safe only if you know that an event could not be delivered that would invoke yet another instance of the blocking callback routine. XtAppPending does not tell you how many events of a particular type are waiting, so it could be one or many.

SEE ALSO

Routines: XtAppMainLoop, XtAppNextEvent, XtAppPeekEvent, XtDispatchEvent,
          XtAppProcessEvent, XtAppAddInput, XtAppAddTimeOut

XtAppProcessEvent (R3)

Processes a single X event, timeout, signal or alternate input source

SYNOPSIS

```
void XtAppProcessEvent( app_context, input_mask )
        XtAppContext                 app_context;
        XtInputMask                  input_mask;
```

ARGUMENTS

app_context	in	Application context in which events are to be handled.
input_mask	in	Bitwise OR of XtIMXEvent, XtIMTimer, XtIMSignal (R6) and/or XtIMAlternateInput, specifying acceptable input type(s) to be processed. The symbolic value XtIMAll is the bitwise OR of all types.

DESCRIPTION

XtAppProcessEvent processes the next X event, alternate input event, signal callback (R6), or expired timeout in the specified application context. Only a single event, which must match the input mask, is processed. If *input_mask* specifies multiple input types, it is undefined which type will be processed. If no input is found matching the input mask, XtAppProcessEvent blocks until there is.

XtAppProcessEvent processes alternate input events by calling the callback routine registered with XtAppAddInput. Timeouts are processed by calling the callback routine registered with XtAppAddTimeOut. Signals are processed by calling the callback routine registered with XtAppAddSignal (R6). X events are processed with XtDispatchEvent.

USAGE

XtAppProcessEvent is used by applications that supply their own implementation of XtAppMainLoop. XtAppProcessEvent is often used together with XtAppPending to build a non-blocking event loop that clears the event queue. This might also be done to establish priority in handling certain kinds of event; for example, all alternate input sources might be cleared before any X events are processed.

```
XtAppContext context;
while(XtAppPending(context) && XtIMAlternateInput){
  XtProcessEvent(context, XtIMAlternateInput);
}
```

CAUTION

If you write your own main loop using XtProcessEvent, you should generally check to see what kinds of input are waiting with XtAppPending. Timeouts and signal callbacks, despite their presumed urgency, will not be processed unless you set the mask bit that says to handle them.

SEE ALSO

Routines: XtAppMainLoop, XtAppNextEvent, XtAppPeekEvent, XtAppPending, XtDispatchEvent, XtAppAddInput, XtAppAddTimeOut, XtAppAddSignal

XtAppReleaseCacheRefs (R4)

Frees a reference to a resource conversion result

SYNOPSIS

```
void XtAppReleaseCacheRefs( app_context, refs )
        XtAppContext                    app_context;
        XtCacheRef                      *cache_refs;
```

ARGUMENTS

app_context	in	Application context within which resource converters are registered.
cache_refs	in	NULL-terminated list of conversion cache references to be released.

DESCRIPTION

XtAppReleaseCacheRefs decrements the reference count for each resource conversion result described by a cache reference in *cache_refs*. If the reference count for a particular conversion result reaches zero, the Intrinsics call the XtDestructor procedure registered for that conversion by XtSetTypeConverter or XtAppSetTypeConverter, and the conversion result is removed from the cache.

USAGE

When a toolkit resource is converted with a new-format type converter, the results of a particular conversion may be cached for future reference. If the same conversion is requested at a later time, the result is available without the possible computational overhead and round-trips to the server required to perform the conversion again. If a type converter is registered with a *cache_type* argument modified by XtCacheRefCount, a cached value is maintained only as long as there are outstanding references to it.

XtAppReleaseCacheRefs is used only if you explicitly wish to track the resource conversion cache reference count. This is rare; very few converters really benefit from caching, and the Intrinsics normally track cache reference counts internally (see XtSetTypeConverter). The only way you could get a cache reference explicitly would be to XtCallConverter. There is seldom a reason for normal applications to use this routine, so the opportunities to use XtAppReleaseCacheRefs are equally rare.

CAUTION

None

SEE ALSO

Routines: XtCallConverter, XtConvertAndStore, XtSetTypeConverter,
        XtAppSetTypeConverter

XtAppSetErrorHandler   **(R3)**

Registers a toolkit low-level error handler

SYNOPSIS

```
XtErrorHandler XtAppSetErrorHandler( app_context, error_handler )
        XtAppContext              app_context;
        XtErrorHandler            error_handler;
```

ARGUMENTS

app_context   in   Application context within which error handler applies.

error_handler   in   New error handler to be established.

DESCRIPTION

XtAppSetErrorHandler establishes a new error handler within the scope of the specified application context, and returns a pointer to the previously-installed error handler. When a toolkit severe error condition is detected (that is, the application or a toolkit internal routine calls XtAppError) control is passed to the specified procedure.

USAGE

Error handler procedures are of type XtErrorHandler (see Appendix B), and are expected to display an error message when called, and then exit. The currently-registered error handler is invoked with XtAppError. The Intrinsics automatically register a default error handler that logs the supplied message to stderr and calls exit().

   If you must perform other actions, such as neatly closing files or terminating network connections, you may register an application-specific error handler with XtAppSetErrorHandler. Since a toolkit error usually implies a serious condition, an error handler should report the error and then exit. XtAppSetErrorHandler returns the address of the previously-registered error handler so that it may be re-registered at a future time, if desired. Handlers to be invoked on non-fatal conditions are registered with XtAppSetWarningHandler.

CAUTION

An application-supplied error handler should exit; otherwise, your application may try to continue execution on serious toolkit errors. You are responsible for properly defining error and warning conditions, and treating them appropriately.

   In the Release 3 Intrinsics, this routine was defined as type void, and did not return the previously-registered handler.

SEE ALSO

Routines: XtAppError, XtAppErrorMsg, XtAppSetErrorMsgHandler

XtAppSetErrorMsgHandler (R3)

Registers a toolkit high-level error message handler

SYNOPSIS

```
XtErrorMsgHandler XtAppSetErrorMsgHandler(app_context, error_msg_handler)
        XtAppContext                app_context;
        XtErrorMsgHandler           error_msg_handler;
```

ARGUMENTS

app_context	in	Application context within which error message handler applies.
error_msg_handler	in	New error message handler to be established.

DESCRIPTION

XtAppSetErrorMsgHandler establishes a new error message handler within the scope of the specified application context, and returns a pointer to the previously installed error message handler. When a toolkit severe error condition is detected (that is, the application or a toolkit internal routine calls XtAppErrorMsg) control is passed to the specified procedure.

USAGE

An error message handler provides a more robust interface for error reporting than a simple error handler. Whereas an error handler simply logs the message that it is given, an error message handler accesses a resource database, looks up the appropriate error message for a specified condition, and edits it to include specific details. This approach provides for easier internationalization and customization of error messages.

XtAppErrorMsg invokes the currently-registered error message handler. The Intrinsics automatically register a default error message handler which looks up "standard" error messages and then calls XtAppError, passing the constructed message. Error messages are defined by default in the file /usr/lib/X11/XtErrorDB, and are retrieved from the resource database with XtAppGetErrorDatabaseText.

If you need to perform other actions you may register an application-specific error message handler with XtAppSetErrorMsgHandler. Error message handlers are of type XtErrorMessageHandler (see Appendix B). XtAppSetErrorMsgHandler returns the address of the previously-registered error message handler so that it may be re-registered at a future time, if desired. Message handlers to be invoked on non-fatal conditions are registered with XtAppSetWarningMsgHandler.

CAUTION

An application-supplied error message handler should exit, or pass control to the current error handler by calling XtAppError. Otherwise, your application may try to continue execution on a serious toolkit errors. You are responsible for properly defining error and warning conditions, and treating them appropriately.

In the Release 3 Intrinsics, this routine was defined as type void, and did not return the previously-registered handler.

SEE ALSO

Routines: XtAppError, XtAppErrorMsg, XtAppSetErrorHandler,
        XtAppGetErrorDatabase, XtAppGetErrorDatabaseText

XtAppSetExitFlag   **(R6)**

Tells XtAppMainLoop to stop and return as soon as it is safe to do so

SYNOPSIS

```
void XtAppSetExitFlag( app_context )
        XtAppContext                    app_context;
```

ARGUMENTS

app_context   in   Application context.

DESCRIPTION

XtAppSetExitFlag sets a flag that is checked by XtAppMainLoop immediately after each event dispatch. This flag is normally False. If the exit flag is set to True, XtAppMainLoop exits. Calling XtAppSetExitFlag expresses the application's desire to exit the main loop as soon as it is safe to do so.

USAGE

In the pre-R6 Intrinsics, XtAppMainLoop loops forever. This is a problem for applications that want to perform rundown functions before an exit, and do not wish to simply call exit() from within a callback routine. It is also an issue for multi-threaded applications in which it may not be safe to simply exit without synchronizing with other threads. XtAppSetExitFlag tells the Intrinsics that you would like to return from XtAppMainLoop. XtAppMainLoop returns as soon as the current event dispatch is complete. If you write your own variant of a main loop, you should check the exit flag periodically with XtAppGetExitFlag and return if it has been set True.

In threaded applications, a thread that wishes to know whether another thread has expressed a desire to exit can call XtAppGetExitFlag to see if the exit flag has been set. By checking, a thread might avoid performing a time-consuming operation that would be superfluous in the face of an impending exit.

CAUTION

None

SEE ALSO

Routines: XtAppGetExitFlag

XtAppSetFallbackResources   (R4)

Sets fallback resources to use if application defaults file is not found

SYNOPSIS

```
void XtAppSetFallbackResources( app_context, spec_list )
        XtAppContext              app_context;
        String                    *fallback_resources;
```

ARGUMENTS

app_context	in	Application context in which fallback resources should apply.
fallback_resources	in	NULL-terminated array of strings specifying resources in resource-file format.

DESCRIPTION

XtAppSetFallbackResources registers a list of resource definitions to be used in place of the class-specific resource file if the actual file cannot be found or cannot be opened when a display is initialized in the application context.

USAGE

In an effort to make software development easier and installations more flexible, developers are encouraged to specify many resources in a program's class-specific resource file, often called the "app-defaults" file. Unfortunately, this is one more file to keep track of. If it cannot be loaded at run time, perhaps due to a system administration problem, an application could be deprived of a great deal of important information, including the geometry of controls, labels on buttons, etc.

Fallback resources are used to define a minimal set of resources that would render a program usable even if its defaults file is misplaced or inaccessible. Usually you'll construct the fallback resources as a static list of strings that mirror the application defaults file. The string list must be terminated by a NULL string.

XtAppSetFallbackResources should be called explicitly before you call XtOpenDisplay to open the display, but is called implicitly if you pass fallback resources to XtAppInitialize or XtOpenApplication (R6). Fallback resources override a widget's default resource values, but are overridden by values declared in other resource files, command-line arguments or widget creation/manipulation arglists.

CAUTION

XtAppSetFallbackResources must be called before XtOpenDisplay or XtDisplayInitialize, but must be called after XtCreateApplicationContext. The fallback resource list must be terminated by a NULL string, or a system error will result. Fallback resources are "all or nothing"; they are not used if an application's class-specific resource file is found, even if this file holds bad values, or no values at all.

SEE ALSO

Routines: XtAppInitialize, XtOpenDisplay, XtDisplayInitialize

XtAppSetSelectionTimeout   (R3)

Sets value of selection timeout

SYNOPSIS

```
void XtAppSetSelectionTimeout( app_context, timeout )
        XtAppContext                  app_context;
        unsigned long                 timeout;
```

ARGUMENTS

app_context	in	Application context within which the timeout value applies.
timeout	in	Selection timeout in milliseconds.

DESCRIPTION

XtAppSetSelectionTimeout sets the selection timeout value, expressed in milliseconds. The timeout value set by XtAppSetSelectionTimeout is valid in the specified application context.

USAGE

The selection timeout is the interval, expressed in milliseconds, within which applications must respond to each another when using the toolkit selection mechanism. If a request for the selection is not honored within the selection timeout, the Intrinsics cancel the request. The initial timeout value is set by the "selectionTimeout" application resource and defaults to five seconds if not otherwise specified.

The selection timeout may be adjusted upwards if server communications are slow, or if the server or application engines are overloaded. It could also be set to a very high value while debugging code that performs toolkit selection, when the requester or owner might be expected to linger in breakpoints. The current value of the selection timeout may be queried with XtAppGetSelectionTimeout.

CAUTION

Setting the selection timeout value too high can adversely impact an application if selection cannot be accomplished for reasons other than an overloaded system. Setting the timeout value too low may render an application incapable of receiving the selection from other applications.

SEE ALSO

Routines: XtAppGetSelectionTimeout

XtAppSetTypeConverter (R4)

Registers a new-format resource type converter

SYNOPSIS

```
void XtAppSetTypeConverter( app_context, from_type, to_type, converter,
    convert_args, num_args, cache_type, destructor )
        XtAppContext              app_context;
        String                    from_type;
        String                    to_type;
        XtTypeConverter           converter;
        XtConvertArgList          convert_args;
        Cardinal                  num_args;
        XtCacheType               cache_type;
        XtDestructor              destructor;
```

ARGUMENTS

app_context	in	Application context within which converter is registered.
from_type	in	String identifying the source data type for the conversion, e.g. "String", or the symbolic constant XtRString.
to_type	in	String identifying the destination data type for the conversion, e.g. "Int", or the symbolic constant XtRInt.
converter	in	Resource type converter to be registered.
convert_args	in	Argument specifying how to compute additional arguments to be supplied to the converter, or NULL.
num_args	in	Number of additional arguments supplied to the converter by *convert_args*, or zero if none.
cache_type	in	Specifies whether conversion result is saved for later reference. Possible values: XtCacheNone, XtCacheAll, XtCacheByDisplay. May be modified by ORing with XtCacheRefCount.
destructor	in	Procedure called to release this type of resource when the reference count for a particular conversion goes to zero.

DESCRIPTION

XtAppSetTypeConverter registers a new-format resource type converter within the application context specified by *app_context*. All other arguments are used as they are in XtSetTypeConverter.

USAGE

Type converters are usually registered by a widget programmer to provide for the conversion of widget-specific resource types. This allows the toolkit to convert the strings found in resource files to the appropriate internal representation when a widget is created. Widgets register converters when the first widget of a particular class is created, or when an application programmer calls XtInitializeWidgetClass. If you define your own data types for application resources, you should register converters for these types before calling XtGetApplicationResources.

Type converters are usually registered for all application contexts with `XtSetTypeConverter`. `XtAppSetTypeConverter` may be used if a converter should be specific to a particular application context. For more information about type converters see the discussion under `XtSetTypeConverter`.

CAUTION

See `XtSetTypeConverter`.

SEE ALSO

Routines: `XtAppReleaseCacheRefs, XtCallbackReleaseCacheRefList, XtCallbackReleaseCacheRef, XtCallConverter, XtConvertAndStore, XtSetTypeConverter`

XtAppSetWarningHandler (R3)

Registers a toolkit low-level warning handler

SYNOPSIS

```
XtErrorHandler XtAppSetWarningHandler( app_context, warning_handler )
        XtAppContext                    app_context;
        XtErrorHandler                  warning_handler;
```

ARGUMENTS

app_context   in   Application context within which warning handler applies.

warning_handler in   ·   New warning handler to be established.

DESCRIPTION

DESCRIPTION

XtAppSetWarningHandler establishes a new warning handler within the scope of the specified application context, and returns a pointer to the previously-installed warning handler. When a toolkit non-fatal error condition is detected (that is, the application or a toolkit internal routine calls XtAppWarning) control is passed to the specified procedure.

USAGE

Warning handlers are of type XtErrorHandler (see Appendix B), and are expected to display a message when called. The currently-registered warning handler is invoked with XtAppWarning. The Intrinsics automatically register a default warning handler that logs the supplied message to stderr and returns.

If you must perform other actions, such as neatly closing files or terminating network connections, you may register an application-specific warning handler with XtAppSetWarningHandler. Since a toolkit warning usually implies a recoverable condition, a warning handler should report the error, take fixup action if appropriate, and then return. XtAppSetWarningHandler returns the address of the previously-registered warning handler so that it may be re-registered at a future time, if desired. Handlers to be invoked on fatal conditions are registered with XtAppSetErrorHandler.

CAUTION

You are responsible for properly distinguishing between error and warning conditions, and treating them appropriately. In the Release 3 Intrinsics, this routine was defined as type void, and did not return the previously-registered handler.

SEE ALSO

Routines: XtAppSetWarningMsgHandler, XtAppWarning, XtAppWarningMsg

XtAppSetWarningMsgHandler　　　(R3)

Registers a toolkit high-level warning message handler

SYNOPSIS

```
XtErrorMsgHandler XtAppSetWarningMsgHandler( app_context,
    warning_msg_handler )
        XtAppContext              app_context;
        XtErrorMsgHandler         warning_msg_handler;
```

ARGUMENTS

app_context　　　　　in　　　Application context within which warning message handler is to be established.

warning_msg_handler　in　　　New warning message handler to be established.

DESCRIPTION

`XtAppSetWarningMsgHandler` establishes a new warning message handler within the scope of the specified application context, and returns a pointer to the previously installed warning message handler. When a toolkit warning condition is detected (that is, when the application or a toolkit internal routine calls `XtAppWarningMsg`) control is passed to the specified procedure.

USAGE

A warning message handler provides a more robust interface for error reporting than a simple warning handler. Whereas a warning handler simply logs the message that it is given, a warning message handler accesses a resource database, looks up the appropriate warning message for a specified condition, and edits it to include specific details. This approach provides for more robust internationalization and customization of warning messages.

　　Warning message handlers are of type `XtErrorMsgHandler` (see Appendix B). The currently-registered warning message handler is invoked by a call to `XtAppWarningMsg`. The Intrinsics automatically register a default warning message handler which looks up "standard" warning messages and then calls `XtAppWarning` to take further action, including displaying the message. Warning messages are usually defined in the file `/usr/lib/X11/XtErrorDB`, and are retrieved from the resource database with `XtAppGetErrorDatabaseText`.

　　If you need to perform other actions you should register application-specific warning message handlers with `XtAppSetWarningMsgHandler`. `XtAppSetWarningMsgHandler` returns the address of the previously-registered warning message handler so that it may be re-registered at a future time, if desired. Message handlers to be invoked on fatal conditions are registered with `XtAppSetErrorMsgHandler`.

CAUTION

You are responsible for properly distinguishing error and warning conditions, and treating them appropriately. In the Release 3 Intrinsics, this routine was defined as type `void`, and did not return the previously-registered handler.

SEE ALSO

Routines:　`XtAppGetErrorDatabaseText, XtAppSetWarningHandler, XtAppWarning,`
　　　　　`XtAppWarningMsg`

XtAppUnlock   **(R6)**

Unlocks thread access to an application context and all related displays and widgets

SYNOPSIS

```
void XtAppUnlock( app_context )
        XtAppContext                    app_context;
```

ARGUMENTS

app_context   in   The application context to be unlocked.

DESCRIPTION

XtAppUnlock releases a lock formerly imposed on an application context by XtAppLock. A thread may assert a lock more than once, and the locks are cumulative. A thread must release the lock as many times as it has acquired it before the lock can be acquired other threads.

USAGE

XtAppLock and XtAppUnlock may be used to construct thread-safe toolkit programs. Before taking any action that would affect the application context, a display or a widget, a thread is expected to call XtAppLock. After a successful completion of the change, the thread must call XtAppUnlock. This is done internally by the Intrinsics routines that access such structures, so there is usually no need for you to call XtAppUnlock. The exceptions are applications that call resource converters directly, and cases in which it is desirable to have a series of Intrinsics routines act as an atomic operation. Special widget access functions that do not use the normal Intrinsics methods, but go straight to widget data structures, must be sure to acquire the lock before doing so.

CAUTION

Locking is enforced only if participating threads follow the convention of acquiring the lock with XtAppLock before accessing the locked data structures. There is really nothing to stop a thread from accessing a locked structure if it ignores the convention and accesses it directly. Threads that access locked structures through the normal Intrinsics routines (XtManageChild, XtSetValues, etc.) do not have to worry about this, because the Intrinsics routines themselves enforce the convention. Threaded applications must call XtToolkitThreadInitialize to initialize thread support before calling XtAppLock or XtAppUnlock.

SEE ALSO

Routines: XtToolkitThreadInitialize, XtAppLock, XtProcessLock,
           XtProcessUnlock

XtAppWarning

(R3)

Calls the toolkit low-level warning handler

SYNOPSIS

```
void XtAppWarning( app_context, message )
        XtAppContext                    app_context;
        String                          message;
```

ARGUMENTS

app_context   in   Application context in which warning handler is established.

message   in   NULL-terminated string specifying warning message to be displayed or logged.

DESCRIPTION

XtAppWarning calls the warning handler currently registered with XtAppSetWarningHandler in the specified application context, or the default warning handler if none has been registered. XtAppWarning returns after the specified warning message is displayed or logged.

USAGE

You can call XtAppWarning to report a simple warning message to the user. Control is passed to the currently-registered warning handler, which takes responsibility for displaying the message as appropriate to the system. Since a warning implies a recoverable condition, a warning handler reports the message, takes fixup action if appropriate, and then returns.

   The Intrinsics automatically register a default warning handler, which logs the warning message to stderr and returns. If you need to perform other actions you may register application-specific warning handlers with XtAppSetWarningHandler.

   XtAppWarning is useful for debugging, but the final version of an application should generally use XtAppWarningMsg instead, as it permits user-customized messages.

CAUTION

XtAppWarning should be used sparingly, as it assumes by default that the user has a console connected to stderr. It is usually reserved for conditions that cannot be reported reliably through an application's normal user interface. Ordinary warnings regarding data entry errors, etc. should be presented in the user interface proper, perhaps in a long-term message area of the main window.

SEE ALSO

Routines: XtAppSetWarningHandler, XtAppWarningMsg, XtAppSetWarningMsgHandler

XtAppWarningMsg (R3)

Calls the toolkit high-level warning message handler

SYNOPSIS

```
void XtAppWarningMsg( app_context, name, type, class, default, params,
    num_params )
        XtAppContext                app_context;
        String                      name;
        String                      type;
        String                      class
        String                      default;
        String                      *params;
        Cardinal                    *num_params;
```

ARGUMENTS

app_context	in	Application context in which warning message handler is established.
name	in	Resource name of message, e.g. "invalidChild".
type	in	Secondary resource name of message, e.g. "xtManageChildren".
class	in	Resource class of message, e.g. "XtToolkitError".
default	in	Default message to display if no match is found.
params	in	Pointer to a list of strings to be substituted in the warning message when it is output.
num_params	in	Pointer to a variable specifying the number of strings in *params*.

DESCRIPTION

XtAppWarningMsg calls the warning message handler currently registered with XtAppSetWarningMsgHandler in the specified application context, or the default warning message handler if none has been registered. The warning message handler displays the message generated from the arguments, and then returns. The default warning message handler constructs a warning message by consulting the error database (usually merged from /usr/lib/X11/XtErrorDB), and then returns.

Warning message handlers usually retrieve the message for a given *name*, *type* and *class* of warning by calling XtAppGetErrorDatabaseText. All toolkit warnings have the class "XtToolkitError". If an entry is not found to match the specified *name* and *type*, the *default* argument message text is used. Since a toolkit warning usually implies a recoverable condition, a warning message handler usually issues the appropriate warning message and then calls XtAppWarning to take fixup action, if any.

Parameters specified in *params* are substituted into the warning text string using printf() formatting conventions. For example, if the entry in the error database resource file is:

```
name.type:  Warning message with one "%s" string substitution
```

the first string in *params* would be substituted for the "%s" in the message.

USAGE

XtAppWarningMsg is used to report a warning message to the user. Control is passed to the currently-registered warning message handler, which takes responsibility for displaying the message as appropriate to the system. Since a warning implies a recoverable condition, a warning message handler reports the message, takes fixup action if appropriate, and then returns.

A warning message handler provides a more robust interface for error reporting than a simple warning handler. A warning handler simply logs the message that it is given, while a warning message handler accesses a resource database of messages, looks up the appropriate message for a specified condition, and edits it to include specific details. This approach provides for easier internationalization and customization of messages.

Warning message handler procedures are of type XtErrorMsgHandler. The Intrinsics automatically register a default warning message handler that looks up "standard" error messages and then calls XtAppWarning to take further action, including displaying the message. If you need to perform other actions you may register an application-specific warning message handler with XtAppSetWarningMsgHandler.

CAUTION

XtAppWarningMsg should be used sparingly, as it assumes by default that the user has a console connected to stderr. It is usually reserved for conditions that cannot be reported reliably through an application's normal user interface. Ordinary warnings regarding data entry errors, etc. should be presented in the user interface proper, perhaps in a long-term message area of the main window.

SEE ALSO

Routines: XtAppGetErrorDatabaseText, XtAppSetWarningMsgHandler, XtAppWarning

XtAugmentTranslations (R3)

Nondestructively adds translations to a widget's translation table

SYNOPSIS

```
void XtAugmentTranslations( w, translations )
        Widget                          w;
        XtTranslations                  translations;
```

ARGUMENTS

w   in   Widget to receive new translations; must be of class Core or any subclass thereof.

translations   in   Compiled translation table.

DESCRIPTION

XtAugmentTranslations non-destructively merges the specified translations into the existing widget translations, ignoring any #replace, #augment or #override directive that may have been specified in the translation string. If a new translation specifies an event sequence that matches one found in the widget's existing translations, the previously-existing translation remains intact.

USAGE

Every widget has a translation table that defines events or event sequences to be detected, and the actions that are executed in response. Default translations are defined by the widget class, but you can augment these so that the widget will invoke application-defined action procedures. If the actions supplied by a widget are documented, you may also change the translation table to alter the widget's response to input. This is often used to modify the behavior of text widgets to mimic a preferred editing style.

To augment a widget's translations, first define a new translation table in the plaintext format described in Appendix D, and then compile it to its internal format with XtParseTranslationTable. The compiled table is non-destructively merged into the widget's existing translation table with XtAugmentTranslations. This leaves any matching translations unchanged in the widget, so the new behavior is added to the widget without displacing any of its existing behavior.

To resolve the actions referenced in an augmented translation, the toolkit first searches any action tables registered by the widget itself, its superclasses and its ancestors in the widget tree. Action tables registered with XtAppAddActions are searched last.

Translations may be merged destructively with XtOverrideTranslations. A widget's translation table may be replaced entirely by calling XtSetValues and passing a compiled table as the new value of the widget's XtNtranslations resource.

CAUTION

None

SEE ALSO

Routines: XtAppAddActions, XtOverrideTranslations, XtParseTranslationTable, XtUninstallTranslations

XtBuildEventMask   **(R3)**

Returns a widget's current event mask

SYNOPSIS

```
EventMask XtBuildEventMask( w )
        Widget                          w;
```

ARGUMENTS

w   in   Widget for which event mask is returned; must be of class Core or any
                            subclass thereof.

DESCRIPTION

XtBuildEventMask returns the event mask representing all the event types that are selected by the
widget. The event mask will be a bitwise OR of any of the event masks listed in Table 9-2. By default, a
widget selects for all event types registered with non-raw event handlers, declared in its translation table, or
installed as an accelerator. A widget automatically updates its event mask when event handlers or
translations are added or removed.

USAGE

XtBuildEventMask is seldom used by application programmers, though it could possibly be helpful in
debugging to see just what events a given widget is waiting for. Its main use is in widget implementation
code to support widgets that call XChangeActivePointerGrab to update the cursor shape during a
grab.

CAUTION

None

SEE ALSO

Routines: XtAddEventHandler, XtAddRawEventHandler, XtInsertEventHandler,
        XtInsertRawEventHandler, XtRemoveEventHandler,
        XtRemoveRawEventHandler

XtCallAcceptFocus (R3)

Calls a widget's accept_focus procedure, if any

SYNOPSIS

```
Boolean XtCallAcceptFocus( w, time )
        Widget                          w;
        Time                            *time;
```

ARGUMENTS

w   in   Widget which is asked to accept focus; must be of class Core or any subclass thereof.

time   in   Specifies the server time of the X event causing the accept focus.

DESCRIPTION

XtCallAcceptFocus calls the specified widget's *accept_focus* class procedure. If the widget's *accept_focus* field is NULL, XtCallAcceptFocus returns False. Otherwise, XtCallAcceptFocus returns whatever the widget's *accept_focus* procedure returns; a value of True implies that the widget actually took keyboard focus by calling XSetInputFocus. Keyboard focus in this case is implemented at the server, and forces non-grabbed keyboard input to the specified widget's window.

USAGE

XtCallAcceptFocus is called to ask a widget to accept the server input focus if it is interested in doing so. It is rarely called in applications, since other client-side methods have largely supplanted the need to assign focus at the server level.

CAUTION

Calling XtCallAcceptFocus does not guarantee that the widget's window will get the input focus. XSetInputFocus is called only if the widget's *accept_focus* procedure does so. This is an area of great variance between toolkits. In some toolkits (e.g. DECwindows XUI) the widget takes focus; in others (e.g. Athena, OSF/Motif) it does nothing.

In practice, most newer toolkits provide alternate methods for providing keyboard traversal. These are generally implemented on the client side to avoid round trips to the server and other headaches associated with trying to direct server input focus to the appropriate window. OSF/Motif, for example, provides the toolkit-specific routine XmProcessTraversal, which should be used instead of XtCallAcceptFocus. Athena widgets expect you to call XtSetKeyboardFocus.

SEE ALSO

Routines: XtSetKeyboardFocus

XtCallActionProc

(R4)

Calls any registered action procedure directly

SYNOPSIS

```
void XtCallActionProc( w, action, event, params, num_params )
        Widget                          w;
        String                          action;
        XEvent                          *event;
        String                          *params;
        Cardinal                        num_params;
```

ARGUMENTS

w	in	Widget ID specifying action tables to be searched for the named action; must be of class Core or any subclass thereof. This widget ID is passed to action procedure when it is invoked.
action	in	String specifying a named action to be invoked.
event	in	Pointer to the XEvent structure to be passed to the action procedure.
params	in	Array of strings specifying parameters to be delivered to the action procedure.
num_params	in	Number of parameters in *params* argument.

DESCRIPTION

XtCallActionProc invokes the named action in the context of widget *w*. XtCallActionProc searches for the action in all action tables registered by the specified widget, its ancestors and superclasses. Action tables previously registered with XtAppAddActions or XtAddActions are searched last. The named action is invoked passing the specified widget ID, event pointer and parameters. If the named action cannot be found, XtCallActionProc issues a warning message and returns.

USAGE

XtCallActionProc is used to invoke an action procedure from within some other procedure. For example, XtCallActionProc can be used in cases in which one action procedure needs to conditionally execute another. XtCallActionProc can also be used in a callback to replay actions recorded by an action hook proc.

CAUTION

Because the named action is invoked directly, rather than through translation management, you are responsible for making sure that the *event* (synthesized or real), *params* and *num_params* arguments are appropriate.

SEE ALSO

Routines: XtAddActions, XtAppAddActions, XtAugmentTranslations, XtOverrideTranslations, XtAppAddActionHook

XtCallbackExclusive (R3)

Built-in callback routine to pop up a Shell and grab the input stream

SYNOPSIS

```
void XtCallbackExclusive( w, client_data, call_data )
        Widget                        w;
        XtPointer                     client_data;
        XtPointer                     call_data;
```

ARGUMENTS

w	in	Widget that called back (unused).
client_data	in	Widget ID of the shell to be popped up; must be a Shell subclass.
call_data	in	Widget-specific callback data (unused).

DESCRIPTION

XtCallbackExclusive is a convenience callback routine that calls XtPopup on the Shell widget specified by *client_data*, with XtPopup's *grab_kind* argument specified as XtGrabExclusive. The *call_data* argument is ignored by this routine.

USAGE

In many styles of user interface, a widget callback is used to cause a shell widget to be popped up. A common example is using the activation callback from a pushbutton widget to pop up a menu or dialog box shell. XtCallbackExclusive is a built-in callback routine that saves you the trouble of writing a special callback routine simply to pop up a widget.

The callback routine XtCallbackExclusive may be added to a widget's callback list with XtAddCallback. The *client_data* argument to XtAddCallback must specify the ID of the Shell widget to be popped up, cast as type XtPointer. When XtCallbackExclusive is called, it pops up the specified shell, with *grab_kind* of XtGrabExclusive.

The built-in callback routines XtCallbackNone and XtCallbackNonexclusive pop up a Shell with *grab_kind*s of XtGrabNone and XtGrabNonexclusive, respectively. The built-in callback routine XtCallbackPopdown pops down a widget from a callback list.

CAUTION

XtCallbackExclusive is always called by registering it in a widget callback list and is never called directly.

SEE ALSO

Routines: XtCallbackNone, XtCallbackNonexclusive, XtCallbackPopdown, XtPopup

XtCallbackNone   **(R3)**

Built-in callback routine to pop up a Shell

SYNOPSIS

```
void XtCallbackNone( w, client_data, call_data )
        Widget                        w;
        XtPointer                     client_data;
        XtPointer                     call_data;
```

ARGUMENTS

w	in	Widget that called back (unused).
client_data	in	Widget ID of the shell to be popped up; must be a Shell subclass.
call_data	in	Widget-specific callback data (unused).

DESCRIPTION

XtCallbackNone is a convenience callback routine that calls XtPopup on the Shell widget specified by *client_data*, with XtPopup's *grab_kind* argument specified as XtGrabNone. The *call_data* argument is ignored by this routine.

USAGE

In many styles of user interface, a widget callback is used to cause a shell widget to be popped up. A common example is using the activation callback from a pushbutton widget to pop up a menu or dialog box shell. XtCallbackNone is a built-in callback routine provided to save you the trouble of writing a special callback routine simply to pop up a widget.

The callback routine XtCallbackNone may be added to a widget's callback list with XtAddCallback. The *client_data* argument to XtAddCallback must specify the ID of the Shell widget to be popped up, cast as type XtPointer. When XtCallbackNone is called, it pops up the specified shell with *grab_kind* of XtGrabNone.

The built-in callback routines XtCallbackExclusive and XtCallbackNonexclusive pop up a Shell with *grab_kind*s of XtGrabExclusive and XtGrabNonexclusive, respectively. The built-in callback routine XtCallbackPopdown pops down a widget from a callback list.

CAUTION

XtCallbackNone is always called by registering it in a widget callback list and is never called directly.

SEE ALSO

Routines: XtCallbackExclusive, XtCallbackNonexclusive, XtCallbackPopdown,
            XtPopup

XtCallbackNonexclusive (R3)

Built-in callback routine to pop up a Shell and grab the input stream

SYNOPSIS

```
void XtCallbackNonexclusive( w, client_data, call_data )
        Widget                    w;
        XtPointer                 client_data;
        XtPointer                 call_data;
```

ARGUMENTS

w	in	Widget that called back (unused).
client_data	in	Widget ID of the shell to be popped up; must be a Shell subclass.
call_data	in	Widget-specific callback data (unused).

DESCRIPTION

XtCallbackNonexclusive is a convenience callback routine that calls XtPopup on the Shell widget specified by *client_data*, with XtPopup's *grab_kind* argument specified as XtGrabNonexclusive. The *call_data* argument is ignored by this routine.

USAGE

In many styles of user interface, a widget callback is used to cause a shell widget to be popped up. A common example is using the activation callback from a pushbutton widget to pop up a menu or dialog box shell. XtCallbackNonexclusive is a built-in callback routine that saves you the trouble of writing a special callback routine simply to pop up a widget.

The callback routine XtCallbackNonexclusive may be added to a widget's callback list with XtAddCallback. The *client_data* argument to XtAddCallback must specify the ID of the Shell widget to be popped up, cast as type XtPointer. When XtCallbackNonexclusive is called, it pops up the specified shell with *grab_kind* of XtGrabNonexclusive.

The built-in callback routines XtCallbackNone and XtCallbackExclusive pop up a Shell with *grab_kind*s of XtGrabNone and XtGrabExclusive, respectively. The built-in callback routine XtCallbackPopdown pops down a widget from a callback list.

CAUTION

XtCallbackNonexclusive is always called by registering it in a widget callback list and is never called directly.

SEE ALSO

Routines: XtCallbackExclusive, XtCallbackNone, XtCallbackPopdown, XtPopup

XtCallbackPopdown   **(R3)**

Built-in callback routine to pop down a Shell

SYNOPSIS

```
void XtCallbackPopdown( w, client_data, call_data )
        Widget                      w;
        XtPointer                   client_data;
        XtPointer                   call_data;
```

ARGUMENTS

w   in   Widget that is calling back (unused).

client_data   in   Pointer to XtPopdownIDRec structure specifying a shell widget to pop
                                   down and the "enable widget" that helped pop it up.

call_data   in   Widget-specific callback data (unused).

DESCRIPTION

XtCallbackPopdown is a convenience callback routine which pops down a shell. The *client_data* is a
pointer to a structure of XtPopdownIdRec, in which the *shell_widget* field identifies the shell to be popped
down, and the *enable_widget* field identifies a widget that is to be set sensitive. The *call_data* argument is
ignored by this routine.

USAGE

In many styles of user interface, a widget callback is used to cause a shell widget to be popped down. A
common example is using the activation callback from a pushbutton widget to pop down a dialog box shell.
XtCallbackPopdown is a built-in callback routine that saves you the trouble of writing a special callback
routine simply to pop down a widget.
     The callback routine XtCallbackPopdown may be added to a widget's callback list with
XtAddCallback. The *client_data* argument to XtAddCallback must specify a pointer to an
XtPopdownIDRec structure, cast as type XtPointer. The XtPopdownIDRec defines the widget ID of
the shell to be popped down, and the "enable widget", which is presumably the widget whose actions
originally popped up the shell. When XtCallbackPopdown is called, it pops down the specified Shell
widget and removes it from the grab list, then sets the enable widget sensitive.
     The built-in callback routines XtCallbackNone, XtCallbackNonexclusive and
XtCallbackExclusive are provided to pop up a Shell with *grab_kind* of XtGrabNone,
XtGrabNonexclusive and XtGrabExclusive, respectively.

CAUTION

XtCallbackPopdown is always called by registering it in a widget callback list and is never called
directly.

SEE ALSO

Routines: XtCallbackExclusive, XtCallbackNone, XtCallbackNonexclusive,
           XtPopdown

XtCallbackReleaseCacheRef (R4)

Built-in callback routine to free a reference to a type conversion result

SYNOPSIS

```
void XtCallbackReleaseCacheRef( w, client_data, call_data )
        Widget                  w;
        XtPointer               client_data;
        XtPointer               call_data;
```

ARGUMENTS

w	in	Object with which the resource is associated.
client_data	in	Conversion cache entry to be released.
call_data	in	Widget-specific callback data (unused).

DESCRIPTION

XtCallbackReleaseCacheRef is a convenience callback routine that decrements the reference count of a resource conversion result. The *client_data* argument to XtAddCallback must specify an XtCacheRef, cast as type XtPointer. The *call_data* argument is ignored by this routine.

USAGE

XtCallbackReleaseCacheRef is used internally by the Intrinsics, which bind it to widgets' XtNdestroyCallback list to release conversion cache references for those widgets when they are destroyed. Application programs should rarely have a use for it.

CAUTION

XtCallbackReleaseCacheRef is always called by registering it in a widget callback list with XtAddCallback, and is never called directly. You should never remove all callbacks from a widget's XtNdestroyCallback list, as this may affect whether resources are released properly.

SEE ALSO

Routines: XtAppReleaseCacheRefs, XtAppSetTypeConverter, XtCallbackReleaseCacheRefList, XtCallConverter, XtConvertAndStore, XtSetTypeConverter

XtCallbackReleaseCacheRefList   (R4)

Built-in callback routine to free multiple references to type conversion results

SYNOPSIS

```
void XtCallbackReleaseCacheRefList(object, client_data, call_data)
        Widget                      object;
        XtPointer                   client_data;
        XtPointer                   call_data;
```

ARGUMENTS

w	in	Object with which the resources are associated.
client_data	in	Pointer to NULL-terminated list of conversion cache entries to be released.
call_data	in	Widget-specific callback data (unused).

DESCRIPTION

XtCallbackReleaseCacheRefList is a convenience callback routine that decrements the reference counts of a list of resource conversion results. The *client_data* argument must specify a pointer to a NULL-terminated list of XtCacheRefs, cast as type XtPointer. The *call_data* argument is ignored by this routine.

USAGE

XtCallbackReleaseCacheRefList is used internally by the Intrinsics, which bind it to the XtNdestroyCallback of widgets to release conversion cache references for those widgets when they are destroyed. Application programs should rarely have a use for it.

CAUTION

XtCallbackReleaseCacheRefList is always called by registering it in a widget callback list with XtAddCallback, and is never called directly. You should never remove all callbacks from a widget's XtNdestroyCallback list, as this may affect whether resources are released properly.

SEE ALSO

Routines: XtAppReleaseCacheRefs, XtAppSetTypeConverter,
            XtCallbackReleaseCacheRefList, XtCallConverter, XtConvertAndStore,
            XtSetTypeConverter

XtCallCallbackList   (R4)

Calls the routines in a callback list

SYNOPSIS

```
void XtCallCallbackList( w, callbacks, call_data )
        Widget                      w;
        XtCallbackList              callbacks;
        XtPointer                   call_data;
```

ARGUMENTS

w	in	Widget ID to be passed as the first argument to each callback routine in the callback list; must be of class Object or any subclass thereof.
callbacks	in	Specifies the callback list to execute.
call_data	in	Data to be passed as the third argument to each callback routine in the callback list.

DESCRIPTION

XtCallCallbackList executes each callback routine in the specified callback list, in the order in which it is found in the list. The specified widget ID and *call_data* are passed to each callback routine, together with the individual *client_data* registered with each routine in the callback list. If *callbacks* is NULL, XtCallCallbackList returns immediately.

USAGE

XtCallCallbackList is used in widget implementation code when the widget wants to invoke its callbacks. The *call_data* is passed to each callback procedure on the list, and is usually a pointer to a widget class-specific data structure.

The *callbacks* argument must specify a widget or object resource declared with a representation type of XtRCallback. Despite what the function prototype says, *callbacks* is not really a simple list of XtCallbackRecs, but a compiled form of the callback list. XtCallCallbackList is rarely if ever called by application programmers. To invoke a list of callbacks outside of widget code, call XtCallCallbacks instead.

CAUTION

XtCallCallbackList cannot be used to invoke a simple list of XtCallbackRecs.

SEE ALSO

Routines: XtAddCallback, XtAddCallbacks, XtCallCallbacks, XtRemoveCallback, XtRemoveCallbacks

XtCallCallbacks **(R3)**

Calls the routines in a widget's callback list

SYNOPSIS

```
void XtCallCallbacks( w, callback_name, call_data )
        Widget                 w;
        String                 callback_name;
        XtPointer              call_data;
```

ARGUMENTS

w	in	Widget containing the callbacks to be invoked; must be of class Object or any subclass thereof. This ID is passed as first argument to each callback routine in the callback list.
callback_name	in	Resource name of the callback list to be called, e.g. "destroyCallback" or the symbolic constant XtNdestroyCallback.
call_data	in	Data to be passed as the third argument to each callback routine in the callback list.

DESCRIPTION

XtCallCallbacks executes all callback routines in the specified list, in the order in which they are found in the list. The specified widget ID and *call_data* are passed to each callback routine, together with the individual *client_data* registered with each routine in the callback list. If no callback routines are found in the specified list, XtCallCallbacks returns immediately. If a callback list of the specified name is not found, XtCallCallbacks issues a warning.

USAGE

XtCallCallbacks is used in older widget implementation code when the widget wants to invoke its callbacks. The *call_data* is passed to each callback procedure on the specified list, and is usually a pointer to a widget class-specific data structure. XtCallCallbacks may in special cases be called by application programmers to simulate the action of a widget.

CAUTION

Generally speaking, there is no way to guarantee the order in which callback routines appear in a callback list. This is because successive calls to XtAddCallback(s) and XtRemoveCallback(s) may reorder the callback list in unpredictable ways. Also, cooperating widgets in a particular toolkit may add and remove callback routines without the knowledge of the application programmer.

SEE ALSO

Routines: XtAddCallback, XtAddCallbacks, XtCallCallbackList, XtRemoveCallback, XtRemoveCallbacks

XtCallConverter (R4)

Calls a new-format resource type converter directly

SYNOPSIS

```
Boolean XtCallConverter( display, converter, convert_args, num_args,
    from, to, cache_ref )
            Display              *display;
            XtTypeConverter      converter;
            XrmValue             *convert_args;
            Cardinal             num_args;
            XrmValue             *from;
            XrmValue             *to;
            XtCacheRef           *cache_ref;
```

ARGUMENTS

display	in	Display with which the conversion is associated.
converter	in	Converter procedure to be called to perform the conversion.
convert_args	in	A list of additional arguments required to perform the conversion, or NULL if none are required.
num_args	in	Number of additional arguments in *convert_args*, or zero if none.
from	in	Pointer to an XrmValue structure describing input value .
to	in/out	Pointer to an XrmValue structure to receive the converted value.
cache_ref	in/out	Address of a variable into which to return the cache ID for the conversion value.

DESCRIPTION

XtCallConverter calls the specified type converter directly. If the converter has previously been called with the same input values and failed, XtCallConverter returns False immediately. If the required conversion has already been performed successfully and the result has been cached, the cached value and size are returned in the *to* argument. If the required conversion has not been performed, or was not cached, the specified converter is called and the conversion result is returned in the *to* argument. XtCallConverter returns True if the conversion was performed successfully.

If additional run-time arguments are required by the specified converter, the caller is expected to provide them in the *convert_args* array. The caller must know which arguments the converter expects, if any.

The caller is responsible for allocating the storage pointed to by the *from, to* and *cache_ref* arguments. Specifically, the caller must provide a buffer large enough to hold the conversion result in the *to* argument. If the caller does not supply a large enough buffer, XtCallConverter returns False and the required size is returned in the *size* field of the *to* argument. If *to.addr* is specified as NULL, the converter allocates sufficient private storage for the conversion result and returns a pointer to the result in *to.addr*. The caller is expected to copy the conversion result into application storage immediately, and not modify it in any way.

If the converter was originally registered with the XtCacheRefCount modifier, and the value returned in *cache_ref* is non-NULL, the caller should store the *cache_ref* value and decrement the cache reference count with XtAppReleaseCacheRefs when the conversion value is no longer needed. *cache_ref* should be specified as NULL if the caller is unwilling to store the value.

USAGE

Values specified in resource files are automatically converted to the appropriate data type when a widget is created or when you call XtGetApplicationResources.   You would probably never call XtCallConverter directly. If you really needed to perform a dynamic conversion you would more likely call XtConvertAndStore to avoid the trouble of explicitly managing resource cache reference counts or convert args.

XtCallConverter is usually used inside a resource converter that wants to perform part of its conversion by calling another resource converter. For example, if you wrote a converter that could read a drawing file and allocate a Pixmap, it would also have to allocate Pixel values for every color in the picture. Rather than handling this itself, the converter might simply call another converter to handle the Pixel conversion. Presumably, converters have knowledge of each other's needs, and would know the appropriate *convert_args*.

CAUTION

Often it pays to use Xlib routines to deal with server resources, particularly if you use lots of them and dynamically create and destroy them. If you call XtCallConverter, you can manage reference counts yourself so that the server resources can be freed when you no longer require the conversion value. However, you must know what additional arguments the converter expects so you can pass them explicitly. These may or may not be documented.

SEE ALSO

Routines: XtAppReleaseCacheRefs, XtAppSetTypeConverter,
             XtCallbackReleaseCacheRef, XtCallbackReleaseCacheRefList,
             XtConvertAndStore, XtSetTypeConverter

XtCalloc   (R3)

Allocates memory for a fixed-size array

SYNOPSIS

```
char *XtCalloc( num, size )
        Cardinal                        num;
        Cardinal                        size;
```

ARGUMENTS

num	in	Number of array elements to allocate.
size	in	Size of each array element in bytes.

DESCRIPTION

XtCalloc allocates enough storage for the specified number of array elements of the specified size, and initializes all values to zero. If there is insufficient storage available to allocate the space, XtCalloc calls XtErrorMsg to log an error and exit.

USAGE

XtCalloc is used in widget implementation code and applications to dynamically allocate arrays of fixed-size elements, which may include callback lists, arglists, or other client data structures. XtCalloc is compatible and interchangeable with its standard C counterpart, calloc(), except that it calls XtErrorMsg on an error.

CAUTION

Call XtFree to free storage allocated by XtCalloc when it is no longer needed.

SEE ALSO

Routines: XtFree, XtMalloc, XtNew, XtNewString, XtRealloc

XtCancelSelectionRequest (R6)

Cancels a bundled section request

SYNOPSIS

```
void XtCancelSelectionRequest( w, selection )
    Widget                          w;
    Atom                            selection;
```

ARGUMENTS

w   in   Widget that had requested the selection; must be of class Core or any subclass thereof.

selection   in   Atom identifying the selection(e.g. XA_PRIMARY).

DESCRIPTION

XtCancelSelectionRequest cancels a pending MULTIPLE target request without sending it and frees storage that had been allocated to the request. Any requests for the same widget and selection queued since the last call to XtCreateSelectionRequest are discarded. A subsequent call to XtSendSelectionRequest will not send the request, and subsequent calls to XtGetSelectionValue, XtGetSelectionValues, XtGetSelectionValueIncr, or XtGetSelectionValuesIncr will not be deferred.

USAGE

Sometimes you may want to request the same selection expressed as multiple targets. XtGetSelectionValues works fine for requesting multiple simple targets. But if your selection targets need to pass parameters with XtSetSelectionParameters, this will not work because XtGetSelectionValues provides no way to collect the multiple parameters before it sends its request.

To support a more robust request for multiple targets, you can call XtCreateSelectionRequest to prepare a request, and then call normal selection routines such as XtGetSelectionValue and XtSetSelectionParameters to add targets to the request. All requests queued since the last call to XtCreateSelectionRequest are bundled into a single request which is finally sent when you call XtSendSelectionRequest. If you decide halfway through preparing a request that it makes no sense to send it, you should call XtCancelSelectionRequest to free the resources allocated to the transfer.

CAUTION

XtSendSelectionRequest is used to send a request for multiple selection targets requiring parameter data. To request "ordinary" multiple selections, the routines XtGetSelectionValues or XtGetSelectionValuesIncr are much simpler to use.

SEE ALSO

Routines: XtCreateSelectionRequest, XtSendSelectionRequest, XtSetSelectionParameters

XtChangeManagedSet (R6)

Changes a Composite widget's set of managed children all at once

SYNOPSIS

```
void XtChangeManagedSet( unmanage_children, num_unmanage_children,
    change_proc, client_data, manage_children, num_manage_children )
    WidgetList                      unmanage_children;
    Cardinal                        num_unmanage_children;
    XtDoChangeProc                  change_proc;
    XtPointer                       client_data;
    WidgetList                      unmanage_children;
    Cardinal                        num_manage_children;
```

ARGUMENTS

unmanage_children	in	List of children to be unmanaged.
num_unmanage	in	Number of children in *unmanage_children*.
change_proc	in	Procedure called between unmanage and manage phases.
client_data	in	Application-supplied data to pass to *change_proc*.
unmanage_children	in	List of children to be managed.
num_manage	in	Number of children in *manage_children*.

DESCRIPTION

XtChangeManagedSet simultaneously manages and unmanages children of a common Composite parent. A child may appear in both the *unmanage_children* and *manage_children* lists. Right after all children in *unmanage_children* have been unmanaged, but before the children in *manage_children* are managed, XtChangeManagedSet calls *change_proc*. If the parent is being destroyed, XtChangeManagedSet returns immediately; if a child is being destroyed, XtChangeManagedSet ignores it. If any child is NULL, or all children do not have the same parent, XtChangeManagedSet issues a warning. If the parent widget is not a subclass of Composite, XtChangeManagedSet issues a fatal error.

USAGE

Use XtChangeManagedSet when you want to remove some children from a layout and replace them with others, or when you want to reset the childrens' geometry. The *change_proc* is of type XtDoChangeProc (see Appendix B) and is used to make changes to children while the parent has the fewest widgets in its managed set. This usually means making geometry changes, taking advantage of the fact that a manager with only a few children is more likely to say yes, and when a child is unmanaged, the Intrinsics internally grant any geometry it wants. One way to enforce a desired layout would be to put all children in *unmanage_children* and *manage_children*, and resize them as you please in *change_proc*.

CAUTION

None

SEE ALSO

Routines: XtManageChild, XtManageChildren, XtUnmanageChild, XtUnmanageChildren

XtCheckSubclass (R3)

Checks widget class of a widget while debugging

SYNOPSIS

```
void XtCheckSubclass( w, widget_class, message )
        Widget                      w;
        WidgetClass                 widget_class;
        String                      message;
```

ARGUMENTS

w	in	Widget or object whose class is to be checked; must be of class Object or any subclass thereof.
widget_class	in	Widget class to test widget against.
message	in	Error message to be displayed if w is not a subclass of *widget_class*.

DESCRIPTION

XtCheckSubclass checks whether the specified widget is a subclass (at any level) of the specified widget class, and issues a fatal error if it is not. XtCheckSubclass is a macro that is only executed if the module has been compiled with the DEBUG compiler symbol defined.

USAGE

XtCheckSubclass is used while debugging widget internals to make sure that an object specified to an Intrinsics routine is of an appropriate class. For application programming you would usually find the routine XtIsSubclass more useful, since it is called even if the DEBUG flag is not defined, and allows you to take more considered action than a simple exit().

CAUTION

None

SEE ALSO

Routines: XtClass, XtIsSubclass, XtSuperclass

XtClass

(R3)

Determines the class of a widget

SYNOPSIS

```
WidgetClass XtClass( w )
        Widget                          w;
```

ARGUMENTS

w   in   The widget whose class is to be queried; must be of class Object or any subclass thereof.

DESCRIPTION

XtClass returns a pointer to the specified object's class record.

USAGE

XtClass is usually used in manager widget implementation code to determine whether a newly managed child is of an appropriate class. The returned value may be tested against a known class pointer constant. XtClass may also be used in application code to test the class of a widget before performing some class-specific operation on it:

```
if (XtClass(mywidget) == xmPushButtonWidgetClass){
    /* do something related to a push button */
}
```

CAUTION

None

SEE ALSO

Routines: XtCheckSubclass, XtIsSubclass, XtSuperclass, XtIs<*Class*>

XtCloseDisplay

(R3)

Closes a connection to an X server and frees its resources

SYNOPSIS

```
void XtCloseDisplay( display )
        Display                        *display;
```

ARGUMENTS

display   in   Display to be closed.

DESCRIPTION

XtCloseDisplay terminates the specified connection to an X server and removes it from its application context, releasing any server resources associated with the connection. The display is closed as it is safe to do so - that is, as soon as the Intrinsics have returned from any event dispatch. The destructors for any resources cached with cache type XtCacheByDisplay are called just before the display connection is terminated, and may release server or other resources.

USAGE

You may call XtCloseDisplay to selectively close down a display connection and continue executing. If all displays are to be closed, you should call XtDestroyApplicationContext instead.

CAUTION

Widgets associated with the display are not explicitly destroyed by XtCloseDisplay, but are pretty useless since there is no way to re-associate them with a display. Widgets should be destroyed with XtDestroyWidget before calling XtCloseDisplay, so as to invoke any callbacks on their XtNdestroyCallback lists, and free their client-side storage.

SEE ALSO

Routines: XtDestroyApplicationContext, XtOpenDisplay, XtSetTypeConverter

XtConfigureWidget (R3)

Explicitly reconfigures a widget and its window

SYNOPSIS

```
void XtConfigureWidget( w, x, y, width, height, border_width )
        Widget                    w;
        Position                  x;
        Position                  y;
        Dimension                 width;
        Dimension                 height;
        Dimension                 border_width;
```

ARGUMENTS

w	in	Widget to be resized and positioned; must be of class RectObj or any subclass thereof.
x	in	New X position of widget in parent's coordinate system.
y	in	New Y position of widget in parent's coordinate system.
width	in	New width of widget.
height	in	New height of widget.
border_width	in	New border width of widget.

DESCRIPTION

XtConfigureWidget unilaterally sets a new width, height, border width, and position for the specified widget, without calling its parent's geometry management routines. If the specified widget is realized, XtConfigureWidget also issues an XConfigureWindow request to resize and position the widget's window. XtConfigureWidget returns immediately if the specified geometry values are the same as the widget's old ones.

USAGE

XtConfigureWidget is called only within a manager widget's implementation code, to change the size of a managed child. You should never call it directly in applications. To reconfigure a widget in normal applications, call XtSetValues specifying the appropriate geometry-related resource values.

CAUTION

Never call XtConfigureWidget to reposition a widget, as it does not give the widget or its parent a chance to respond to the change.

SEE ALSO

Routines: XtMakeGeometryRequest, XtMoveWidget, XtQueryGeometry,
        XtResizeWidget

XtConvert

(R3O)

Looks up and calls a resource type converter

SYNOPSIS

```
void XtConvert( w, from_type, from, to_type, to )
        Widget                      w;
        String                      from_type;
        XrmValue                    *from;
        String                      to_type;
        XrmValue                    *to;
```

ARGUMENTS

w	in	Widget with which conversion is associated; must be of class Object or any subclass thereof.
from_type	in	String identifying the source data type for the conversion, e.g. "String", or symbolic constant XtRString.
from	in	Pointer to XrmValue structure supplying the value to be converted.
to_type	in	String identifying the destination data type for the conversion, e.g. "lnt", or symbolic constant XtRInt.
to	in/out	Pointer to XrmValue structure to receive the conversion result.

DESCRIPTION

XtConvert looks up the resource type converter registered to convert *from_type* to *to_type*, computes any addition arguments needed, and then calls XtDirectConvert (if it is an old-format converter) or XtCallConverter (if it is a new-format converter) to perform the conversion.

USAGE

XtConvert is an obsolete routine provided for backwards compatibility with older versions of the Intrinsics; new widgets or applications should use new-format resource converters and should call XtConvertAndStore in the rare cases where a conversion must be invoked directly.

CAUTION

XtConvert is provided for backwards compatibility with earlier versions of the Intrinsics, and is superseded in the R4 and later Intrinsics by the routine XtConvertAndStore. XtConvert does not return a status; by convention, if a conversion fails, *to.addr* is returned as NULL. The caller is expected to immediately copy the return value to new storage, as it may point to static storage in the converter. XtConvert gives no control over how resources are cached or if they are cached.

SEE ALSO

Routines: XtCallConverter, XtConvertAndStore, XtDirectConvert

XtConvertAndStore (R4)

Looks up and calls a resource type converter

SYNOPSIS

```
Boolean XtConvertAndStore( w, from_type, from, to_type, to )
        Widget                      w;
        String                      from_type;
        XrmValue                    *from;
        String                      to_type;
        XrmValue                    *to;
```

ARGUMENTS

w	in	Object identifying display and application context associated with the conversion; must be of class Object or any subclass thereof.
from_type	in	String identifying the source data type for the conversion, e.g. "String", or symbolic constant XtRString.
from	in	Pointer to an XrmValue structure describing the input value.
to_type	in	String identifying the destination data type for the conversion, e.g. "Int", or symbolic constant XtRInt.
to	in/out	Pointer to an XrmValue structure to receive the converted value.

DESCRIPTION

XtConvertAndStore looks up the required new-format or old-format type converter in the application context associated with the specified object or widget *w*. If there is no converter registered for *from_type* to *to_type* conversion, or if the converter has previously been called with the same input values and failed, XtConvertAndStore returns False immediately. If the required conversion has already been performed successfully and the result has been cached, the cached value and size are returned in the *to* argument. If the required conversion has not been performed, or was not cached, the required converter is called and the result is returned in the *to* argument. Any additional arguments needed by the converter are computed by the Intrinsics based on the *convert_args* supplied when the converter was registered. XtConvertAndStore returns True if the conversion succeeds.

The caller is responsible for allocating the storage pointed to by the *from* and *to* arguments. Specifically, the caller should provide a buffer large enough to hold the conversion result in the *to* argument. If the caller does not supply a large enough buffer, XtConvertAndStore returns False and the required size is returned in the *size* field of the *to* argument. However, if *to.addr* is specified as NULL, the Intrinsics allocate sufficient private storage for the conversion result. The caller is expected to copy the conversion result into application storage immediately, as it may point to static storage owned by the converter.

Converters may be registered such that they cache conversion values. If the converter was originally registered with the XtCacheRefCount modifier, and returns an XtCacheRef value, the Intrinsics automatically add the built-in callback routine XtCallbackReleaseCacheRef to the XtNdestroyCallback list of the specified widget or object *w*. This frees the conversion cache reference when the specified object is destroyed.

USAGE

Values specified in resource files are automatically converted to the appropriate data type when a widget is created or when you call `XtGetApplicationResources`. You will rarely call `XtConvertAndStore` directly, but may do so if a specific conversion must be requested. If the conversion does not employ one of the standard converters provided by the Intrinsics (see Chapter 6), you are responsible for making sure that the required converter is registered with `XtAppSetTypeConverter` or `XtSetTypeConverter`.

CAUTION

Because `XtConvertAndStore` binds callback routines to a widget's `XtNdestroyCallback` list, you should never remove all callbacks from this list. This also implies that any server resources allocated by a call to `XtConvertAndStore` are not freed until the associated widget is destroyed. Calling `XtConvertAndStore`, then, is not an efficient way to dynamically allocate fonts, colors, etc. Often it pays to use Xlib routines to deal with server resources, particularly if you use lots of them and dynamically create and destroy them.

SEE ALSO

Routines: `XtAppSetTypeConverter`, `XtCallConverter`, `XtSetTypeConverter`

XtConvertCase (R3)

Returns upper and lower-case equivalents of a KeySym

SYNOPSIS

```
void XtConvertCase( display, keysym, lower_return, upper_return )
        Display                     *display;
        KeySym                      keysym;
        KeySym                      *lower_return;
        KeySym                      *upper_return;
```

ARGUMENTS

display	in	Pointer to Display associated with keysym to be converted.
keysym	in	Keysym to be converted.
lower_return	in/out	Returned lower-case equivalent of keysym.
upper_return	in/out	Returned upper-case equivalent of keysym.

DESCRIPTION

XtConvertCase accepts a keysym and returns its upper-case and lower-case keysym equivalents. XtConvertCase calls the case converter currently registered with XtRegisterCaseConverter to perform the conversion, or the default case converter if no other converter is registered.

USAGE

This routine may be called to convert an input keysym to lower or upper-case. This is done automatically as Key events are processed through translation management, so you won't need to call this explicitly very often. XtConvertCase expects a keysym; inside an action procedure that processes keyboard input, you can call XtGetActionKeysym to retrieve the keysym that was just entered. If you are parsing keyboard events directly through event handlers, you must convert the keycode in the incoming event to a keysym with XtTranslateKeycode, XLookupString, or an application-supplied routine before calling XtConvertCase.

CAUTION

None

SEE ALSO

Routines: XtRegisterCaseConverter, XtTranslateKeycode

XtCreateApplicationContext (R3)

Creates a new application context

SYNOPSIS

XtAppContext XtCreateApplicationContext()

ARGUMENTS

None

DESCRIPTION

XtCreateApplicationContext creates a new application context and returns its ID.

USAGE

The application context holds global information about an application and its input sources, including the list of open displays, the grab list, and the lists of signal callbacks, alternate input sources, timeouts, and work procedures. An application context is a required argument to many toolkit routines.

You will usually use one of the convenience routines XtAppInitialize or XtOpenApplication (R6) instead of calling XtCreateApplicationContext explicitly.

If you do not use the convenience routines, XtCreateApplicationContext must be called after XtToolkitInitialize, but before any call to XtOpenDisplay or XtDisplayInitialize. An application context may be destroyed with XtDestroyApplicationContext, which closes all open displays and releases any server resources associated with the application context.

CAUTION

XtAppMainLoop does not handle multiple application contexts, and it is nearly impossible to write a private main loop that does handle multiple application contexts reliably. It is not necessary to create multiple application contexts to handle multiple displays; the main loop handles multiple displays in the same application context without modification. An application context is a required argument to all routines that start with the letters "XtApp". These routines replace earlier routines that used a default application context implicitly (see XtInitialize).

SEE ALSO

Routines: XtAppCreateShell, XtAppInitialize, XtDestroyApplicationContext, XtToolkitInitialize, XtWidgetToApplicationContext

XtCreateApplicationShell (O)

Creates a parentless shell widget to root an application widget tree

SYNOPSIS

```
Widget XtCreateApplicationShell( name, widget_class, args, num_args )
        String                          name;
        WidgetClass                     widget_class;
        ArgList                         args;
        Cardinal                        num_args;
```

ARGUMENTS

name	in	Resource name for widget to be created, e.g. "myApp".
widget_class	in	Class pointer specifying class of widget to be created. Must be subclass of Shell (usually `applicationShellWidgetClass`).
args	in	An array of Args specifying initial resource values for the new application shell.
num_args	in	Number of name/value pairs in *args*.

DESCRIPTION

`XtCreateApplicationShell` creates a shell of the specified class on the specified display. The shell has a NULL parent and is used to root an application widget tree.

USAGE

See `XtAppCreateShell`.

CAUTION

`XtCreateApplicationShell` is an obsolete routine provided for backwards compatibility with the Release 2 Intrinsics. It uses the default application context created by `XtInitialize`, which must be called first. This routine is superseded in the R3 and later Intrinsics by `XtAppCreateShell`.

SEE ALSO

Routines: `XtAppCreateShell, XtInitialize`

XtCreateManagedWidget   **(R3)**

Creates and manages a normal child widget

SYNOPSIS

```
Widget XtCreateManagedWidget( name, widget_class, parent, args, num_args)
        String                    name;
        WidgetClass               widget_class;
        Widget                    parent;
        ArgList                   args;
        Cardinal                  num_args;
```

ARGUMENTS

name	in	Resource name for the new widget, e.g. "myWidget".
widget_class	in	Class pointer specifying the type of widget to create, e.g. `xmPushButtonWidgetClass`, to get an OSF/Motif XmPushButton widget.
parent	in	Widget ID of parent; must be of class Composite or any subclass thereof.
args	in	An array of Args specifying resources to override declarations in resource files or the command line.
num_args	in	Number of name/value pairs in *args*.

DESCRIPTION

`XtCreateManagedWidget` is a convenience routine that creates a normal child widget and immediately manages it. Input arguments are used as they are in `XtCreateWidget`. If *widget_class* or *parent* is NULL, `XtCreateManagedWidget` issues a fatal error.

USAGE

`XtCreateManagedWidget` is a convenience routine that replaces separate calls to `XtCreateWidget` and `XtManageChild`. You can use `XtCreateManagedWidget` if a new widget should be visible as soon as it is created. `XtVaCreateManagedWidget` is the varargs variant of this routine.

CAUTION

If you are creating many children of the same parent, it is more efficient to create them with `XtCreateWidget` and then manage them all together by calling `XtManageChildren`.

SEE ALSO

Routines: `XtCreateWidget, XtManageChild, XtManageChildren,`
            `XtVaCreateManagedWidget`

XtCreatePopupShell   (R3)

Creates a pop-up Shell widget

SYNOPSIS

```
Widget XtCreatePopupShell( name, widget_class, parent, args, num_args )
        String                          name;
        WidgetClass                     widget_class;
        Widget                          parent;
        ArgList                         args;
        Cardinal                        num_args;
```

ARGUMENTS

name	in	Resource name for widget to be created, e.g. "myShell".
widget_class	in	Class pointer specifying class of widget to be created; must be a subclass of Shell, e.g. `transientShellWidgetClass`.
parent	in	Widget ID of parent widget; must be of class Core or any subclass thereof.
args	in	An array of Args specifying resources to override declarations in resource files or the command line.
num_args	in	Number of name/value pairs in *args*.

DESCRIPTION

`XtCreatePopupShell` creates and initializes a shell of the specified class and adds it to its parent's list of pop-up children, returning the widget ID of the new shell. The arglist supplies initial resource values, and overrides any conflicting values declared in resource files or command-line arguments. The specified *name* may be non-unique. If *widget_class* or *parent* is NULL, `XtCreatePopupShell` issues a fatal error.

USAGE

`XtCreatePopupShell` is used to create pop-up widgets such as menus and dialog boxes. Shells created with `XtCreatePopupShell` are added to the parent's list of pop-up children, which is distinct from the list of normal children maintained by a Composite parent. Shells may have non-Composite parents, and never invoke geometry management when they are mapped. Shells are mapped and unmapped with `XtPopup`/`XtPopdown` instead of `XtManageChild`/`XtUnmanageChild`.

The input arglist is usually declared as a static array of type Arg, and is filled in with repeated calls to `XtSetArg`. Shells created with `XtCreatePopupShell` may be destroyed with `XtDestroyWidget`. `XtVaCreatePopupShell` is the varargs variant of `XtCreatePopupShell`.

CAUTION

Widget_class must specify a subclass of Shell; however, the parentless shell used to root a widget tree must be created with `XtAppCreateShell` instead of `XtCreatePopupShell`. If the *name* argument is not unique, loosely-bound declarations in resource files may inadvertently refer to more than one widget.

SEE ALSO

Routines: XtAppCreateShell, XtCreateWidget, XtDestroyWidget, XtPopup,
            XtPopdown, XtVaCreatePopupShell

XtCreateSelectionRequest (R6)

Initializes a bundled selection request

SYNOPSIS

```
void XtCreateSelectionRequest( requester, selection )
    Widget                              requester;
    Atom                                selection;
```

ARGUMENTS

requester	in	Widget ID of selection requester; must be of class Core or any subclass thereof.
selection	in	Atom identifying selection to be requested.

DESCRIPTION

XtCreateSelectionRequest prepares to send a request for the MULTIPLE selection target. After the call to XtCreateSelectionRequest, subsequent calls to XtGetSelectionValue, XtGetSelectionValues, XtGetSelectionValueIncr, XtGetSelectionValuesIncr or XSetSelectionParameters are deferred if they reference the same selection and widget. The individual requests resulting from these calls are bundled into a single request for MULTIPLE targets that is sent when the requester calls XtSendSelectionRequest.

USAGE

Sometimes you may want to request the same selection expressed as multiple targets. XtGetSelectionValues works fine for requesting multiple simple targets. But this will not work if your selection targets need to pass parameters with XtSetSelectionParameters, because XtGetSelectionValues provides no way to assemble multiple parameters before it sends its request.

To support a more robust request for multiple targets, you can call XtCreateSelectionRequest to prepare a request, and then call normal selection routines such as XtGetSelectionValue and XtSetSelectionParameters to add targets to the request. All requests queued since the last call to XtCreateSelectionRequest are bundled into a single request for the MULTIPLE target, which is sent when you finally call XtSendSelectionRequest. If you decide midway through preparing a request that it makes no sense to send it, you should call XtCancelSelectionRequest to free the resources allocated to the transfer.

Bundling the selection request like this is the only way to send a request for the MULTIPLE target that also includes parameterized requests. To set parameters for particular selection requests, call XtSetSelectionParameters before each call to XtGetSelectionValue that requests a parameterized target. This is an advanced form of selection and will rarely be needed by ordinary applications.

CAUTION

To request "ordinary" multiple selections, the routines XtGetSelectionValues or XtGetSelectionValuesIncr are much simpler to use.

SEE ALSO

Routines: XtSendSelectionRequest, XtCancelSelectionRequest, XtSetSelectionParameters

XtCreateWidget (R3)

Creates a normal child widget

SYNOPSIS

```
Widget XtCreateWidget(name, widget_class, parent, args, num_args)
        String                          name;
        WidgetClass                     widget_class;
        Widget                          parent;
        ArgList                         args;
        Cardinal                        num_args;
```

ARGUMENTS

name	in	Resource name for widget to be created, e.g. "myWidget".
widget_class	in	Class pointer specifying the type of widget to be created, e.g. xmLabelWidgetClass to get an OSF/Motif Label widget.
parent	in	Widget ID of parent; must be of class Object or any subclass thereof.
args	in	An array of Args specifying resources to override declarations in resource files or the command line.
num_args	in	Number of resource name/value pairs in *args*.

DESCRIPTION

XtCreateWidget creates and initializes a widget of the specified class, and returns its widget ID. The arglist supplies initial resource values for the new widget, and overrides any conflicting values declared in resource files or command-line arguments. The specified *name* may be non-unique. If *widget_class* or *parent* is NULL, XtCreatePopupShell issues a fatal error.

USAGE

XtCreateWidget is used to create all normal (non-Shell) widgets. Acceptable values for the *widget_class* argument are supplied in the header files for your widget set. Technically, any widget can have children, but the parent must be a subclass of Composite if you expect to manage the child so it can be seen. The input arglist is usually declared as a static array of type Arg, and is filled in with repeated calls to XtSetArg.

The *name* is used to reference the new widget in resource files. The fully-qualified name of any resource is constructed by concatenating the application name, the names of all the widget's ancestors in superior-to-inferior order, the widget's own name and the resource name, separated by periods.

Widgets created with XtCreateWidget may be destroyed with XtDestroyWidget. XtVaCreateWidget is the varargs variant of this routine.

CAUTION

XtCreateWidget cannot be used to create widgets that are subclasses of Shell; to create pop-up windows, call XtCreatePopupShell instead. If a non-unique name is specified, loosely-bound declarations in resource files may inadvertently refer to more than one widget.

SEE ALSO

Routines: XtAppCreateShell, XtCreateManagedWidget, XtCreatePopupShell, XtDestroyWidget, XtVaCreateWidget

XtCreateWindow   **(R3)**

Creates a widget's window

SYNOPSIS

```
void XtCreateWindow( w, window_class, visual, attribute_mask, attributes)
        Widget                          w;
        unsigned int                    window_class;
        Visual                          *visual;
        XtValueMask                     attribute_mask;
        XtSetWindowAttributes           *attributes;
```

ARGUMENTS

w	in	Widget that defines geometry of window to be created; must be of class Core or any subclass thereof.
window_class	in	Specifies the Xlib window class - `InputOutput`, `InputOnly` or `CopyFromParent`.
visual	in	Specifies the Xlib window visual type (usually `CopyFromParent`).
attribute_mask	in	Mask specifying attributes to set in the `XCreateWindow` call.
attributes	in	Pointer to data structure specifying window attribute values.

DESCRIPTION

`XtCreateWindow` is a convenience interface for the Xlib routine `XCreateWindow`. The geometry, depth and screen of the window are taken from the specified widget's resource fields. The *attributes* and *attribute_mask* arguments are used exactly as in the `XCreateWindow`.

USAGE

`XtCreateWindow` is a convenience routine used in widget implementation code to create a widget's window. The widget is given a chance to do this at realization time. `XtCreateWindow` should not be called by application programmers.

CAUTION

`XtCreateWindow` is a widget internal routine and should not be called by application programmers.

SEE ALSO

Routines: `XtRealizeWidget, XtUnrealizeWidget`

XtDatabase   (R3)

Returns the per-display resource database

SYNOPSIS

```
XrmDatabase XtDatabase( display )
        Display                         *display;
```

ARGUMENTS

display   in   Specifies an open display for which database is requested.

DESCRIPTION

XtDatabase returns the resource database built by XtDisplayInitialize and associated with the specified display.

USAGE

A resource database is maintained for each open display and each screen of a display. The contents of these databases are built from a variety of sources, including resource files, command-line arguments and properties found on the display's root window (see XtDisplayInitialize).

When widgets are created. their resources are automatically loaded from their associated database. Likewise, XtGetApplicationResources retrieves application resources from the appropriate database, so you will rarely need to access a resource database directly.

If you want to explicitly examine or add resource definitions, you can use the Xlib "Xrm" routines to manipulate the resource database. The database returned by XtDatabase holds resources that would be common to all screens of the specified display. In versions of the Intrinsics prior to R5, the per-display database is the only database, and is used for all screens of a display. In R5 and R6, the screen-specific database returned by XtScreenDatabase is a superset of the per-display database, and holds resources that would be searched by applications displaying on a particular screen.

CAUTION

This database is built when the display is initialized with XtDisplayInitialize, or one of the routines that calls it (XtOpenDisplay, XtAppInitialize, XtOpenApplication). If the display has not been initialized, the results of XtDatabase are undefined in releases prior to R5, and NULL in releases R5 and greater.

SEE ALSO

Routines: XtAppInitialize, XtDisplayInitialize, XtOpenDisplay,
           XtScreenDatabase

XtDestroyApplicationContext   **(R3)**

Destroys an application context

SYNOPSIS

```
void XtDestroyApplicationContext( app_context )
        XtAppContext                    app_context;
```

ARGUMENTS

app_context   in   The application context to be destroyed.

DESCRIPTION

XtDestroyApplicationContext destroys the specified application context and closes any displays associated with it. The application context is destroyed as soon as it is safe to do so; if XtDestroyApplicationContext is called from within an event dispatch (e.g. from a callback procedure), the application context is not destroyed until the dispatch is complete.

USAGE

XtDestroyApplicationContext is seldom used since most applications have only a single application context and need it until the application exits. You should use it only if you have multiple application contexts and need to close one. To exit an application, you would usually just call exit() from within a callback routine. In R6, exit handling is improved - you can use XtAppSetExitFlag to set a flag that causes XtAppMainLoop to return. Code that performs clean-up activities can then be placed after XtAppMainLoop.

CAUTION

Widgets associated with the application context are not explicitly destroyed by XtDestroyApplicationContext, but are pretty useless since there is no way to re-associate them with a display. Widgets should be destroyed with XtDestroyWidget before calling XtDestroyApplicationContext, so as to invoke any callbacks on their XtNdestroyCallback lists and free their storage.

SEE ALSO

Routines: XtCreateApplicationContext

XtDestroyGC (O)

Frees a reference to a shared GC

SYNOPSIS

```
void XtDestroyGC( w, gc )
        Widget                          w;
        GC                              gc;
```

ARGUMENTS

w   in   Widget specifying display for which shared GC is valid; must be of class Object or any subclass thereof.

gc   in   Identifier of shared GC returned by XtGetGC or XtAllocateGC.

DESCRIPTION

XtDestroyGC frees a reference to a shared GC previously allocated with XtGetGC or XtAllocateGC. The toolkit maintains a reference count for each shared GC, and sends a request to the server to free the real GC when the last user releases it.

USAGE

See XtReleaseGC.

CAUTION

XtDestroyGC is an obsolete routine provided for backwards compatibility with earlier releases of the Intrinsics. It should not be called in applications. This function has been replaced in the R4 and later Intrinsics by XtReleaseGC, which is more portable and whose name better describes the actual function of the routine.

SEE ALSO

Routines: XtAllocateGC, XtGetGC, XtReleaseGC

XtDestroyWidget

(R3)

Destroys a widget and frees its resources

SYNOPSIS

```
void XtDestroyWidget( w )
        Widget                      w;
```

ARGUMENTS

w   in   Widget to be destroyed; must be of class Object or any subclass thereof.

DESCRIPTION

XtDestroyWidget recursively destroys the specified widget and all of its normal and pop-up descendants. The Intrinsics destroy the widget(s) as soon as it is safe to do so, and free any client and server resources associated with the destroyed widget(s). All widgets have a "destroy" callback list, identified by the resource XtNdestroyCallback. Any routines on this list are called just before the widget is finally destroyed.

USAGE

XtDestroyWidget is used to destroy a widget that is no longer needed. If you wish to perform additional processing when a widget is destroyed, you can register one or more procedures with the widget's XtNdestroyCallback. The Intrinsics take advantage of this to make sure that cached resource values are released when a widget that references them is destroyed (see XtCallbackReleaseCacheRef).

XtDestroyWidget may be called at any time - even within an event dispatch (e.g. a callback procedure). The widget(s) are not actually destroyed until all processing associated with the current event dispatch is complete. Thus, a widget's callback may safely destroy the widget itself, its parent, ancestors, siblings or descendants. However, this also means that the same widget could conceivably be destroyed multiple times within a single event dispatch. If XtDestroyWidget sees that the specified widget is currently being destroyed it simply returns. The XtNdestroyCallback will only be called once per widget that gets destroyed.

CAUTION

Widget creation and destruction takes a relatively long time, and should not be used as a substitute for managing and unmanaging (or mapping/unmapping) widgets. In most cases, widgets should be destroyed only when you are sure that they will never be used again, or when client or server memory resources are very scarce.

Callbacks on the XtNdestroyCallback list are invoked only by XtDestroyWidget. If a widget is destroyed by any other agent (such as simply exiting the application), these callbacks are not invoked.

If all of the widgets in a given application context are destroyed but XtAppMainLoop has not exited, your application can be left in a state in which it is waiting for events but there are no windows to deliver them nor widgets to process them.

SEE ALSO

Routines: XtAppCreateShell, XtCreatePopupShell, XtCreateWidget,
            XtManageChild, XtRealizeWidget, XtUnmanageChild, XtUnrealizeWidget

XtDirectConvert (R3O)

Calls an old-format resource type converter directly

SYNOPSIS

```
void XtDirectConvert( converter, args, num_args, from, to_return)
        XtConverter                converter;
        XrmValue                   *convert_args;
        Cardinal                   num_args;
        XrmValue                   *from;
        XrmValue                   *to;
```

ARGUMENTS

converter	in	Old-format resource converter to be called.
convert_args	in	Pointer to a list of additional arguments required to perform conversion, or NULL if none are needed.
num_args	in	Number of additional arguments provided, or zero if none are needed.
from	in	Pointer to an XrmValue structure describing the input value .
to	in/out	Pointer to an XrmValue structure to receive the converted value.

DESCRIPTION

XtDirectConvert first checks the conversion cache to see if the specified conversion has already been performed. If the *from* value has been previously converted and cached, the cached value is returned in *to*. Otherwise, XtDirectConvert invokes the specified old-format resource converter to convert the *from* value (expressed in the converter source type) to the *to* value (expressed in the converter destination type), passing any arguments specified by *args* and *num_args*. The converted value is returned by the converter in *to*, and the result is cached for later reference.

USAGE

See XtCallConverter.

CAUTION

This routine is superseded by XtCallConverter in the R4 and later Intrinsics. The resource converter to be invoked is specific to the *from/to* type conversion, and the caller is responsible for ensuring that the *from* value and *convert_args* are appropriate to the specific converter. XtDirectConvert does not return a status. By convention, if the conversion fails, the converter logs a warning message and the *addr* field of the returned *to* argument is NULL.

SEE ALSO

Routines: XtAppAddConverter, XtAddConverter, XtConvert

XtDisownSelection   **(R3)**

Voluntarily releases selection ownership

SYNOPSIS

```
void XtDisownSelection( w, selection, time )
        Widget                    w;
        Atom                      selection;
        Time                      time;
```

ARGUMENTS

w	in	Widget that owns selection; must be of class Core or any subclass thereof.
selection	in	Atom identifying which selection is disowned, e.g. XA_PRIMARY if disowning primary selection; XA_SECONDARY if disowning secondary selection, etc.
time	in	Timestamp specifying when the selection ownership is relinquished; this should be the timestamp of the event that triggered the decision to give up the selection, or the symbolic value CurrentTime.

DESCRIPTION

XtDisownSelection releases ownership of the specified selection. Requests for this selection that arrive after XtDisownSelection is called are not delivered. However, any incremental transfers in progress when XtDisownSelection is called are allowed to run to completion. If a transfer in progress completes after the call to XtDisownSelection, the *done_proc* registered by XtOwnSelection or XtOwnSelectionIncremental will be called.

USAGE

An application or widget volunteers to own a selection by calling XtOwnSelection or XtOwnSelectionIncremental. This registers routines to be called when the selection is requested. When an application is no longer interested in providing the selection, XtDisownSelection releases selection ownership. The *time* argument should be the timestamp from with the event that triggered the decision to cancel ownership.

If you disown the selection, you are responsible for providing any appropriate visual feedback to the user to indicate that the selection is no longer owned.

CAUTION

Selection ownership may also be lost involuntarily because another widget or application has requested it. If this occurs, the Intrinsics call the *lose_selection_proc* registered by a previous call to XtOwnSelection or XtOwnSelectionIncremental.

SEE ALSO

Routines: XtGetSelectionValue, XtGetSelectionValueIncremental,
            XtGetSelectionValues, XtGetSelectionValuesIncremental,
            XtOwnSelection, XtOwnSelectionIncremental

XtDispatchEvent (R3)

Dispatches an X event to the widget tree for processing

SYNOPSIS

```
Boolean XtDispatchEvent( event )
        XEvent                          *event;
```

ARGUMENTS

event   in   Pointer to event structure to be processed.

DESCRIPTION

XtDispatchEvent sends an X event to the toolkit to be processed. The widget to which the event is dispatched is determined from the window ID in the event structure, the state of the grab list (see XtAddGrab), and any keyboard forwarding in effect (see XtSetKeyboardFocus). If the receiving widget requests it, XtDispatchEvent compresses Expose, PointerMotion and EnterNotify/LeaveNotify events.

XtDispatchEvent records the timestamp of the event (if it has one), then checks the widget's list of event handlers and calls each handler registered for the event type being processed. If the event is of a type referenced in the widget's translation table, it is also processed through translation management, and may invoke action procedures or callbacks. XtDispatchEvent returns False if no event handlers are found that accept the specified event, and returns True if the event is passed to at least one event handler.

USAGE

XtDispatchEvent is normally called internally by XtAppMainLoop to handle X events received from the user interface. You can call XtDispatchEvent directly if you write your own version of the main loop. Usually the event to be dispatched is a real event returned by XtAppNextEvent, but you could also dispatch synthetic events to simulate user input.

CAUTION

Event handlers are called before action procedures, but the Intrinsics do not define the order in which individual event handlers or callback routines are executed. If an event dispatch results in a widget invoking callback routines, XtDispatchEvent does not return until the last of these callbacks returns.

SEE ALSO

Routines: XtAddEventHandler, XtAddGrab, XtAppMainLoop,
           XtDispatchEventToWidget, XtInsertEventHandler, XtMainLoop,
           XtRemoveEventHandler, XtRemoveGrab, XtLastTimestampProcessed,
           XtSetKeyboardFocus, XtLastEventProcessed

XtDispatchEventToWidget   **(R6)**

Dispatches an X event to a specific widget for processing

SYNOPSIS

```
Boolean XtDispatchEventToWidget( w, event )
        Widget                   w;
        XEvent                   *event;
```

ARGUMENTS

w	in	Widget that should handle the event; must be of class Core or any subclass thereof.
event	in	Pointer to event structure to be processed.

DESCRIPTION

XtDispatchEventToWidget sends an X event to a specific widget for processing. Expose events are compressed, if the receiving widget has requested it, and cause the widget's *expose* procedure to be called to refresh its graphics. VisibilityNotify events are also processed internally and update the widget's internal state.

XtDispatchEventToWidget then checks the widget's list of event handlers and calls each handler registered for the event type being processed. If the event is of a type referenced in the widget's translation table, it is also processed through translation management, and may invoke action procedures or callbacks. XtDispatchEventToWidget returns False if the event could not be processed, and True if it was processed in some way.

USAGE

You would call XtDispatchEventToWidget only if you supply your own event dispatcher for extension events, or if you write your own main loop that dispatches events selectively to widgets. These cases are rare, and if you write your own main loop you would usually call XtDispatchEvent instead. Usually the event to be dispatched is a real event returned by XtAppNextEvent, but you could also dispatch synthetic events to simulate user input.

CAUTION

Event handlers are called before action procedures, but the Intrinsics do not define the order in which individual event handlers or callback routines are executed. If an event dispatch results in a widget invoking callback routines, XtDispatchEvent does not return until the last of these callbacks returns.

SEE ALSO

Routines: XtAddEventHandler, XtAddGrab, XtAppMainLoop, XtInsertEventHandler, XtMainLoop, XtRemoveEventHandler, XtRemoveGrab

XtDisplay   (R3)

Returns a widget's display pointer

SYNOPSIS

```
Display *XtDisplay( w )
      Widget                        w;
```

ARGUMENTS

w   in   Widget for which the display pointer is requested; must be of class Core
                                   or any subclass thereof.

DESCRIPTION

XtDisplay returns a pointer to the Display structure associated with the specified widget.

USAGE

XtDisplay is often used in callback routines, event handlers and action procedures to derive a display
pointer from the widget ID supplied as the first argument. This may be used in Xlib drawing and resource
management routines, such as XCreatePixmapFromBitmapData or XDrawLine. XtDisplay may
also be used together with Xlib information macros such as XDefaultScreenOfDisplay(display)
to retrieve information about the server. To derive the display associated with a windowless object, call
XtDisplayOfObject instead.

CAUTION

None

SEE ALSO

Routines: XtScreen, XtWindow

XtDisplayInitialize

(R3)

Initializes a display and loads the resource databases

SYNOPSIS

```
void XtDisplayInitialize( app_context, display, app_name, app_class,
    options, num_options, argc, argv )
        XtAppContext        app_context;
        Display             *display;
        String              app_name;
        String              app_class;
        XrmOptionDescRec    *options;
        Cardinal            num_options;
        Cardinal            *argc;
        String              *argv;
```

ARGUMENTS

app_context	in	The application context to which the display should be assigned.
display	in	The previously-opened display to be initialized.
app_name	in	The application resource name, e.g. "myApp".
app_class	in	The application resource class, e.g. "MyApp".
options	in	Pointer to a list of option description records describing command-line options that set resource values.
num_options	in	Number of option descriptors in *options*.
argc	in/out	Pointer to variable specifying argument count provided to main() at image activation; returns number of unparsed arguments.
argv	in/out	Argument vector provided to main() at image activation; returns unparsed arguments.

DESCRIPTION

XtDisplayInitialize adds a display that was previously opened with XOpenDisplay to the specified application context. The per-display and per-screen resource databases are then built by combining the following sources, in descending order of precedence:

- Arguments from the application command line (*argc* and *argv*).
- The user environment resource file ($ENVIRONMENT or $HOME/.Xdefaults-<*host*>).
- Per-screen resources from the SCREEN_RESOURCES property on the root window of the screen. These are usually established with the xrdb utility. SCREEN_RESOURCES is only used by R5 or greater releases of the Intrinsics, and are only merged in the per-screen resource database.
- Per-display resources from the RESOURCE_MANAGER property on the default root window of the display. These are usually established with the xrdb utility. The file $HOME/.Xdefaults is used if the property is not found.
- The user-specific, application-specific resource file, usually $HOME/*app_class*
- The system-wide, application-specific resource file, usually /usr/lib/X11/app-defaults/*app_class*

These sources were discussed in Chapter 6. The following sections provide more detail on how they are found and used.

The tricky part is how `XtDisplayInitialize` decides where to look for the files that it needs. The Intrinsics want to provide a way for you to organize multiple resource files by application, user, language, the nature of your display, etc. and control which are loaded at run time. This way, two users of the same program binary could reference different resource files, and see the application customized to their needs.

The Intrinsics search for each resource file by constructing a list of filenames and testing them in order until a file is found. This is done in concert with the routine `XtResolvePathname`, and is controlled by the values of certain environment variables and application resources.

Environment variables:

- `$HOME`   User's home directory
- `$LANG`   A language specification string (see below)
- `$XAPPLRESDIR`   A base directory name for finding the user defaults file
- `$XENVIRONMENT`   A complete file name for the user environment file
- `$XUSERFILESEARCHPATH`   A colon-delimited list of paths, with substitution characters, used to find the application-specific, user-specific resources
- `$XFILESEARCHPATH`   A colon-delimited list of paths, with substitution characters, used to find the application-specific, system-wide resources

Application resources:

- `.xnlLanguage`   A language specification to override $LANG
- `.customization`   A user-defined "customization" string to convey more information about the environment; e.g. "-24true" to imply that a 24-plane TrueColor workstation is being used, or "-mono" to imply a monochrome workstation.

All of these are intended to be strings that could be interpreted as a path, a directory, a piece of a filename, or a file suffix. The Intrinsics assemble the components in various ways to find the appropriate resource files. File names are constructed by substituting strings derived from the application resources for substitution characters found in the paths. The most common substitutions used in XFILESEARCHPATH and XUSERFILESEARCHPATH are:

- %N   The application class name - usually the string you pass to `XtAppInitialize`
- %C   Value of the `.customization` application resource
- %L   Language string associated with the specified display
- %l   "Language" part of the display's language string
- %t   "Territory" part of the display's language string
- %c   "Codeset" part of the display's language string

Sometimes, the Intrinsics search an implementation-dependent default path. This is tailored by system vendors as appropriate to a particular platform. After all, the "right" place to look for a resource file would not be the same on a UNIX system and an MS-DOS system. Sometimes the default path is decided by `XtDisplayInitialize`, and sometimes by `XtResolvePathname`. Without going into details of the exact code used to load the resource databases, here is how `XtDisplayInitialize` searches for its resource files:

`XtDisplayInitialize` first loads a temporary resource database from the RESOURCE_MANAGER property found on the root window of the specified display, or the user's `$HOME/.Xdefaults` file if that property is not found. Now, it tries to find a language specification by examining the command line for the -xnlLanguage option or a -xrm option specifying the application resource ".xnlLanguage" (Class: ".XnlLanguage"). If nothing is found on the command line, the previously-loaded resources from .Xdefaults are searched for the required resource.

In releases of the Intrinsics greater than or equal to R5, the Intrinsics next check to see if a language proc has been set with XtSetLanguageProc. If there is a language proc, the toolkit assumes that you are serious about internationalization; it calls the language proc, passing the language specification, or the empty string "" if no specification was found. The language proc is expected to enable localization support for the requested language and return the language string (see XtLanguageProc, Appendix B). This string does not have to be the same as the language specification (but often is).

If there is no registered language proc, or if you're using a release of the Intrinsics prior to R5, the Intrinsics assume that you want "poor-man's" internationalization support. That is, you might have language-specific resource files, but you won't receive any other special support for the locale. The value of the .xnlLanguage resource, if found, is used as the language string. Otherwise, the value of the LANG environment variable is used, or if that is not defined, the empty string "".

The language string is implementation-dependent, and is intended to convey information about the language, its dialect, and the set of characters required to write it. In practical use, it is usually of the form "*language_territory.codeset*", where *language* is an abbreviation for the national language, *territory* is an abbreviation for a locality, and *codeset* is the encoding used to describe characters in that locale. An example might be "en_US.8859-1", indicating English as used in the United States, employing an ISO Latin-1 encoding. However, as mentioned before, this is implementation-dependent, so the same locale on another system might be expressed by the string "EN_USA.88591" The parts of the language string are substituted into the paths used by XtDisplayInitialize as shown in the substitution list above.

The following sections discuss the paths searched by XtDisplayInitialize for each of its important resource files:

- The system-wide, application-specific resource file ("app defaults"), or fallback resources:
  - On POSIX-based systems this usually defaults to /usr/lib/X11/app-defaults/*app_class*.
  - Actually, XtDisplayInitialize calls XtResolvePathname with the arguments (*display*, "app-defaults", NULL, NULL, NULL, NULL, 0, NULL), which lets XtResolvePathname choose its own path to search for the file. This is controlled by the environment variable XFILESEARCHPATH, but after seeing the reference page for XtResolvePathname, you may wonder where it does *not* look.
  - If no application defaults file is found, XtDisplayInitialize merges any fallback resources specified by XtAppSetFallbackResources or XtAppInitialize.
- The user-specific, application-specific resource file
  - On POSIX-based systems this usually defaults to $HOME/*app_class*.
  - Actually, XtDisplayInitialize calls XtResolvePathname with the arguments (*display*, NULL, NULL, NULL, <*path*>, NULL, 0, NULL), where <path> is determined as follows:
  - If the environment variable XUSERFILESEARCHPATH is defined, this is passed as the *path* argument to XtResolvePathname.
  - If XUSERFILESEARCHPATH is undefined but XAPPLRESDIR is defined, the Intrinsics search an implementation-dependent default path that includes the value of XAPPLRESDIR plus various substitutions.

>	$XAPPLRESDIR with	%C, %N, %L	or	%C, %N, %l, %, t, %c
>	$XAPPLRESDIR with	%C, %N, %l		
>	$XAPPLRESDIR with	%C, %N		
>	$XAPPLRESDIR with	%N, %L	or	%N, %l, %, t, %c
>	$XAPPLRESDIR with	%N, %l		
>	$XAPPLRESDIR with	%N		
>	$HOME with	%N		

Users often assume that if XAPPLRESDIR is defined, then the resource file will be in $XAPPLRESDIR/*AppClass*; in reality, this is one of the last places searched.

- If neither XUSERFILESEARCHPATH nor XAPPLRESDIR is defined, the Intrinsics try:

  > $HOME with %C, %N, %L or %C, %N, %l, %, t, %c
  > $HOME with %C, %N, %l
  > $HOME with %C, %N
  > $HOME with %N, %L or %N, %l, %, t, %c
  > $HOME with %N, %l
  > $HOME with %N

- The user defaults file:
  - $HOME/.Xdefaults
- The host-specific user environment file:
  - If the environment variable XENVIRONMENT is defined, it is used as the full name of the file
  - If XENVIRONMENT is not defined, the Intrinsics look for a file named $HOME/.Xdefaults-*host*, where *host* is the name of the machine the client is running on.

In the end, the resource database holds definitions from all the sources listed at the start of this section. This database is searched by the Intrinsics when creating widgets or fetching application resources with XtGetApplicationResources. In versions of the Intrinsics greater than R4, there are two resource databases - a display-specific database and a screen-specific database. The screen-specific database holds resources that would apply to a client running on a particular screen of a display. The per-display database holds resources that would apply to any client connecting to the server.

USAGE

XtDisplayInitialize is called automatically by XtAppInitialize, XtOpenDisplay and XtOpenApplication (R6), so you would probably never call XtDisplayInitialize directly. However, it's important to understand where it looks when building the resource database.

CAUTION

None

SEE ALSO

Routines: XtAppInitialize, XtAppSetFallbackResources, XtCloseDisplay, XtOpenDisplay

XtDisplayOfObject

(R4)

Returns an object's display pointer

SYNOPSIS

```
Display *XtDisplayOfObject( object )
        Widget                      object;
```

ARGUMENTS

object   in   Widget or object for which display pointer is requested; must be of class
                                Object or any subclass thereof.

DESCRIPTION

XtDisplayOfObject returns a pointer to the Display structure associated with the nearest windowed relative of the specified object. If the specified object is a subclass (at any level) of Core, XtDisplayOfObject is identical in function to XtDisplay.

USAGE

XtDisplayOfObject is often used in widget or object callbacks to derive a display pointer from the widget ID supplied as the first argument. This may be used in Xlib drawing and resource management routines, such as XCreatePixmapFromBitmapData or XDrawLine, or with Xlib information macros such as XDefaultScreenOfDisplay(display) to retrieve information about the server. XtDisplayOfObject is also used in the implementation code for windowless objects, which must use their relative's window for drawing.

CAUTION

None.

SEE ALSO

Routines: XtScreenOfObject, XtWindowOfObject

XtDisplayStringConversionWarning (R4)

Logs an error message generated by a String resource conversion

SYNOPSIS

```
void XtDisplayStringConversionWarning( display, from_value, to_type )
        Display                       *display;
        String                        from_value;
        String                        to_type;
```

ARGUMENTS

display	in	Pointer to display with which conversion is associated.
from_value	in	String specifying source data which could not be converted.
to_type	in	String specifying the failed destination data type, e.g. "Int" or the symbolic constant XtRInt.

DESCRIPTION

XtDisplayStringConversionWarning issues a warning message by calling XtAppWarningMsg with *name* equal to "conversionError", *type* equal to "string", *class* equal to "XtToolkitError" and the default message string "Cannot convert *from_value* to *to_type*"

USAGE

XtDisplayStringConversionWarning is a convenience routine called by new-format resource converters when a resource value of type String cannot be converted to the appropriate type. It is employed by the Intrinsics built-in resource converters, and you can use it if you write application-specific resource converters. To issue other types of warnings, you should call XtAppWarningMsg directly.

CAUTION

None

SEE ALSO

Routines: XtAppSetTypeConverter, XtAppWarningMsg, XtSetTypeConverter

XtDisplayToApplicationContext   **(R4)**

Returns the application context associated with a display

SYNOPSIS

```
XtAppContext XtDisplayToApplicationContext( display )
        Display                         *display;
```

ARGUMENTS

display   in   Pointer to open display.

DESCRIPTION

`XtDisplayToApplicationContext` returns the application context in which the specified display is registered.

USAGE

`XtDisplayToApplicationContext` is most commonly used in resource converter implementation code to supply the application context argument required by `XtAppWarningMsg`. This is necessary because resource type converters are provided with a display pointer, but not an application context, when they are invoked. You seldom use this routine for anything else.

CAUTION

None

SEE ALSO

Routines: `XtOpenDisplay`

XtError (O)

Calls the toolkit low-level error handler

SYNOPSIS

```
void XtError( message )
        String                          message;
```

ARGUMENTS

message   in   Error message to be reported.

DESCRIPTION

XtError calls the error handler currently registered by XtSetErrorHandler in the default application context, or the default error handler if none has been registered. The toolkit default error handler simply displays the specified message to stderr and then exits.

USAGE

XtError is called by toolkit internal routines that cannot derive the application context of the caller. Application programmers should call XtAppError or XtAppErrorMsg instead.

CAUTION

XtError is an obsolete routine supplied for backwards compatibility with earlier versions of the Intrinsics, and is superseded by XtAppError in the Release 3 and later Intrinsics. XtError uses the default application context established by XtInitialize, which must be called first.

SEE ALSO

Routines: XtAppError, XtInitialize, XtSetErrorHandler

XtErrorMsg

(O)

Calls the toolkit high-level error handler

SYNOPSIS

```
void XtErrorMsg( name, type, class, default, params, num_params )
        String              name;
        String              type;
        String              class;
        String              default;
        String              *params;
        Cardinal            *num_params;
```

ARGUMENTS

name	in	Resource name of message, e.g. "invalidClass".
type	in	Secondary resource name of message, e.g. "xtPopup".
class	in	Resource class of message, e.g. "XtToolkitError".
default	in	Default message to display if no match is found.
params	in	Pointer to a list of string values to be substituted in the error message when it is output.
num_params	in	Pointer to a variable specifying number of string values in *params*.

DESCRIPTION

XtErrorMsg calls the error message handler currently registered by XtSetErrorMsgHandler in the default application context, or the default error message handler if none has been registered. The error message handler reports the message generated from the arguments, and then exits.

USAGE

XtErrorMsg is called by toolkit internal routines that cannot derive the application context of the caller. Application programmers should call XtAppErrorMsg instead.

CAUTION

XtErrorMsg is an obsolete routine supplied for backwards compatibility with earlier versions of the Intrinsics, and is superseded by XtAppErrorMsg in the Release 3 and later Intrinsics. XtErrorMsg uses the default application context established by XtInitialize, which must be called first.

SEE ALSO

Routines: XtAppErrorMsg, XtInitialize, XtSetErrorMsgHandler

XtFindFile (R4)

Searches for a file in a permuted path

SYNOPSIS

```
String XtFindFile( path, substitutions, num_substitutions, predicate )
        String                    path;
        SubstitutionRec           *substitutions;
        Cardinal                  num_substitutions;
        XtFilePredicate           predicate;
```

ARGUMENTS

path	in	A string specifying a series of potential filenames delimited by colons, and including substitution characters.
substitutions	in	Pointer to a list of substitution-character/string pairs to be used to permute the path.
num_substitutions	in	Number of character/string combinations supplied in *substitutions*.
predicate	in	Specifies a routine called to determine whether a synthesized filename is appropriate, or NULL to use the default predicate.

DESCRIPTION

XtFindFile searches for a file by name, using substitutions to permute the path. A "substitution character" in the *path* argument is indicated by a preceding percent sign "%". For example, in the path "/usr/users/%t/defaults", "%t" indicates that the letter "t" is a substitution character. Each time a substitution character is found, the list of *substitutions* is checked for strings to substitute for this character.

A path may include any number of substitution characters, as long as they are all specified in *substitutions*. The string "%%" implies a percent sign which should not be substituted. The string "%:" implies a colon which is part of the path and should not be interpreted as a delimiter between file names.

Each filename in *path* is permuted using the specified substitutions, each time passing the resulting string to the specified XtFilePredicate callback. The XtFilePredicate callback returns True when the permuted string matches the appropriate filename; the criteria used by *predicate* to determine whether a filename is "appropriate" are its own. The default predicate is named TestFile and returns True if the file exists, is readable and is not a directory. The string specifying the file's full path is returned by XtFindFile. If no string yields a True return from *predicate*, XtFindFile returns NULL.

USAGE

You can use XtFindFile to look up files with stylized path names. This is used by the Intrinsics to find Internationalized versions of resource files, which usually reside in related directories. For example, the English and French-language equivalent resource files for an application might "/usr/lib/X11/app-defaults/en_US/Appl" and "/usr/lib/X11/app-defaults/fr_FR/Appl".

CAUTION

The filename returned by XtFindFile should be freed with XtFree when non longer needed.

SEE ALSO

Routines: XtResolvePathname

XtFree

Frees memory associated with most toolkit data types

SYNOPSIS

```
void XtFree( pointer )
        char                         *pointer;
```

ARGUMENTS

pointer   in   Pointer to a block of storage to free.

DESCRIPTION

XtFree releases a block of allocated storage for reuse. It performs the same function as the "C" language runtime routine free(), but simply returns if *pointer* is NULL.

USAGE

XtFree is used to free blocks of memory dynamically allocated by Intrinsics routines for Strings, ArgLists, type-conversion results, etc. These include but are not limited to the following:

- ArgLists returned by XtMergeArgLists
- XtVarArgsLists returned by XtVaCreateArgsList
- XtResourceLists returned by XtGetResourceList and XtGetConstraintResourceList
- Selection values returned with XtGetSelectionValue, XtGetSelectionValues, etc.
- Filenames returned by XtFindFile or XtResolvePathname
- Lists of keycodes returned by XtKeysymToKeycodeList
- Certain resource values returned by XtGetValues
- Action tables returned by XtGetActionList
- Lists of displays returned by XtGetDisplays
- Other blocks allocated with XtMalloc, XtNew, XtRealloc, XtCalloc or XtNewString

XtFree is fully compatible and interchangeable with its standard C counterpart, free(), except that it simply returns if passed a NULL pointer.

CAUTION

If dynamically-allocated storage is not freed, application memory usage may grow without bound as your application runs ("memory leaks"). In extreme cases, this can adversely affect application (and system) performance.

XtFree must not be used to free storage owned by the Intrinsics themselves. Examples are keysym lists returned by XtGetKeysymTable and strings returned by XtGetApplicationNameAndClass or XtName.

XtFree cannot be used to free data structures that themselves contain pointers to data. XtFree does not know how to free the embedded pointed-to data and will leave blocks of allocated memory. Structures that cannot be freed with XtFree include Widgets, XFontStructs and OSF/Motif XmStrings. To free such structures, use the type-specific deallocation routine, e.g. XmStringFree.

SEE ALSO

Routines: XtCalloc, XtMalloc, XtNew, XtNewString, XtRealloc

XtGetActionKeysym (R4)

Reports the KeySym that invoked an action procedure

SYNOPSIS

```
KeySym XtGetActionKeysym( event, modifiers_return )
        XEvent                          *event;
        Modifiers                       *modifiers_return;
```

ARGUMENTS

event	in	Pointer to an XEvent structure.
modifiers_return	in/out	Returns modifiers that caused the translation match, if non-NULL.

DESCRIPTION

XtGetActionKeysym may be called inside action procedures that are invoked by a KeyPress or KeyRelease event. If the specified *event* is that which invoked the action procedure, XtGetActionKeysym retrieves the cached keysym and modifiers corresponding to the Key event. If *event* is a KeyPress or KeyRelease, but does not match the triggering event, XtGetActionKeysym calls XtTranslateKeycode and returns the results. Otherwise, XtGetActionKeysym returns NoSymbol and does nothing with *modifiers_return*.

USAGE

XtGetActionKeysym is provided as a convenience for action procedures that are invoked by a Key event and need to examine the keysym and/or modifiers derived from the triggering event. For performance, the Intrinsics cache this information until the action procedure returns. XtGetActionKeysym lets you avoid repeating the processing that was just performed by the Intrinsics to match the translation entry.

If the action procedure invokes another action procedure directly by calling XtCallActionProc, the nested action procedure may also call XtGetActionKeysym. Calling XtGetActionKeysym outside of an action procedure is equivalent to calling XtTranslateKeycode.

CAUTION

The information returned by XtGetActionKeysym is preserved by the Intrinsics only for the duration of the action procedure within which it is called.

SEE ALSO

Routines: XtTranslateKeycode

XtGetActionList   **(R5)**

Retrieves the names of actions supported by a widget class

SYNOPSIS

```
void XtGetActionList( class, actions_return, num_actions_return )
     WidgetClass                    class;
     XtActionList                   *actions_return;
     Cardinal                       *num_actions_return;
```

ARGUMENTS

class	in	Class pointer (e.g. xmPushButtonWidgetClass) specifying widget class.
actions_return	in/out	Pointer to variable in which to return a pointer to the action table.
num_actions_return	in/out	Pointer to variable in which to return the number of actions in the table.

DESCRIPTION

XtGetActionList retrieves the default action list provided by the specified widget class. If the class is not initialized, or is not a subclass of Core, or does not define any actions, *actions_return* will be NULL and *num_actions_return* will be zero.

USAGE

XtGetActionList is used in widget implementation code to allow a subclass to access the action procedures of its superclass. Since it doesn't tell you what the action procedures actually do or what parameters they expect, this routine is seldom used in normal applications. It might be utilized to explore an unfamiliar toolkit if no documentation were available, but this would be tricky work at best.

If you were writing a graphical user interface editor, it could be used to verify that actions referenced by the user in a translation table actually existed in the context of a particular widget. In that case, the editor wouldn't have to know the meaning of an action to allow a user to reference it.

CAUTION

Free the returned action list with XtFree when it is no longer needed.

SEE ALSO

Routines: None

XtGetApplicationNameAndClass (R4)

Retrieves the application resource name and class

SYNOPSIS

```
void XtGetApplicationNameAndClass( display, name_return, class_return )
        Display                         *display;
        String                          *name_return;
        String                          *class_return;
```

ARGUMENTS

display	in	Specifies an open display.
name_return	in/out	Returned string specifying application resource name.
class_return	in/out	Returned string specifying application resource class.

DESCRIPTION

XtGetApplicationNameAndClass returns the application name and class declared when the specified display was initialized. If the specified *display* has been closed or was never initialized, the results are undefined.

USAGE

If the application name was specified by the RESOURCE_NAME environment variable or the −name command-line option, XtGetApplicationNameAndClass can be used to determine the resource name used to root application resources.

CAUTION

The returned strings are owned by the Intrinsics and must not be modified or freed by the application. If the caller wants a private copy, the strings can be copied with XtNewString.

SEE ALSO

Routines: XtDisplayInitialize, XtOpenDisplay

XtGetApplicationResources   (R3)

Fetches values for application variables from the resource database

SYNOPSIS
```
void XtGetApplicationResources( object, base, resources, num_resources,
    args, num_args )
        Widget                      object;
        XtPointer                   base;
        XtResourceList              resources;
        Cardinal                    num_resources;
        ArgList                     args;
        Cardinal                    num_args;
```

ARGUMENTS

object	in	Specifies the root of resource names; the database associated with this object is searched. Must be of class Object or any subclass thereof.
base	in/out	Base address of data structure to receive resource values.
resources	in	Pointer to a list of resource description records.
num_resources	in	Number of resource definitions in *resources*.
args	in	An array of Args specifying resource values to override values found in the resource database.
num_args	in	Number of override Args in *args*.

DESCRIPTION

XtGetApplicationResources fetches values from the resource database and stores them in the specified data buffer, which is usually an application-specific data structure. The resource list declares resource names, classes and types, and the offset from the base address at which they are to be stored.

The *object* argument specifies the database to be searched, and the root for naming the application resources. For example, if *object* has the fully-qualified resource name "myApp.myMain.defaults", and *resources* specifies a resource named "data", the database would be searched for a specification matching "myApp.myMain.defaults.data". *Object* need not be managed or realized, and may in fact be a dummy object that does nothing but provide a resource name for attaching the application resources. Often, though, *object* specifies the application shell.

USAGE

XtGetApplicationResources lets you retrieve values for application variables from the resource database, which lets the user declare them in resource files just like widget resources. The resource list is usually a static array of type XtResource; it describes the resource names, types and default values for fields in the structure, and the location in the structure where the fetched values are to be stored.

The Intrinsics convert resource values expressed as strings to the appropriate type when they are fetched. If an application-specific data type is required, you must register a type converter which can perform the necessary String-to-*Type* conversion (see XtAppSetTypeConverter) before calling XtGetApplicationResources.

The input arglist is usually declared as a static array of type Arg, and is filled in with repeated calls to XtSetArg. Values in *args* override default values declared in *resources* or found in the resource database.

XtVaGetApplicationResources is the varargs variant of this routine.

CAUTION

XtGetApplicationResources may overwrite the specified resource list with an equivalent representation in an internal format so as to optimize access time if the list is used repeatedly. The resource list must be allocated in writeable storage and the caller must not try to modify it after the call to XtGetApplicationResources, if it is to be used again.

SEE ALSO

Routines: XtAppSetTypeConverter, XtSetArg, XtVaGetApplicationResources

XtGetClassExtension

(R6)

Returns a pointer to a class extension record

SYNOPSIS

```
XtPointer XtGetClassExtension( object_class, byte_offset, type, version,
    record_size)
        WidgetClass         object_class
        Cardinal            byte_offset
        XrmQuark            type
        long                version
        Cardinal            record_size
```

ARGUMENTS

object_class	in	Object class containing the extension record.
byte_offset	in	Offset of extension list from beginning of class record.
type	in	Specifies the *record_type* of the class extension.
version	in	Minimum acceptable version of class extension record to qualify for a match.
record_size	in	Minimum acceptable length of class extension record to qualify for a match, or 0 if any will do.

DESCRIPTION

XtGetClassExtension returns a pointer to the class extension record identified by the arguments.

USAGE

This routine is used in widget internals and is not called by application programmers. Sometimes widget writers have to add fields to a widget class after it has already been designed, and perhaps after it has been subclassed by other widget classes. To allow this without forcing all subclasses to be recompiled, the last field in a widget class record is usually an *extension* field, to which a linked list of *extension records* may be attached. In general, subclasses don't have to know that these fields exist, but subclasses that do wish to access these fields can do so by calling XtGetClassExtension.

CAUTION

None

SEE ALSO

Routines: None

XtGetConstraintResourceList   (R4)

Retrieves the list of constraint resources supported by a Constraint widget

SYNOPSIS

```
void XtGetConstraintResourceList( widget_class, resources, num_resources)
        WidgetClass               widget_class;
        XtResourceList            *resources;
        Cardinal                  *num_resources;
```

ARGUMENTS

widget_class   in   Widget class for which constraint resource list is requested; must be objectClass or any subclass thereof.

resources   in/out   Pointer to variable to receive address of returned array of resource description records.

num_resources   in/out   Pointer to integer variable to receive number of resources in list.

DESCRIPTION

If *widget_class* is a subclass of Constraint, XtGetConstraintResourceList returns an array of XtResource structs describing the constraint resources supplied by the specified widget class. If called before the specified class has been initialized (that is, before the first widget of that class or one of its subclasses is instantiated) XtGetConstraintResourceList returns only the resources associated specifically with that subclass. If called after the class has been initialized, it returns the merged constraint resource list that includes resources supplied by all of the superclasses of *widget_class*. If the class is not a subclass of Constraint, the returned *resources* are NULL and *num_resources* is zero.

USAGE

When a Constraint widget is given children, it attaches a set of its constraint resources to each child. These supplement the resources normally supported by the child, and may be set or queried by calling XtSetValues or XtGetValues on the child. The Constraint parent uses these resources to maintain and specify complex geometry management information about its children. To find out what constraint resources a Constraint widget attaches to its children, call XtGetConstraintResourceList on the Constraint parent.

Since the resource list doesn't tell you what the resources mean or how they are used, this routine is seldom used in normal applications. It might be utilized to explore an unfamiliar toolkit if no documentation were available, but this would be tricky work at best. However, if you were writing a graphical user interface editor or an Editres-type client, you could use it to report which resources apply to a particular widget. In that case, the editor wouldn't have to know the meaning of a resource to allow a user to set it.

CAUTION

XtGetConstraintResourceList dynamically allocates storage for the returned resource list. The returned resource list should be freed with XtFree when no longer needed.

SEE ALSO

Routines: XtFree, XtGetResourceList

XtGetDisplays

(R6)

Retrieves the list of displays associated with the specified application context

SYNOPSIS

```
void XtGetDisplays( context, disp_return, num_disp_return )
    XtAppContext                    context;
    Display                         ***disp_return;
    Cardinal                        *num_disp_return;
```

ARGUMENTS

context	in	Application context for which displays are requested.
disp_return	in/out	Pointer to a variable in which an array of display pointers is returned.
num_disp_return	in/out	Pointer to a variable in which the number of displays is returned.

DESCRIPTION

XtGetDisplays retrieves the list of open displays associated with the application context.

USAGE

XtGetDisplays is seldom called directly by applications. It is most often used by debugging tools, resource editors or other external agents that you link into your program. Such tools may wish to do something on a display-by-display basis but don't know which displays you opened. However, if the tool has access to the application context it can get the list of open displays with XtGetDisplays. To make the opposite transformation and return the application context associated with a display, call XtDisplayToApplicationContext.

CAUTION

The list of displays should be freed with XtFree when it is no longer required.

SEE ALSO

Routines: XtDisplayToApplicationContext, XtCreateApplicationContext, XtOpenDisplay

XtGetErrorDatabase   (O)

Returns the error message database

SYNOPSIS

XrmDatabase *XtGetErrorDatabase()

ARGUMENTS

None

DESCRIPTION

XtGetErrorDatabase returns the address of the resource database from which toolkit error and warning messages are extracted. This resource database is merged on POSIX-based systems from the resource file /usr/lib/X11/XtErrorDB.

USAGE

See XtAppGetErrorDatabase.

CAUTION

Note that this routine, unlike XtDatabase or XtScreenDatabase, returns the *address* of an XrmDatabase. The error database is not actually merged until the first call to XtGetErrorDatabaseText.

XtGetErrorDatabase is an obsolete routine supplied for backwards compatibility with earlier versions of the Intrinsics, and is superseded by XtAppGetErrorDatabase in the Release 3 and later Intrinsics. XtGetErrorDatabase uses the default application context established by XtInitialize, which must be called first.

SEE ALSO

Routines: XtAppGetErrorDatabase, XtGetErrorDatabaseText, XtInitialize

XtGetErrorDatabaseText   **(O)**

Fetches a message from the message database

SYNOPSIS

```
void XtGetErrorDatabaseText( name, type, class, default, buffer_return,
    buffer_size )
            String                          name;
            String                          type;
            String                          class;
            String                          default;
            String                          buffer_return;
            int                             buffer_size;
```

ARGUMENTS

name	in	Resource name of message to be retrieved, e.g. "invalidClass".
type	in	Secondary resource name of message, e.g. "xtPopup".
class	in	Resource class of message to be retrieved, e.g. "XtToolkitError".
default	in	Default message to be returned if the requested message is not found.
buffer_return	in/out	Address of buffer to hold returned message string.
buffer_size	in	Size of *buffer_return*, in bytes.

DESCRIPTION

XtGetErrorDatabaseText retrieves the error or warning message specified by *name*, *type* and *class* from the default error database, which on POSIX-based systems is merged from the file /usr/lib/X11/XtErrorDB on the first call to XtGetErrorDatabaseText.

USAGE

See XtAppGetErrorDatabaseText.

CAUTION

XtGetErrorDatabaseText is an obsolete routine supplied for backwards compatibility with earlier versions of the Intrinsics, and is superseded by XtAppGetErrorDatabaseText in the Release 3 and later Intrinsics. XtGetErrorDatabaseText uses the default application context established by XtInitialize, which must be called first.

SEE ALSO

Routines: XtAppGetErrorDatabaseText, XtInitialize

XtGetGC (R3)

Allocates a shared, read-only GC

SYNOPSIS

```
GC XtGetGC( w, value_mask, values )
        Widget                          w;
        XtGCMask                        value_mask;
        XGCValues                       *values;
```

ARGUMENTS

w   in   Widget specifying screen and depth for which GC is valid; must be of
                                class Object or any subclass thereof.

value_mask   in   Mask specifying which GC fields are specified by *values*.

values   in   Pointer to XGCValues data structure defining initial GC values.

DESCRIPTION

XtGetGC returns a shared, read-only GC with the specified GC values. If a GC with the requested values does not already exist, a new one is created and maintained by the Intrinsics. If a previously-allocated GC exists with the requested values, its reference count is incremented by one and its ID is returned.

USAGE

Graphics Contexts (GCs) are server objects that control the attributes of drawing primitives. Shared GCs are a toolkit client-side optimization which decreases server resource utilization when many widgets use the same graphic rendition, and could therefore use the same GC. Shared GCs are mainly used in widget implementation code, when it is likely that many widgets in a toolkit will use the same colors, fonts and patterns to draw their graphics. Shared GCs may also be used by application programmers in an effort to decrease the number of server resources required by application graphics code.

You can reserve a shared read-only GC by calling XtGetGC. If a GC with the appropriate values has already been created by an earlier call to XtGetGC, the Intrinsics return the resource ID of the previously-allocated GC, and increment its reference count. If new and unique GC values are specified, the server is asked to create a new GC, and the GC values are cached for later reference.

Shared GCs allocated with XtGetGC are considered read-only, and must never be directly modified with Xlib routines. If a shared GC with modifiable fields is desired, call XtAllocateGC. XtReleaseGC should be called to release a reference to a shared GC when it is no longer needed. When the last reference to a shared GC is released, the GC is destroyed.

CAUTION

"Shared" GCs are implemented strictly within a single client; neither the Intrinsics nor Xlib provide mechanisms for sharing GCs between clients.

SEE ALSO

Routines: XtAllocateGC, XtDestroyGC, XtReleaseGC

XtGetKeyboardFocusWidget   **(R6)**

Finds the widget that will process keyboard events

SYNOPSIS

```
Widget XtGetKeyboardFocusWidget ( source_widget )
    Widget                          source_widget;
```

ARGUMENTS

source_widget   in   Widget for which keyboard forwarding information is requested.

DESCRIPTION

XtGetKeyboardFocusWidget returns the widget that would finally handle a keyboard event forwarded by the specified source widget. If no forwarding has been requested with XtSetKeyboardFocus, XtGetKeyboardFocusWidget returns the ID of *source_widget*.

USAGE

XtSetKeyboardFocus is used to redirect keyboard input in a widget subtree to a particular widget. This lets the keyboard "stick" to that widget even if the pointer is not located directly over it. It is commonly used to assign focus to a particular text widget in a data-entry form or a dialog box.

A manager widget may call XtSetKeyboardFocus internally to forward focus to one of its children. If that child is itself a manager widget, the focus may be forwarded yet again. This can go on to arbitrarily deep levels.

XtGetKeyboardFocusWidget is called by widget writers or advanced application writers to determine which widget would be responsible for processing keyboard events at a particular moment in time. This information might be used to construct a private main loop that forwards other kinds of event types to the focus widget, too, or takes other special action based on which widget has focus.

CAUTION

There are a variety of ways in which toolkits may negotiate which widget is to receive keyboard events. XtGetKeyboardFocusWidget only works if the focus was set with XtSetKeyboardFocus. It will not necessarily yield the correct answer when used with toolkits that assign the focus through other methods, including XSetInputFocus or private methods. OSF/Motif focus is assigned with XmProcessTraversal, and Motif programs should call XmGetFocusWidget to find the widget with keyboard focus.

SEE ALSO

Routines: XtSetKeyboardFocus

XtGetKeysymTable (R4)

Returns the default KeyCode-to-KeySym conversion table

SYNOPSIS

```
KeySym *XtGetKeysymTable( display, min_keycode, keysyms_per_code )
        Display                     *display;
        KeyCode                     *min_keycode;
        int                         *keysyms_per_code;
```

ARGUMENTS

display	in	Display for which mapping table is requested.
min_keycode	in/out	Pointer to variable to receive the minimum keycode valid for the display.
keysyms_per_code	in/out	Pointer to variable to receive the number of keysyms per keycode in the returned table.

DESCRIPTION

XtGetKeysymTable returns a pointer to the keysym table that is used by the Intrinsics to perform keycode-to-keysym translation for the specified display. In the returned table, *keysyms_per_code* keysyms are defined for each keycode. The set of keysyms mapping to a given keycode x start at the index (x - *min_keycode*) * *keysyms_per_code*. Any entry in the table with no corresponding keysym holds the value NoSymbol. Keycodes with values less than *min_keycode* are invalid for the specified display. The maximum value of a keycode is 255.

USAGE

This routine is used in keycode-to-keysym translators, and is rarely called by application programmers. It could be used by applications that wish to parse Key events directly through event handlers.

A Key event holds a keycode that tells which physical key (e.g. top row, third key) was pressed. The mapping of physical keys to keycodes is fixed and specific to a keyboard make and model. Prior to further processing, a keycode is usually translated into a keysym, which is a vendor-neutral encoding describing the symbol associated with that key (e.g. the symbol "A" - see <X11/keysymdef.h>). Modifier keys (e.g. Shift, Ctrl, etc.) may affect which keysym should be mapped to a particular keycode. Therefore, the server also reports any modifier keys that were active when the Key was pressed.

The default mapping between keycodes and keysyms is known to the server and reported to clients when they first connect. It is expressed as a table with multiple keysym entries for each keycode. Columns in the table represent the translation resulting from the keycode with various combinations of modifiers. The Intrinsics' default keycode-to-keysym translator consults this table while parsing Key events through translation management. If you wish to view the table directly you can call XtGetKeysymTable.

CAUTION

The storage pointed to by XtGetKeysymTable is owned by the Intrinsics and must not be written, modified or freed. You should not save the returned pointer and reference it repeatedly, since the tables may change before the next event dispatch. Instead, call XtGetKeysymTable explicitly each time the table needs to be referenced.

SEE ALSO

Routines: XtSetKeyTranslator, XtTranslateKeycode

XtGetMultiClickTime   **(R4)**

Returns the timeout value used to distinguish repeated events

SYNOPSIS

```
int XtGetMultiClickTime( display )
        Display                          *display;
```

ARGUMENTS

display   in   Pointer to Display for which multi-click time is valid.

DESCRIPTION

XtGetMultiClickTime returns the time, expressed in milliseconds, used to determine whether multiple events of the same type are to be interpreted as a repeated event when matching an entry containing a repeat count in a translation table.

USAGE

The toolkit translation manager distinguishes between single events (e.g. pointer button clicks) and repeated events which should be treated as an entity. This distinction is necessary to allow double-clicks, triple-clicks (and so on) to be defined as translations. Such translations are declared in a translation table by specifying an event with a repeat count. Example; a double-click on button 1:

```
    <Btn1Up>(2):  SelectLine()
```

The "multi-click time" is the period of time within which each succeeding similar event must be processed to be considered part of a repeated event. XtGetMultiClickTime returns the current value of the multi-click time, so that it may be reported to the user or saved as a default. The routine XtSetMultiClickTime is used to set a new value for the multi-click time. The multi-click time can also be set using the application resource "multiClickTime" (Class: "MultiClickTime"), and is loaded by XtDisplayInitialize. The default value is 200 milliseconds.

CAUTION

Multi-click times with very large (>1000 ms.) or small (<100 ms.) values may result in rather eccentric toolkit behavior. If an application depends on repeat counts in translations, the multi-click time should be inspected to ensure that it makes sense.

SEE ALSO

Routines: XtSetMultiClickTime

XtGetResourceList (R3)

Retrieves the list of resources supported by a widget class

SYNOPSIS

```
void XtGetResourceList( widget_class, resources, num_resources )
        WidgetClass                 widget_class;
        XtResourceList              *resources;
        Cardinal                    *num_resources;
```

ARGUMENTS

widget_class	in	Widget class for which resource list is requested; must be objectClass or any subclass thereof.
resources	in/out	Pointer to a variable to receive the address of a returned array of resource records of type XtResource.
num_resources	in/out	Pointer to variable to receive returned number of elements in *resources*.

DESCRIPTION

XtGetResourceList returns the list of resources applicable to the specified widget class. If called before the specified class has been initialized (that is, before the first widget of that class or one of its subclasses is instantiated), XtGetResourceList returns only the new resources associated specifically with that subclass. If called after the class has been initialized, it returns the merged resource list that includes resources for the specified class, and its complete chain of superclasses.

USAGE

XtGetResourceList can be used to query a widget class to see what resources it supports. Its main use is as an internal Intrinsics routine used to implement varargs resources. Since the resource list doesn't tell you what the resources mean or how they are used, this routine is seldom used in normal applications. It might be utilized to explore an unfamiliar toolkit if no documentation were available, but this would be tricky work at best. However, if you were writing a graphical user interface editor or an Editres-type client, you could use it to report which resources apply to a particular widget. In that case, the editor wouldn't have to know the meaning of a resource to allow a user to set it.

CAUTION

XtGetResourceList dynamically allocates storage for the returned resource list. The resource list should be freed when no longer needed with XtFree. XtGetResourceList does not return the list of constraint resources, which may have been attached by a manager parent. To examine these, the widget's parent should be queried with XtGetConstraintResourceList.

SEE ALSO

Routines: XtGetConstraintResourceList, XtGetValues, XtSetValues

XtGetSelectionParameters (R6)

Fetches parameters passed by a selection requester

SYNOPSIS

```
void XtGetSelectionParameters( w, selection, request_id, type_return,
    value_return, length_return, format_return )
    Widget                          w;
    Atom                            selection;
    XtRequestId                     request_id;
    Atom                            *type_return;
    XtPointer                       *value_return;
    unsigned long                   *length_return;
    int                             *format_return;
```

ARGUMENTS

w	in	Widget ID of selection owner; must be of class Core or any subclass thereof.
selection	in	Atom identifying which selection is being processed, e.g. XA_PRIMARY for primary selection; XA_SECONDARY for secondary selection, etc.
request_id	in	Specifies requester ID in case of incremental transfers; Must be NULL for atomic transfers.
type_return	in/out	Pointer to Atom in which property type is returned.
value_return	in/out	Pointer to variable in which a pointer to a list of parameters is returned.
length_return	in/out	Pointer to a variable in which the length of the parameter list (in *format_return* units) is returned.
format_return	in/out	Pointer to a variable in which the format (8, 16 or 32-bit) of the parameters is returned.

DESCRIPTION

XtGetSelectionParameters retrieves parameters sent by the selection requester regarding a selection request. If there are no parameters, NULL is stored into *value_return*. XtGetSelectionParameters may only be called within an XtConvertSelectionProc, or from the first call to an XtConvertSelectionIncr proc with a new *request_id*.

USAGE

Requests for certain selection targets, such as the targets INSERT_PROPERTY and INSERT_SELECTION, require the requester to pass additional parameters that describe more detail about the desired selection.

The selection request event doesn't have enough room for such parameters, so they are passed by placing them in a window property where the selection owner can retrieve them. The property is then referenced in the selection request. Prior to R6, a selection provider had to call XtGetSelectionRequest and examine the request directly. In R6, XtSetSelectionParameters and XtGetSelectionParameters take care of the mechanics of the transfer.

Selection requesters should call XtSetSelectionParameters just before making any selection request that takes additional parameters. Selection owners call XtGetSelectionParameters to retrieve them. There are very few targets that require additional parameters, so these routines are not used very often.

CAUTION

Parameters, if any, are specific to the target of a request; if you intend to perform parameterized selection, you should read the ICCCM carefully to see what is expected for a particular target.

SEE ALSO

Routines: XtSetSelectionParameters

XtGetSelectionRequest **(R4)**

Returns the selection request event that started a selection transfer

SYNOPSIS

```
XSelectionRequestEvent *XtGetSelectionRequest( w, selection, request_id )
    Widget                                  w;
    Atom                                    selection;
    XtRequestId                             request_id;
```

ARGUMENTS

w	in	Widget that currently owns the selection; must be of class Core or any subclass thereof.
selection	in	Atom identifying the selection being processed.
request_id	in	In the case of incremental selections, identifies which request is being processed. Must be specified as NULL for atomic transfers.

DESCRIPTION

XtGetSelectionRequest returns a pointer to the SelectionRequest event that caused a conversion procedure to be called. If no request for the specified selection is pending, XtGetSelectionRequest returns NULL.

USAGE

XtGetSelectionRequest may only be called from within an XtConvertSelectionProc that wants to see the actual event for itself. Prior to R6, this was used to see if parameters were being passed by the requester through a window property referenced in the request. In R6 this is done by the routine XtGetSelectionParameters, so there is rarely a need to call XtGetSelectionRequest.

CAUTION

None

SEE ALSO

Routines: XtOwnSelection, XtOwnSelectionIncremental,
           XtGetSelectionParameters

XtGetSelectionTimeout (O)

Returns the timeout value for toolkit selection communication

SYNOPSIS

unsigned long XtGetSelectionTimeout()

ARGUMENTS

None

DESCRIPTION

XtGetSelectionTimeout returns the selection timeout value, expressed in milliseconds. The timeout value returned by XtGetSelectionTimeout is valid in the default application context established by XtInitialize.

USAGE

See XtAppGetSelectionTimeout.

CAUTION

XtGetSelectionTimeout is an obsolete routine supplied for backwards compatibility with earlier versions of the Intrinsics, and is superseded by XtAppGetSelectionTimeout in the Release 3 and later Intrinsics. XtGetSelectionTimeout uses the default application context established by XtInitialize, which must be called first.

SEE ALSO

Routines: XtAppGetSelectionTimeout, XtAppSetSelectionTimeout,
XtSetSelectionTimeout

XtGetSelectionValue
(R3)

Retrieves the current selection value in a single transfer

SYNOPSIS

```
void XtGetSelectionValue( w, selection, target, get_select_proc,
    client_data, time )
        Widget                          w;
        Atom                            selection;
        Atom                            target;
        XtSelectionCallbackProc         get_select_proc;
        XtPointer                       client_data;
        Time                            time;
```

ARGUMENTS

w	in	Widget making the request for the selection; must be of class Core or any subclass thereof.
selection	in	Atom identifying which selection is requested, e.g. XA_PRIMARY for primary selection; XA_SECONDARY for secondary selection, etc.
target	in	Atom specifying the information desired about the selection, e.g. "TEXT".
get_select_proc	in	Procedure to be called when the selection value is ready
client_data	in	Application-defined data to be passed to *get_select_proc* when it is called.
time	in	Specifies time at which the selection is requested; this should be the timestamp of the event that triggered the call to get the selection; the symbolic value CurrentTime is not acceptable.

DESCRIPTION

XtGetSelectionValue requests the specified selection in a single transfer, expressed in the representation described by *target*. It is the responsibility of the selection owner to convert the selection accordingly. When the selection value is ready to be retrieved, *get_select_proc* is called to accept it. This procedure is called some time after the call to XtGetSelectionValue is made, but may be called before or after XtGetSelectionValue returns. The *client_data* is passed to the callback procedure when it is executed. If the selection fails due to a timeout, *get_select_proc* is called with *type* argument equal to XT_CONVERT_FAIL.

USAGE

XtGetSelectionValue is often called internally by widgets to implement cut and paste without the application having to be explicitly involved. Many text widgets, for example, request the current selection when you press a "paste" button or key. If the selection value must be retrieved explicitly, applications may also call XtGetSelectionValue.

XtGetSelectionValue does not return the selection value directly. Instead, it registers a callback procedure of type XtSelectionCallbackProc (see Appendix B), which is called by the Intrinsics to receive the selection value when it is ready. The *selection* is usually XA_PRIMARY or XA_SECONDARY, which are pre-defined atoms found in <X11/Xatom.h>. If it is the CLIPBOARD atom or an atom describing a private selection, it must be interned with XInternAtom.

The atom describing the target should be interned with XInternAtom. Possible targets and their meanings are discussed in the ICCCM and in Chapter 10. To find out what targets the selection owner could provide, you can call XtGetSelectionValue with a target of "TARGETS".

The *time* argument must be the timestamp of the event that triggered the decision to request the selection. This may be obtained with XtLastTimestampProcessed.

CAUTION

Memory allocated by the Intrinsics for the selection value becomes the property of the selection requester, and should be freed with XtFree when it is no longer needed. See the description of XtSelectionCallbackProc in Appendix B for more information on the responsibilities of the requester. There is no guarantee that the selection owner will be able to convert the selection to the requested target, or that there is a current selection owner at all, so the requester should plan a graceful fallback if the selection value cannot be retrieved.

SEE ALSO

Routines: XtDisownSelection, XtGetSelectionTimeout,
XtGetSelectionValueIncremental, XtGetSelectionValues,
XtGetSelectionValuesIncremental, XtOwnSelection,
XtOwnSelectionIncremental, XtSetSelectionTimeout

XtGetSelectionValueIncremental **(R4)**

Retrieves the current selection value in multiple incremental transfers

SYNOPSIS

```
void XtGetSelectionValueIncremental( w, selection, target,
    get_select_proc, client_data, time )
        Widget                        w;
        Atom                          selection;
        Atom                          target;
        XtSelectionCallbackProc       get_select_proc;
        XtPointer                     client_data;
        Time                          time;
```

ARGUMENTS

w	in	Widget making the request for the selection; must be of class Core or any subclass thereof.
selection	in	Atom identifying which selection is requested, e.g. XA_PRIMARY for primary selection; XA_SECONDARY for secondary selection, etc.
target	in	Atom specifying the information desired about the selection, e.g. "TEXT".
get_select_proc	in	Procedure to be called when the selection value is ready.
client_data	in	Application-defined data to be passed to *get_select_proc* when it is called.
time	in	Specifies time at which the selection is requested; this should be the timestamp of the event that triggered the call to get the selection; the symbolic value CurrentTime is not acceptable.

DESCRIPTION

XtGetSelectionValueIncremental requests that the toolkit retrieve the specified selection through a series of incremental transfers. The arguments are handled as they are in a call to XtGetSelectionValue, but the *get_select_proc* is called repeatedly, each time receiving the specified *client_data* and the next selection segment. The end of a selection transfer is indicated when *get_select_proc* is called with a non-NULL value of length zero.

This procedure is called some time after the call to XtGetSelectionValueIncremental is made, but may be called before or after XtGetSelectionValueIncremental returns. If the selection fails due to a timeout, *get_select_proc* is called with *type* argument equal to XT_CONVERT_FAIL. The callback procedure must decide whether any partially-completed transfer is valid or not.

USAGE

XtGetSelectionValueIncremental is used instead of XtGetSelectionValue when the selection value is likely to be large and too cumbersome to pass in a single transfer, or when the requested selection value may consist of several discrete pieces of data. For example, if the selection is likely to be a collection of graphics objects, it might make sense to receive them one at a time.

CAUTION

Memory allocated by the Intrinsics for the selection value becomes the property of the selection requester, and should be freed with XtFree when it is no longer needed. See the description of XtSelectionCallbackProc in Appendix B for more information on the responsibilities of the requester. There is no guarantee that the selection owner will be able to convert the selection to the requested target, or that there is a current selection owner at all, so the requester should plan a graceful fallback if the selection value cannot be retrieved.

SEE ALSO

Routines: XtDisownSelection, XtGetSelectionTimeout, XtGetSelectionValue,
            XtGetSelectionValues, XtGetSelectionValuesIncremental,
            XtOwnSelection, XtOwnSelectionIncremental, XtSetSelectionTimeout

XtGetSelectionValues

(R3)

Retrieves the current selection value expressed in multiple targets

SYNOPSIS

```
void XtGetSelectionValues( w, selection, targets, count, get_select_proc,
    client_data, time )
        Widget                         w;
        Atom                           selection;
        Atom                           *targets;
        int                            count;
        XtSelectionCallbackProc        get_select_proc;
        XtPointer                      client_data;
        Time                           time;
```

ARGUMENTS

w	in	Widget making the request for the selection; must be of class Core or any subclass thereof.
selection	in	Atom identifying which selection is requested, e.g. XA_PRIMARY for primary selection; XA_SECONDARY for secondary selection, etc.
targets	in	Pointer to a list of Atoms describing information desired about selection, e.g. XA_STRING.
num_targets	in	Number of different target types requested by *targets*.
get_select_proc	in	Procedure to be called when selection values are ready.
client_data	in	Specifies a list of application-defined data values to be passed to *get_select_proc*, each corresponding to an entry in *targets*.
time	in	Timestamp of the event that triggered the decision to get the selection; the symbolic value CurrentTime is not acceptable.

DESCRIPTION

XtGetSelectionValues requests the specified selection expressed in multiple targets, with each target passed in a single transfer. It is the responsibility of the selection owner to convert the current selection to the specified targets. When the values are ready to be retrieved, *get_select_proc* is called *num_targets* times, each time receiving the next entry in the array of *client_data* and the selection value expressed as the next requested target. *Get_select_proc* may be called before or after XtGetSelectionValues returns. If the selection fails due to a timeout, *get_select_proc* is called with type XT_CONVERT_FAIL.

USAGE

XtGetSelectionValues is equivalent to calling XtGetSelectionValue multiple times, but guarantees that the selection owner does not change between the delivery of the selection value in different targets. It should be used instead of XtGetSelectionValue when more than one piece of information is desired regarding the current selection. For example, if you are a debugger requesting the selection from a text editor, you might request the value expressed as both a filename and a line number.

CAUTION

Memory allocated by the Intrinsics for the selection value becomes the property of the selection requester, and should be freed with XtFree when it is no longer needed. See the description of XtSelectionCallbackProc in Appendix B for more information on the responsibilities of the requester. There is no guarantee that the selection owner will be able to convert the selection to the requested target, or that there is a current selection owner at all, so the requester should plan a graceful fallback if the selection value cannot be retrieved.

SEE ALSO

Routines: XtDisownSelection, XtGetSelectionTimeout, XtGetSelectionValue, XtGetSelectionValueIncremental, XtGetSelectionValuesIncremental, XtOwnSelection, XtOwnSelectionIncremental, XtSetSelectionTimeout

XtGetSelectionValuesIncremental   **(R4)**

Retrieves the current selection value as multiple targets in multiple incremental transfers

SYNOPSIS

```
void XtGetSelectionValuesIncremental( w, selection, targets, num_targets,
    get_select_proc, client_data, time )
        Widget                      w;
        Atom                        selection;
        Atom                        *targets;
        int                         num_targets;
        XtSelectionCallbackProc     get_select_proc;
        XtPointer                   client_data;
        Time                        time;
```

ARGUMENTS

w	in	Widget making the request for the selection; must be of class Core or any subclass thereof.
selection	in	Atom identifying which selection is requested, e.g. XA_PRIMARY for primary selection; XA_SECONDARY for secondary selection, etc.
targets	in	Pointer to a list of Atoms specifying requested data types of selection, e.g. XA_INT, XA_LINE.
num_targets	in	Number of different target types requested by *targets*.
get_select_proc	in	Procedure to be called when selection is ready.
client_data	in	Application-defined data to be passed to *get_select_proc* when it is executed.
time	in	Specifies time at which the selection is requested; this should be the timestamp of the event that triggered the call to get the selection; the symbolic value CurrentTime is not acceptable.

DESCRIPTION

XtGetSelectionValuesIncremental requests that the toolkit retrieve the specified selection expressed in multiple targets, with each transfer accomplished as a series of incremental transfers. It is the responsibility of the selection owner to convert the current selection to the target data types. When the selection values are ready to be retrieved, *get_select_proc* is called to accept them. The callback procedure is called repeatedly to receive each target as a series of incremental transfers, each time being receiving the corresponding entry in the array of *client_data*. The end of each selection transfer is indicated when *get_select_proc* is called with a non-NULL value of length zero.

USAGE

XtGetSelectionValuesIncremental is equivalent to making multiple sequential calls to XtGetSelectionValueIncremental, but guarantees that the selection source does not change between the delivery of the selection value in different targets. It should be used instead of XtGetSelectionValueIncremental when more than one attribute of the current selection is desired.

CAUTION

Memory allocated by the Intrinsics for the selection value becomes the property of the selection requester, and should be freed with XtFree when it is no longer needed. See the description of XtSelectionCallbackProc in Appendix B for more information on the responsibilities of the requester. There is no guarantee that the selection owner will be able to convert the selection to the requested target, or that there is a current selection owner at all, so the requester should plan a graceful fallback if the selection value cannot be retrieved.

SEE ALSO

Routines: XtDisownSelection, XtGetSelectionTimeout, XtGetSelectionValue,
           XtGetSelectionValues, XtGetSelectionValueIncremental,
           XtOwnSelection, XtOwnSelectionIncremental, XtSetSelectionTimeout

XtGetSubresources   **(R3)**

Fetches values for resources not maintained in a widget's instance record

SYNOPSIS
```
void XtGetSubresources( w, base, name, class, resources, num_resources,
    args, num_args )
        Widget              w;
        XtPointer           base;
        String              name;
        String              class;
        XtResourceList      resources;
        Cardinal            num_resources;
        ArgList             args;
        Cardinal            num_args;
```

ARGUMENTS

w	in	Widget owning the subresources to be set; must be of class Object or any subclass thereof.
base	in/out	Base address of data structure to receive values.
name	in	Resource name of widget subpart.
class	in	Resource class of widget subpart.
resources	in	Pointer to a list of resource description records.
num_resources	in	Number of resource definitions in *resources*.
args	in	An array of Args specifying explicit resource values to override values found in database.
num_args	in	Number of name/value pairs in *args*.

DESCRIPTION

XtGetSubresources constructs the complete resource name of each specified subpart resource by concatenating the application name (declared in XtOpenDisplay or XtDisplayInitialize), the names of all the widget's ancestors in order from top to bottom, the subpart name, and the resource name, separated by periods. The resource database associated with *w* is searched for matching resource values, which are placed in the subpart data structure as specified by *resources*. Resource values specified by *args* override values found in the database.

USAGE

Widgets may maintain data structures which are not part of the widget instance record. These are considered "non-widget" data structures, and are not automatically initialized by the Intrinsics. To initialize these data structures, a widget must explicitly call XtGetSubresources. It is given the opportunity to do so at creation time. XtVaGetSubresources is the varargs variant of this routine. To update the state of subpart resources, call XtSetSubvalues.

XtGetSubresources is used in widget implementation code and is not called by application programmers. To set values in application data structures using resource files you should call XtGetApplicationResources instead.

CAUTION

None.

SEE ALSO

Routines: XtGetApplicationResources, XtVaGetSubresources, XtSetSubvalues, XtGetSubvalues

XtGetSubvalues   **(R3)**

Queries values of resources not maintained in a widget's instance record

SYNOPSIS

```
void XtGetSubvalues( base, resources, num_resources, args, num_args )
            XtPointer                   base;
            XtResourceList              resources;
            Cardinal                    num_resources;
            ArgList                     args;
            Cardinal                    num_args;
```

ARGUMENTS

base	in	Base address of data structure from which to retrieve resource values.
resources	in	Pointer to list of resource description records declaring names, types and offsets of resource fields.
num_resources	in	Number of resource definitions in *resources*.
args	in/out	An array of Args specifying which resources are to be queried, and the addresses of variables into which values are to be returned.
num_args	in	Number of resource name/address pairs in *args*.

DESCRIPTION

XtGetSubvalues retrieves the resources specified in *args* from the data structure pointed to by *base*. The XtResourceList *resources* determines where in the data buffer the values are found.

USAGE

XtGetSubvalues is used by widget programmers to retrieve the state of non-widget data structures. The Intrinsics automatically retrieve resource values from fields declared in a widget's instance record when you call XtGetValues. Fields declared in other structures are considered "non-widget" subparts and are not examined automatically. If such fields are to be accessed through resources, they must be retrieved explicitly by the widget programmer with XtGetSubvalues.

The widget programmer has a chance to do this when XtGetValues is invoked on the widget, calling the widget's *get_values_hook* procedure. This passes the arglist constructed by the caller of XtGetValues, which can then be forwarded to XtGetSubvalues.

XtVaGetSubvalues is the varargs variant of XtGetSubvalues. To set the values of non-widget resource fields, call XtSetSubvalues. To load initial resources from the resource database, call XtGetSubresources. XtGetSubvalues is not called by application programmers.

CAUTION

None

SEE ALSO

Routines: XtSetSubvalues, XtVaGetSubvalues, XtGetSubresources

XtGetValues (R3)

Queries widget resource values

SYNOPSIS

```
void XtGetValues( w, args, num_args )
        Widget                          w;
        ArgList                         args;
        Cardinal                        num_args;
```

ARGUMENTS

w	in	Widget from which resource values are to be retrieved; must be of class Object or any subclass thereof.
args	in/out	An array of Args specifying which resources are to be queried, and the addresses of variables into which values are to be returned.
num_args	in	Number of resource name/address pairs in *args*.

DESCRIPTION

XtGetValues retrieves resource values from the specified widget. Any value field specified in *args* must be a pointer to the variable in which to store the returned resource value. If a NULL return address is passed in *args,* XtGetValues issues a fatal error. If a NULL arglist is passed but *num_args* is greater than zero, XtGetValues issues a warning.

Valid resource names are widget class-specific. If XtGetValues is passed a resource name that the specified widget does not support, that name is simply ignored. Other valid resource names in *args* will be responded to. If the widget's parent is a subclass of Constraint, XtGetValues can return the values of any constraint resources attached to widget.

USAGE

XtGetValues is used to query the state of a widget. You usually construct the input arglist by statically declaring an array of Args and calling XtSetArg repeatedly. To set the state of a widget, use XtSetValues. XtVaSetValues and XtVaGetValues are the varargs variants of these routines, and are often easier to use.

CAUTION

If resources are retrieved that have values of pointer type, a widget may allocate new storage for the pointed-to data. If it does, the caller is responsible for freeing this storage when it is no longer required. For example, the XmNvalue resource of a Motif text widget is a char*. If you request this value, the text widget allocates new memory, makes a copy of its internal buffer and returns a pointer to the copy. The pointed-to storage must later be freed with XtFree. Unfortunately, the toolkit specification does not dictate whether widgets must copy pointed-to data or not, so read your widget manpages carefully.

If *num_args* does not match the number of name/value pairs actually set in *args*, unpredictable errors may result.

SEE ALSO

Routines: XtFree, XtSetValues, XtVaGetValues

XtGrabButton

(R4)

Registers a passive server-side grab on a pointer button

SYNOPSIS

```
void XtGrabButton( w, button, modifiers, owner_events, event_mask,
    pointer_mode, keyboard_mode, confine_to, cursor )
        Widget              w;
        int                 button;
        Modifiers           modifiers;
        Boolean             owner_events;
        unsigned int        event_mask;
        int                 pointer_mode;
        int                 keyboard_mode;
        Window              confine_to;
        Cursor              cursor;
```

ARGUMENTS

w	in	Widget specifying the window for which grab is asserted; must be of class Core or any subclass thereof.
button	in	Pointer button to be grabbed, or AnyButton.
modifiers	in	Key modifiers associated with button. AnyModifier, or any bitwise OR of: ShiftMask, LockMask, ControlMask, Mod1Mask, Mod2Mask, Mod3Mask, Mod4Mask, Mod5Mask.
owner_events	in	True if pointer events should be reported normally; False if pointer events are to be reported with respect to grab window.
event_mask	in	Event mask specifying which types of pointer events are to be delivered to the application during the grab.
pointer_mode	in	Specifies how pointer events are to be processed during the grab; may be GrabModeSync or GrabModeAsync.
keyboard_mode	in	Specifies how keyboard events are to be processed during the grab; may be GrabModeSync or GrabModeAsync.
confine_to	in	Window in which pointer should be confined during grab, or None.
cursor	in	New cursor to display during grab, or None.

DESCRIPTION

XtGrabButton establishes a passive grab on the specified button. If the widget is realized, XtGrabButton calls XGrabButton using the widget's window as the grab window, and passes all other arguments exactly as in the Xlib call. If the widget is not realized, XGrabButton is called as soon as it does become realized and its window is mapped. If the widget is unrealized and realized repeatedly, XGrabButton is called again each time it becomes realized.

In the future, if the Intrinsics receive an event that triggers the grab, but this event is discarded or remapped to a widget other than the grabbing widget, XUngrabPointer is called automatically to release the grab. However, if a pointer grab is already in progress, the grab is not released.

USAGE

A passive grab becomes activated when the specified pointer button (together with any modifiers) is pressed, and remains active until the button is released (regardless of the state of any modifiers). A button grab ensures that the grab window receives pointer input, even if the pointer in the meantime is moved to another window. There is seldom a need to grab a button explicitly, since the server automatically enforces an asynchronous pointer grab for you when any button is pressed. Moreover, menu widgets in most toolkits do the right thing automatically where grabs are concerned.

Synchronous grabs (with *pointer_mode* and/or *keyboard_mode* set to GrabModeSync) are sometimes used to halt event delivery during a grab, while the state of an application and its windows is changed. Event processing resumes when the client calls XAllowEvents or XUngrabPointer. However, there are many complications to grabs.

In the rare cases where a grab is necessary (see Chapter 9), XtGrabButton and XtUngrabButton should be used rather than their Xlib equivalents, XGrabButton and XUngrabButton, since the Intrinsics routines handle the request properly whether the widget is realized or not. The toolkit routines also cause the grab to be released automatically if there is a modal cascade when the grab goes into effect, but widget *w* is not in the active set. This way, the toolkit does not hang waiting for an event to be processed that can't be delivered.

CAUTION

Grabs established by XtGrabButton are implemented in the server, and should not be confused with grabs implemented on the client side via the grab list and XtAddGrab. Server-side grabs should only be employed when it is absolutely necessary for you to control the delivery of events to the exclusion of other clients. You should always approach grabs with caution, and should only grab a button, key, the pointer or keyboard when absolutely required.

SEE ALSO

Routines: XtRegisterGrabAction, XtUngrabButton

XtGrabKey

Registers a passive server-side grab on a key

SYNOPSIS

```
void XtGrabKey( w, keycode, modifiers, owner_events, pointer_mode,
    keyboard_mode )
        Widget                          w;
        KeyCode                         keycode;
        Modifiers                       modifiers;
        Boolean                         owner_events;
        int                             pointer_mode;
        int                             keyboard_mode;
```

ARGUMENTS

w	in	Widget specifying window for which grab is asserted; must be of class Core or any subclass thereof.
keycode	in	Keycode specifying which key on the physical keyboard is grabbed.
modifiers	in	Key modifiers associated with button. AnyModifier, or any bitwise OR of: ShiftMask, LockMask, ControlMask, Mod1Mask, Mod2Mask, Mod3Mask, Mod4Mask, Mod5Mask.
owner_events	in	True if pointer events should be reported normally; False if pointer events are to be reported with respect to grab window.
pointer_mode	in	Specifies how pointer events are to be processed during the grab; may be GrabModeSync or GrabModeAsync.
keyboard_mode	in	Specifies how keyboard events are to be processed during the grab; may be GrabModeSync or GrabModeAsync.

DESCRIPTION

XtGrabKey establishes a passive grab on the specified key. If the widget is realized, XtGrabKey calls XGrabKey using the widget's window as the grab window, and the specified arguments exactly as in the Xlib call. If the widget is not realized, XGrabKey is called as soon as it does become realized and its window is mapped. If the widget is unrealized and realized repeatedly, XGrabKey is called again each time it is realized.

In the future, if the Intrinsics receive an event that triggers the grab, but this event is discarded or remapped to a widget other than the grabbing widget, XUngrabPointer is called automatically to release the grab. However, if a pointer grab is already in progress, the grab is not released.

USAGE

A passive grab becomes activated when the specified key (together with any specified modifiers) is pressed while the focus is assigned to widget *w* or one of its normal descendants, and remains active until the specified key is released (regardless of the state of any modifiers). The grab ensures that *w* receives the specified KeyPress event, and all keyboard input while the grab is active.

There is seldom a need to grab a key explicitly. In the few cases where a key grab is appropriate (see Chapter 9), it is usually better to register a grab action with XtRegisterGrabAction. Since a grab is asserted for a device-specific keycode, this saves you the trouble of having to figure out which physical keys are really used for particular symbols or functions.

In the even rarer cases where you want to grab a key explicitly, XtGrabKey and XtUngrabKey should be used rather than their Xlib equivalents, XGrabKey and XUngrabKey, since the Intrinsics routines handle the request properly whether the widget is realized or not. The toolkit routines also cause the grab to be released automatically if there is a modal cascade when the grab goes into effect, but widget *w* is not in the active set. This way, the toolkit does not hang waiting for an event to be processed that can't be delivered.

CAUTION

Grabs established with XtGrabKey are implemented in the server, and should not be confused with grabs implemented on the client side via the grab list and XtAddGrab. Server-side grabs should only be employed when it is absolutely necessary for you to control the delivery of events to the exclusion of other clients. You should always approach grabs with caution, and should only grab a button, key, the pointer or keyboard when absolutely required.

SEE ALSO

Routines: XtRegisterGrabAction, XtUngrabKey

XtGrabKeyboard (R4)

Asserts an active server-side grab on the keyboard

SYNOPSIS

```
int XtGrabKeyboard( w, owner_events, pointer_mode, keyboard_mode, time )
        Widget                          w;
        Boolean                         owner_events;
        int                             pointer_mode;
        int                             keyboard_mode;
        Time                            time;
```

ARGUMENTS

w	in	Widget specifying window for which grab is asserted; must be of class Core or any subclass thereof.
owner_events	in	True if keyboard events should be reported normally; False if keyboard events are to be reported with respect to grab window.
pointer_mode	in	Specifies how pointer events are to be processed during the grab; may be GrabModeSync or GrabModeAsync.
keyboard_mode	in	Specifies how keyboard events are to be processed during the grab; may be GrabModeSync or GrabModeAsync.
time	in	Time at which grab is effective; may be an event timestamp or the symbolic constant CurrentTime.

DESCRIPTION

XtGrabKeyboard establishes an active grab on the keyboard. If w is realized, XtGrabKeyboard calls XGrabKeyboard using the widget's window as the grab window, and returns a value of GrabNotViewable, AlreadyGrabbed, GrabFrozen, GrabInvalidTime or GrabSuccess, depending on the results of the grab. All other input arguments are treated exactly as in the Xlib call. The specified *time* is used by the server to arbitrate whether a grab succeeds. If w is not realized XtGrabKeyboard immediately returns GrabNotViewable and no grab is performed.

USAGE

If you grab the keyboard, you get exclusive access to all keyboard events for a period of time. This could be used to prevent eavesdropping by other X clients when entering sensitive data. Toolkit applications should call XtGrabKeyboard and XtUngrabKeyboard rather than their Xlib equivalents, XGrabKeyboard and XUngrabKeyboard, as the Intrinsics routines perform properly whether the widget is realized or not.

CAUTION

Grabs established by XtGrabKeyboard are implemented in the server, and should only be used when it is necessary to receive input to the exclusion of other clients. You must release the grab with XtUngrabKeyboard as soon as you can. If there are widgets on the grab list, beware! Establishing a keyboard grab for a widget that is not in the active set is usually wrong, as the widget will not get the events.

SEE ALSO

Routines: XtUngrabKeyboard

XtGrabPointer   (R4)

Asserts an active server-side grab on the pointing device

SYNOPSIS

```
int XtGrabPointer( w, owner_events, event_mask, pointer_mode,
    keyboard_mode, confine_to, cursor, time )
        Widget                          w;
        Boolean                         owner_events;
        unsigned int                    event_mask;
        int                             pointer_mode;
        int                             keyboard_mode;
        Window                          confine_to;
        Cursor                          cursor;
        Time                            time;
```

ARGUMENTS

w	in	Widget specifying window for which grab is asserted; must be of class Core or any subclass thereof.
owner_events	in	True if pointer events should be reported normally; False if pointer events are to be reported with respect to grab window.
event_mask	in	Event mask specifying which types of pointer events are to be delivered to the application during the grab.
pointer_mode	in	Specifies how pointer events are to be processed during the grab; may be GrabModeSync or GrabModeAsync.
keyboard_mode	in	Specifies how keyboard events are to be processed during the grab; may be GrabModeSync or GrabModeAsync.
confine_to	in	Window in which pointer should be confined during grab, or None.
cursor	in	New cursor to display during the grab, or None.
time	in	Time at which grab is effective; may be an event timestamp or the symbolic constant CurrentTime.

DESCRIPTION

If the specified widget is realized, XtGrabPointer initiates an active grab on the pointer by calling XGrabPointer, and returns a value of GrabNotViewable, AlreadyGrabbed, GrabFrozen, GrabInvalidTime or GrabSuccess, depending on the results of the grab. The widget's window is specified as the grab window, and all other arguments are used exactly as they are in the corresponding Xlib routine. If the grab is successful, XtGrabPointer immediately grabs all input from the pointer to the exclusion of other clients, and keeps the grab until it is released with XtUngrabPointer. If w is not realized XtGrabPointer immediately returns GrabNotViewable and no grab is performed.

USAGE

Pointer grabs are sometimes done by special clients that implement "drag and drop" and rubberbanding operations that traverse other windows (see Chapter 9). There is rarely a need for an ordinary application to assert an active pointer grab. Toolkit applications that really must grab should use XtGrabPointer and

XtUngrabPointer rather than their Xlib equivalents, XGrabPointer and XUngrabPointer, since the Intrinsics routines handle the request properly whether the widget is realized or not.

CAUTION

Grabs established by XtGrabPointer are implemented in the server, and should only be employed when it is absolutely necessary to control the delivery of events to the exclusion of other clients. Grabbing the pointer keeps other clients from receiving pointer input, so you must remember to release the grab with XtUngrabPointer as soon as you can. If there are widgets on the grab list, beware! Establishing a pointer grab for a widget that is not in the active set is usually wrong, as the widget will not get the events.

SEE ALSO

Routines: XtUngrabPointer

XtHasCallbacks   (R3)

Queries the state of a widget's callback list

SYNOPSIS

```
XtCallbackStatus XtHasCallbacks( w, callback_name )
        Widget                     w;
        String                     callback_name;
```

ARGUMENTS

w   in   Widget whose callback list should be checked; must be of class Object
                            or any subclass thereof.

callback_name   in   Resource name of callback list to be queried, e.g. "destroyCallback" or
                            the symbolic constant XtNdestroyCallback.

DESCRIPTION

XtHasCallbacks examines the specified callback list and returns a value of XtCallbackHasSome if
the list currently has callbacks, XtCallbackHasNone if there are no callbacks registered on the list, and
XtCallbackNoList if the widget does not have a list by that name.

USAGE

The Intrinsics use XtHasCallbacks internally to determine whether an attempt should be made to invoke
callbacks registered in the specified callback list. This is used as an optimization; if there are no callbacks, a
few machine cycles can be saved by not bothering to try. It is rarely used in applications.

CAUTION

None

SEE ALSO

Routines: XtAddCallback, XtAddCallbacks, XtRemoveAllCallbacks,
           XtRemoveCallback, XtRemoveCallbacks

XtHooksOfDisplay (R6)

Returns the ID of a hook registration object

SYNOPSIS

```
Widget XtHooksOfDisplay( display )
    Display                         *display;
```

ARGUMENTS

display   in   Display for which hook registration object is valid.

DESCRIPTION

XtHooksOfDisplay returns the ID of an implementation-dependent hook registration object. Resources of the Hook object are callbacks that are invoked when toolkit operations are conducted. These can be used to log toolkit activities.

USAGE

XtHooksOfDisplay is a routine intended for widget writers or application programmers that need to log toolkit operations, perhaps as a debugging aid, or to report them to external agents such as resource editors. The Hook object returned by XtHooksOfDisplay is a non-windowed subclass of Object. It has no parent and only a subset of the Intrinsics routines can be used with it. The Hook object is implementation-dependent and may support different callbacks on different systems.

CAUTION

None

SEE ALSO

Routines: None

XtInitialize (O)

Obsolete convenience initialization routine

SYNOPSIS

```
Widget XtInitialize( app_name, app_class, options, num_options, argc,
    argv )
            String                          app_name;
            String                          app_class;
            XrmOptionDescRec                *options;
            Cardinal                        num_options;
            Cardinal                        *argc;
            String                          **argv;
```

ARGUMENTS

app_name	in	Resource name of the application instance , e.g. "myApp".
app_class	in	Resource class of the application , e.g. "MyApp".
options	in	Pointer to a list of option description records specifying command-line options that set resource values.
num_options	in	Number of option descriptors in *options*.
argc	in/out	Pointer to integer specifying argument count provided to main() at image activation; returns number of unparsed arguments remaining after XtInitialize has parsed *argv*.
argv	in/out	Arguments provided to main() at image activation; returns all unparsed arguments.

DESCRIPTION

XtInitialize is an obsolete convenience routine that calls XtToolkitInitialize, XtCreateApplicationContext, XtOpenDisplay and XtAppCreateShell, returning the widget ID of a new application shell. A single "default" application context is created, which is used implicitly by the other obsolete routines listed below. XtInitialize should be called before any of the following routines is referenced.

```
XtMainLoop      XtAddInput      XtError             XtWarning
XtNextEvent     XtAddTimeOut    XtErrorMsg          XtWarningMsg
XtPeekEvent     XtAddWorkProc   XtSetErrorHandler   XtSetWarningHandler
XtPending       XtProcessEvent  XtAddActions        XtSetErrorMsgHandler
XtSetWarningMsgHandler          XtCreateApplicationShell
XtDisplayStringConversionWarning
```

USAGE

XtInitialize is used as a blanket initialization routine by R3 applications supporting a single application context, display and application shell. Though widely used in older programs, and still supported in the R6 Intrinsics, it is superseded by XtAppInitialize (R4 and R5) or XtOpenApplication (R6).

CAUTION

If you use `XtInitialize` to initialize the toolkit, do not call any routines that start with the letters "XtApp".   Similarly, if you use `XtAppInitialize` to initialize the toolkit, or create your application context with `XtCreateApplicationContext`, do not call any of the routines listed above.

SEE ALSO

Routines: `XtAppInitialize, XtOpenApplication (R6)`

XtInitializeWidgetClass (R5)

Initializes a widget's class record without creating any widgets

SYNOPSIS

```
Widget XtInitializeWidgetClass( class )
    WidgetClass                             class;
```

ARGUMENTS

class   in   Specifies widget class to initialize; must be `objectClass` or any subclass thereof.

DESCRIPTION

`XtInitializeWidgetClass` initializes the specified widget class without creating any widgets. This registers resource converters for any special resource types used by the class, and performs any other dynamic initialization required by the class. Any uninitialized superclasses of the specified widget class are also initialized, in superclass-to-subclass order. If the specified widget class was compiled with an incompatible version of the Intrinsics, `XtInitializeWidgetClass` issues a fatal error.

USAGE

`XtInitializeWidgetClass` is usually called to make sure that any special resource type converters supplied by a widget class are in place before fetching application resources of that type. By default, converters supplied by a widget class are registered when the first widget of that class is created. For example, the OSF/Motif `String-to-XmString` converter is registered when you create any OSF/Motif subclass of XmPrimitive or XmManager. If you wanted to fetch an application resource of type `XmString` before you created any widgets, you could call `XtInitializeWidgetClass` to initialize the XmPrimitive class, causing the `String-to-XmString` converter to be registered explicitly.

CAUTION

None

SEE ALSO

Routines: None

XtInsertEventHandler   **(R4)**

Adds an ordered event handler to a widget

SYNOPSIS

```
void XtInsertEventHandler( w, event_mask, nonmaskable, event_handler,
    client_data, position )
        Widget                          w;
        EventMask                       event_mask;
        Boolean                         nonmaskable;
        XtEventHandler                  event_handler;
        XtPointer                       client_data;
        XtListPosition                  position;
```

ARGUMENTS

w	in	Widget to which the event handler is added; must be of class Core or any subclass thereof.
event_mask	in	Mask specifying which X event types the handler should process, e.g. `PointerMotionMask`.
nonmaskable	in	`True` if event handler should be called to handle nonmaskable events (GraphicsExpose, NoExpose, SelectionClear, SelectionRequest, SelectionNotify, ClientMessage, MappingNotify).
event_handler	in	The event handler to be registered.
client_data	in	Application-defined data to be passed to event handler.
position	in	`XtListHead` or `XtListTail`; specifies desired position in event handler list.

DESCRIPTION

`XtInsertEventHandler` registers an event handler to respond to the specified event(s) in widget *w*. It is identical to `XtAddEventHandler` except that it accepts the additional argument *position*. If *position* is `XtListTail`, the event handler is inserted after all previously-registered event handlers in the widget's list of event handlers. If *position* is `XtListHead`, the event handler is inserted before all previously-registered event handlers. If the specified *event_handler/client_data* pair is already registered, the existing event mask is augmented by *event_mask*, and the handler is moved to the requested position in the list.

USAGE

`XtInsertEventHandler` is used instead of `XtAddEventHandler` to register an event handler which must, for some reason, be called before (or after) other handlers invoked for the same event type.

CAUTION

The ordering capability of `XtInsertEventHandler` is not terribly robust, since succeeding calls to `XtAddEventHandler` may reorder the list again. Ordering event handlers should not be considered the "best" way to guarantee the order in which application-specific actions are carried out.

SEE ALSO

Routines: `XtAddEventHandler, XtDispatchEvent, XtRemoveEventHandler`

XtInsertEventTypeHandler (R6)

Add an event handler to respond to extension events

SYNOPSIS

```
void XtInsertEventTypeHandler( w, event_type, select_data, event_handler,
    client_data, position )
        Widget              w;
        int                 event_type;
        XtPointer           select_data;
        XtEventHandler      event_handler;
        XtPointer           client_data;
        XtListPosition      position;
```

ARGUMENTS

w	in	The widget to which the event handler is to be added; must be of class Core or any subclass thereof.
event_type	in	Integer specifying event type for which the handler should be called.
select_data	in	Data required to select events of this type from the server, or NULL.
event_handler	in	The event handler to be registered.
client_data	in	Application-defined data to be passed to event handler.
position	in	XtListHead or XtListTail; specifies desired position in event handler list.

DESCRIPTION

XtInsertEventTypeHandler is similar to XtInsertEventHandler, except that it can register handlers to respond to events that are not part of the core X protocol. The event is specified by the integer value used to identify its type. This is assigned when an extension is initialized.

If *position* is XtListTail, the event handler is inserted after all previously-registered event handlers. If *position* is XtListHead, the event handler is inserted before all previously-registered event handlers in the list. If the specified *event_handler/client_data* pair is already registered the handler is moved to the indicated position in the list.

USAGE

X allows the core protocol to be extended to support new event types, called extension events. XtInsertEventTypeHandler must be used instead of XtAddEventHandler or XtInsertEventHandler to register handlers for extension events. It can also be used to register handlers for ordinary X events, but this is not common.

If *event_type* specifies one of the event types in the core protocol, *select_data* must be a pointer to an event mask, which is used by XSelectInput to select for that event. If *event_type* specifies an extension event, XtRegisterExtensionSelector must be used to register an extension-dependent selector procedure that knows how to request such events from the server. In that case, *select_data* is whatever is expected by the XtExtensionSelectProc registered for that event type. XtInsertEventTypeHandler does not guarantee to copy the *select_data*, so you must ensure that the data remains valid as long as the event handler remains registered with this value of *select_data*.

Position is usually `XtListTail`, unless the program has some important reason to try to place this event handler before (or after) others that are already registered.

CAUTION

The ordering capability of `XtInsertEventTypeHandler` is not terribly robust, since succeeding calls to `XtInsertEventTypeHandler` may reorder the list again. Ordering event handlers should not be considered the "best" way to guarantee the order in which application-specific actions are carried out.

SEE ALSO

Routines: `XtRemoveEventTypeHandler, XtRegisterExtensionSelector`

XtInsertRawEventHandler (R4)

Adds an ordered event handler without adjusting a widget's event mask

SYNOPSIS

```
void XtInsertRawEventHandler( w, event_mask, nonmaskable, event_handler,
    client_data, position )
        Widget                      w;
        EventMask                   event_mask;
        Boolean                     nonmaskable;
        XtEventHandler              event_handler;
        XtPointer                   client_data;
        XtListPosition              position;
```

ARGUMENTS

w	in	Widget to which the event handler is added; must be of class Core or any subclass thereof.
event_mask	in	Mask specifying which X event types the handler should process, e.g. `PointerMotionMask`.
nonmaskable	in	`True` if event handler should be called when nonmaskable events (GraphicsExpose, NoExpose, SelectionClear, SelectionRequest, SelectionNotify, ClientMessage, MappingNotify) are received.
event_handler	in	The event handler to be registered.
client_data	in	Application-defined data to be passed to event handler.
position	in	`XtListHead` or `XtListTail`; specifies desired position in event handler list.

DESCRIPTION

XtInsertRawEventHandler is identical to XtAddRawEventHandler, except that it places the event handler into the widget's list of event handlers at the specified position. If *position* is XtListTail, the event handler is inserted after all previously-registered event handlers. If *position* is XtListHead, the event handler is inserted before all previously-registered event handlers. If the specified *event_handler/client_data* pair is already registered, the handler's event mask is augmented by *event_mask*, and the handler is moved to the requested position. The event mask of the widget's window is not updated.

USAGE

XtInsertRawEventHandler is used to register a raw event handler which must, for some reason, be called before (or after) other previously-registered handlers invoked for the same event type.

CAUTION

The ordering capability of XtInsertRawEventHandler is not terribly robust, since succeeding calls to XtAddEventHandler may reorder the list again. Ordering event handlers should not be considered the "best" way to guarantee the order in which application-specific actions are carried out.

SEE ALSO

Routines: XtAddRawEventHandler, XtDispatchEvent, XtRemoveRawEventHandler

XtInstallAccelerators   **(R3)**

Installs accelerators on the widget that receives the events

SYNOPSIS

```
void XtInstallAccelerators( destination, source )
        Widget                          destination;
        Widget                          source;
```

ARGUMENTS

destination   in   Widget which will detect the events; must be of class Core or any subclass thereof.

source   in   Widget which defines the accelerator translations; must be of class Core or any subclass thereof.

DESCRIPTION

XtInstallAccelerators installs accelerators from widget *source* onto widget *destination*. Actions are bound in the context of the *source* widget, but events to be translated are captured by the *destination* widget.

USAGE

Accelerators are translations that are bound to action procedures in the context of one widget (the source), but receive their events in another (the destination). The most common use is to let Key events received by text widgets invoke the actions of buttons in menus. This lets you activate buttons even if their corresponding menus are not displayed.

Accelerators are first defined in translation table syntax (see Appendix D) and compiled with XtParseAcceleratorTable. The compiled table is then attached to the XtNaccelerators resource of the source widget using XtSetValues. This prepares the source widget to use its actions.

Finally, XtInstallAccelerators is called to bind the accelerators to the widget in which the events are to be trapped. XtInstallAccelerators must be called once for each combination of source and destination widget, so in many cases XtInstallAllAccelerators will be more convenient.

CAUTION

Many modern toolkits handle keyboard accelerators automatically, and do not require that you go through the steps outlined above. For example, OSF/Motif button widgets export the resource XmNaccelerator (not XtNaccelerators), which lets you specify the left-hand side (only) of an accelerator table. The right-hand side is assumed to be the activation action of the button. Installing the accelerators, etc. is handled internally. Such predefined accelerators may be destroyed if you use XtSetValues to replace the XtNaccelerators resource.

In toolkits that do expect you to install accelerators explicitly (e.g. Athena), you must know the action names provided by the widget that you want to accelerate.

It is usually good taste to use non-printing characters (e.g. Ctrl-C) as accelerators, since accelerators are often bound to text widgets that would otherwise want the character themselves. It is also a good idea to display something in the label of the button to let the user know what the accelerator keystroke is.

SEE ALSO

Routines: XtInstallAllAccelerators, XtParseAcceleratorTable

XtInstallAllAccelerators (R3)

Installs accelerators on the widget that receives the events

SYNOPSIS

```
void XtInstallAllAccelerators( destination, source )
        Widget                          destination;
        Widget                          source;
```

ARGUMENTS

destination   in   Widget which will detect the events; must be of class Core or any subclass thereof.

source   in   Root of widget tree which defines the accelerator translations; must be of class Core or any subclass thereof.

DESCRIPTION

XtInstallAllAccelerators recursively descends the widget tree rooted at *source*, installing the accelerators from every widget found there onto the widget *destination*.

USAGE

Accelerators are translations that are bound to action procedures in the context of one widget (the source), but receive their events in another (the destination). The most common use is to let Key events received by text widgets invoke the actions of buttons in menus. This lets you activate buttons even if their corresponding menus are not displayed.

Usually, XtInstallAccelerator is called to bind accelerators to the widget in which the events are to be trapped. XtInstallAllAccelerators is a convenience routine that installs the accelerators from a widget and all of its descendants (an entire menu, for example) in a single call, saving multiple calls to XtInstallAccelerators. XtInstallAccelerators must still be called once for each destination widget. In applications where the sole use of accelerators is to allow Key input to trigger buttons in menus, it may be sufficient to call XtInstallAllAccelerators once just before entering XtAppMainLoop, specifying the application "main" widget as both *source* and *destination*.

CAUTION

See XtInstallAccelerators.

SEE ALSO

Routines: XtInstallAccelerators, XtParseAcceleratorTable

XtIs*<Class>*   **(R4)**

Checks the widget class of an existing widget against a known class

SYNOPSIS

```
Boolean XtIs<Class>( w )
        Widget                        w;
```

ARGUMENTS

w   in   Widget or object for which information is requested.

DESCRIPTION

The following routines accept a widget or object ID, and return `True` if the specified widget is a subclass (at any level) of the Intrinsics-defined class specified by the routine name:

```
XtIsObject              XtIsRectObj          XtIsWidget
XtIsComposite           XtIsConstraint       XtIsShell
XtIsOverrideShell       XtIsWMShell          XtIsVendorShell
XtIsTransientShell      XtIsTopLevelShell    XtIsApplicationShell
XtIsSessionShell (R6)
```

For checking against the Intrinsics-defined classes, these may be faster than calling `XtIsSubclass`.

USAGE

You can use these routines to determine whether an anticipated operation (in a callback routine, for instance) is appropriate to perform on a given widget, based on its class. They are also used internally by the Intrinsics to invoke code specific to a given class of widget. For example, `XtIsComposite` is used in widget implementation code when a widget must take specific action depending on whether its parent or child is Composite. This usually occurs in cases in which, if the parent is Composite, the list of siblings attached to the parent is traversed for information.

When programming in C, these are usually implemented as macros; in other languages, they are implemented as functions. There is no functional difference. Toolkits such as OSF/Motif often provide additional macros or functions that you can use to check toolkit-specific classes (e.g. `XmIsPushButton`).

CAUTION

Do not confuse superclass/subclass relationships with parent/child relationships. Parent/child defines the relationship of widget instances in a particular user-interface widget tree. Superclass/subclass defines how different types of widgets inherit their features and functionality.

SEE ALSO

Routines: `XtIsSubclass`

XtIsManaged (R3)

Checks if a widget is managed

SYNOPSIS

```
Boolean XtIsManaged( w )
        Widget                      w;
```

ARGUMENTS

w   in   Widget or object for which information is requested; must be of class
                                Object or any subclass thereof.

DESCRIPTION

XtIsManaged returns True if the specified widget is a subclass of RectObject and is managed by its
parent, and False if it is not.

USAGE

XtIsManaged is used by the Intrinsics themselves and in widget implementation code when a widget must
take selective action on a child depending on whether or not it is managed. You could use it in application
code to decide whether to undertake some compute-intensive action that could be avoided if a widget is
unmanaged (and thus invisible).

CAUTION

None

SEE ALSO

Routines: XtManageChild, XtManageChildren, XtUnmanageChild,
            XtUnmanageChildren

XtIsRealized

(R3)

Checks if a widget is realized

SYNOPSIS

```
Boolean XtIsRealized( w )
        Widget                          w;
```

ARGUMENTS

w   in   Widget or object for which information is requested; must be of class
                               Object or any subclass thereof.

DESCRIPTION

XtIsRealized returns True if the specified widget is realized. If *w* is a non-windowed object,
XtIsRealized returns True if its nearest windowed relative is realized.

USAGE

A widget does not have a valid window unless and until it has been realized. In applications that use Xlib
calls, it is prudent to verify that a widget is realized before using XtWindow or XtWindowOfObject to
obtain its window ID. Calling Xlib graphics routines with an invalid window ID will cause a fatal protocol
error.

CAUTION

None

SEE ALSO

Routines: XtRealizeWidget, XtUnrealizeWidget, XtWindow, XtWindowOfObject

XtIsSensitive (R3)

Checks if a widget is sensitive to user input

SYNOPSIS

```
Boolean XtIsSensitive( w )
        Widget                          w;
```

ARGUMENTS

w   in   Widget or object for which information is requested; must be of class Object or any subclass thereof.

DESCRIPTION

XtIsSensitive returns True if the specified widget is a subclass of RectObject and is sensitive to user input. If a widget is insensitive, it does not receive events of type KeyPress, KeyRelease, ButtonPress, ButtonRelease, MotionNotify, EnterNotify, LeaveNotify, FocusIn or FocusOut. A widget is sensitive only if both its *sensitive* and *ancestor_sensitive* fields are True.

USAGE

You can use this routine to determine if a widget has been set sensitive or insensitive by a callback routine. XtIsSensitive is used by the Intrinsics to determine whether a widget should have user events dispatched to it. The routine XtSetSensitive is used to set a widget sensitive or insensitive.

CAUTION

Widgets may or may not visually reflect whether they are sensitive.

SEE ALSO

Routines: XtSetSensitive

XtIsSubclass   **(R3)**

Checks if a widget is a subclass of a specified widget class

SYNOPSIS

```
Boolean XtIsSubclass( w, widget_class )
        Widget                          w;
        WidgetClass                     widget_class;
```

ARGUMENTS

w   in   Widget or object for which information is requested; must be objectClass or any subclass thereof.

widget_class   in   Class pointer used to test widget, e.g. compositeWidgetClass.

DESCRIPTION

XtIsSubclass returns True if the specified widget or object is a subclass, at any level, of the specified widget class. It need not be a direct subclass of the specified class.

USAGE

XtIsSubclass is often used in Composite widget implementation code to inspect children and determine how to handle them based on their class. You can also use this routine to determine whether an anticipated operation (in a callback routine, for instance) is appropriate to perform on a given widget, based on its class.

As a convenience, the Intrinsics also provide the following macros which accept a widget or object ID, and return True if the specified widget is a subclass (at any level) of the Intrinsics-defined class specified in the routine name:

```
XtIsObject           XtIsRectObj          XtIsWidget
XtIsComposite        XtIsConstraint       XtIsShell
XtIsOverrideShell    XtIsWMShell          XtIsVendorShell
XtIsTransientShell   XtIsTopLevelShell    XtIsApplicationShell
XtIsSessionShell (R6)
```

For checking against the Intrinsics-defined classes, these routines may be faster than calling XtIsSubclass. Toolkits such as OSF/Motif often provide additional macros or functions that you can use to check toolkit-specific classes (e.g. XmIsPushButton).

CAUTION

Do not confuse superclass/subclass relationships with parent/child relationships. Parent/child defines the relationship of widget instances in a particular user-interface widget tree. Superclass/subclass defines how different types of widgets inherit their features and functionality.

SEE ALSO

Routines: XtSuperclass

XtKeysymToKeycodeList (R4)

Retrieves the list of KeyCodes which could map to a specified KeySym

SYNOPSIS

```
void XtKeysymToKeycodeList( display, keysym, keycodes_return,
    count_return )
        Display                         *display;
        KeySym                          keysym;
        KeyCode                         **keycodes_return;
        Cardinal                        *count_return;
```

ARGUMENTS

display	in	Display for which translation is applicable.
keysym	in	Keysym for which translation is desired.
keycodes_return	in/out	Pointer to variable in which a pointer to a list of keycodes is returned.
count_return	in/out	Pointer to a variable in which the number of keycodes in *keycodes_return* is returned.

DESCRIPTION

XtKeysymToKeycodeList returns the list of keycodes which translate to the specified keysym in the keyboard mapping table associated with *display*.

USAGE

The Intrinsics use XtKeysymToKeycodeList internally to determine which keycode(s) must be grabbed to satisfy a translation that triggers a grab action. Normal applications do not use this routine, but should call XtRegisterGrabAction to register any action procedure that needs to activate key or button grabs.

Key events coming from a server report a keycode that tells which physical key was pressed. During translation, this is parsed into a keysym, which is a vendor-neutral encoding describing the symbol or function associated with that key (e.g. the symbol "2"). Modifier keys (e.g. Shift, Ctrl, Meta, etc.) may affect which keysym is mapped from a particular keycode, so a Key event reports any modifiers which were active when the event was generated.

The mapping between keycodes and keysyms is kept in a table (see XtGetKeysymTable). Several keycodes may translate to the same keysym; for example, the keysym corresponding to the symbol "2" might be generated by a numeric key along the top of the keyboard, or the similar key on a separate numeric keypad. If pressing the "2" key invokes an action that requires control of pointer and keyboard events, a passive grab must be established for *both* physical keys which could translate to the triggering keysym. XtKeysymToKeycodeList returns the list of keycodes that could translate to the specified symbol.

CAUTION

The returned list of keycodes should be freed with XtFree when it is no longer required.

SEE ALSO

Routines: XtGetKeysymTable, XtRegisterGrabAction, XtTranslateKeycode

XtLastEventProcessed   **(R6)**

Returns a pointer to the last X event processed by XtDispatchEvent

SYNOPSIS

```
XEvent *XtLastEventProcessed( display )
        Display                         *display;
```

ARGUMENTS

display   in   Display for which information is requested.

DESCRIPTION

XtLastEventProcessed returns a pointer to the last X event processed for the specified display by XtDispatchEvent. The storage for this event structure is owned by the Intrinsics and must not be modified or freed.

USAGE

XtLastEventProcessed is usually used inside callbacks to fetch the event that triggered the callback. In some toolkits (e.g. Motif) this information is also available through the *call_data* argument. In releases of the Intrinsics prior to R6, it was common to implement a private main loop and cache the event in a global variable so that it could be referenced later.

CAUTION

Callbacks should not assume that the event is of a particular type, since the event that triggers a callback may be modified through translations. Callbacks that read the event should check the type before trying to parse any type-specific event fields.

SEE ALSO

Routines: XtDispatchEvent, XtLastTimestampProcessed

XtLastTimestampProcessed (R4)

Returns the timestamp of the last X event processed by XtDispatchEvent

SYNOPSIS

```
Time XtLastTimestampProcessed( display )
        Display                     *display;
```

ARGUMENTS

display   in   Display for which information is requested.

DESCRIPTION

XtLastTimestampProcessed returns the timestamp of the last KeyPress, KeyRelease, ButtonPress, ButtonRelease, MotionNotify, EnterNotify, LeaveNotify, PropertyNotify or SelectionClear event processed by XtDispatchEvent for the specified display. If no event matching one of the preceding types has yet been dispatched for the specified display, XtLastTimestampProcessed returns zero. The timestamp is in server time.

USAGE

XtLastTimestampProcessed is used to return a server time from an event that triggers toolkit selection or an input device grab. The timestamp is used to resolve which client had ownership of a given display resource when it was referenced. A timestamp must be specified in the following calls:

XtCallAcceptFocus	XtGrabKeyboard
XtUngrabKeyboard	XtGrabPointer
XtUngrabPointer	XtOwnSelection
XtDisownSelection	XtOwnSelectionIncremental
XtGetSelectionValue	XtGetSelectionValues
XtGetSelectionValueIncremental	XtGetSelectionValuesIncremental
XtSendSelectionRequest (R6)	

CAUTION

The timestamp is expressed in server time on the specified display, and does not reflect the time on the client machine or other displays in the same application context. Only the listed event types provide a timestamp, so XtLastTimestampProcessed provides no information about when other events, if any, might have been generated.

SEE ALSO

Routines: XtCallAcceptFocus, XtDisownSelection, XtGetSelectionValue,
            XtGetSelectionValues, XtGetSelectionValueIncremental,
            XtGetSelectionValuesIncremental, XtGrabKeyboard, XtGrabPointer,
            XtOwnSelection, XtOwnSelectionIncremental, XtSendSelectionRequest,
            XtUngrabKeyboard, XtUngrabPointer

XtMainLoop   **(O)**

Obsolete main event processing loop

SYNOPSIS

void XtMainLoop()

ARGUMENTS

None

DESCRIPTION

XtMainLoop starts the event handling loop within the default application context established by XtInitialize. XtMainLoop does not return, but is simply an endless loop of XtNextEvent and XtDispatchEvent.

USAGE

See XtAppMainLoop.

CAUTION

XtMainLoop is an obsolete routine supplied for backwards compatibility with earlier versions of the Intrinsics, and is superseded by XtAppMainLoop in the Release 3 and later Intrinsics. XtMainLoop uses the default application context established by XtInitialize, which must be called first.

SEE ALSO

Routines: XtAddInput, XtAddTimeOut, XtAddWorkProc, XtInitialize, XtNextEvent, XtPeekEvent, XtPending, XtProcessEvent

XtMakeGeometryRequest (R3)

Requests a geometry change from a parent widget

SYNOPSIS

```
XtGeometryResult XtMakeGeometryRequest( w, request, reply )
        Widget                       w;
        XtWidgetGeometry             *request;
        XtWidgetGeometry             *reply;
```

ARGUMENTS

w	in	Widget making the geometry request; must be of class RectObj or any subclass thereof.
request	in	Pointer to data structure specifying requested geometry.
reply	in/out	Pointer to data structure to receive the returned geometry.

DESCRIPTION

If the specified widget is managed and its parent is realized, XtMakeGeometryRequest passes the requested geometry to the parent's geometry handler routine. Depending on the result of the request, XtMakeGeometryRequest returns XtGeometryYes, XtGeometryNo or XtGeometryAlmost. The *reply* argument returns the parent's suggested geometry. If the specified widget's parent is not a subclass of Composite, XtMakeGeometryRequest issues a fatal error.

USAGE

XtMakeGeometryRequest is used in widget implementation code when a widget must ask its parent for a geometry change. It is rarely called directly by application programmers, though it could be used in user interface editors to send a query-only request to a parent to see what its response would be to a proposed change to a child. To change a widget's geometry in ordinary applications, call XtSetValues and specify the appropriate geometry resources.

If the return value is XtGeometryYes, it implies that the requested values were acceptable. The parent or the Intrinsics actually resize the widget, so the child need take no further action. If the result is XtGeometryNo, the request was disallowed, and the child should not ask again. If the result is XtGeometryAlmost, the *reply* argument supplies compromise values suggested by the parent. The child is expected to accept these values by calling XtMakeGeometryRequest again immediately, passing the suggested values in *request*. Otherwise, no geometry adjustment takes place, and it is assumed that the child has decided to live with its old values.

CAUTION

XtMakeGeometryRequest is a widget internal routine and should not be called by normal applications.

SEE ALSO

Routines: XtConfigureWidget, XtMakeResizeRequest, XtMoveWidget,
           XtQueryGeometry, XtResizeWidget

XtMakeResizeRequest (R3)

Requests a resize from parent widget

SYNOPSIS

```
XtGeometryResult XtMakeResizeRequest( w, width, height, width_return,
    height_return )
            Widget                          w;
            Dimension                       width;
            Dimension                       height;
            Dimension                       *width_return;
            Dimension                       *height_return;
```

ARGUMENTS

w	in	Widget making the geometry request; must be of class RectObj or any subclass thereof.
width	in	Desired width.
height	in	Desired height.
width_return	in/out	Pointer to variable to receive width that child actually got.
height_return	in/out	Pointer to variable to receive height that child actually got.

DESCRIPTION

If the specified widget is managed and its parent is realized, XtMakeResizeRequest passes the requested geometry to the parent's geometry handler routine. Depending on the result of the request, XtMakeResizeRequest returns XtGeometryYes, XtGeometryNo or XtGeometryAlmost. The arguments *width_return* and *height_return* return the parent's suggested geometry. If the specified widget's parent is not a subclass of Composite, XtMakeResizeRequest issues a fatal error.

USAGE

XtMakeResizeRequest is used in widget implementation code when a widget must ask its parent for a resize. It is not called directly by application programmers.

If the return value is XtGeometryYes, it implies that the requested values were acceptable. The parent or the Intrinsics actually resize the widget, so the child need no further action. If the result is XtGeometryNo, the request was disallowed, and the child should not ask again. If the result is XtGeometryAlmost, *width_return* and *height_return* supply compromise values suggested by the parent. The child is expected to accept these values (if it wants to) by calling XtMakeResizeRequest again immediately, passing the suggested values for *width* and *height*. Otherwise, no geometry adjustment takes place, and it is assumed that the child has decided to live with its old values.

CAUTION

XtMakeResizeRequest is a widget internal routine and should never be called by normal applications.

SEE ALSO

Routines: XtConfigureWidget, XtMakeGeometryRequest, XtMoveWidget,
XtQueryGeometry, XtResizeWidget

XtMalloc (R3)

Allocates memory

SYNOPSIS

```
char *XtMalloc( size )
        Cardinal                        size;
```

ARGUMENTS

size   in   Size of storage to allocate, in bytes.

DESCRIPTION

XtMalloc returns a pointer to a block of storage of at least the specified size. If there is insufficient storage available to allocate the space, XtMalloc issues an error and exits.

USAGE

XtMalloc is used throughout the Intrinsics and applications to dynamically allocate memory, including space for widget data structures, strings, or other client data structures. XtMalloc is fully compatible and interchangeable with its standard C counterpart malloc(), except that it calls XtErrorMsg on an error. XtMalloc is more portable than malloc(), since it exists on systems that use other means to allocate memory and do not support malloc() directly.

To avoid compiler warnings, the pointer returned by XtMalloc should be cast to the appropriate type before use. To allocate memory for structures or copies of strings, the routines XtNew and XtNewString provide a simpler interface.

CAUTION

Call XtFree to free storage allocated with XtMalloc when it is no longer needed.

SEE ALSO

Routines: XtCalloc, XtFree, XtNew, XtNewString, XtRealloc

XtManageChild

(R3)

Manages a widget and, by default, causes it to be displayed

SYNOPSIS

```
void XtManageChild( w )
        Widget                    w;
```

ARGUMENTS

w   in   Widget to be managed; must be of class RectObj or any subclass
                                 thereof..

DESCRIPTION

XtManageChild adds the specified widget to its parent's managed (displayable) set. If the parent is
realized, the child is also realized. By default, the child widget's window is also mapped, making it visible;
you can override this behavior by calling XtSetMappedWhenManaged on the child with a value of
False. If the parent widget is not a subclass of Composite, XtManageChild issues a fatal error. If the
child is NULL, XtManageChild issues a warning.

USAGE

XtManageChild is used to make a normal (not pop-up) widget child visible on the screen, while invoking
the parent's geometry management routines. The specific visual effect of XtManageChild depends on
how the parent treats managed children. Generally, the parent displays the newly-managed child and
possibly adjusts the geometry of the child and its siblings to make room for it.

A widget may be simultaneously created and managed with XtCreateManagedWidget. If several
children of the same parent must be managed simultaneously, XtManageChildren is more efficient than
multiple calls to XtManageChild. A managed widget may be removed from its parent's managed set by
calling XtUnmanageChild or XtUnmanageChildren. In the R6 Intrinsics, the routine
XtChangeManagedSet can be used to simultaneously manage and unmanage children of the same parent.

CAUTION

Managing or unmanaging a widget that is itself a parent does not change the managed state of its own
children. However, a widget is visible only if all of its ancestors are also managed, realized and mapped. So
unmanaging a parent removes its children from the screen with it.

XtManageChild should never be called for pop-up shells, since pop-up widgets are not included in
the parent's list of normal children and do not invoke geometry management. To make a pop-up shell
visible, call XtPopup. However, note that the OSF/Motif XmDialogShell and XmMenuShell pop
themselves up when their child is managed, so in Motif, shells are controlled by managing and unmanaging
the child of the shell.

SEE ALSO

Routines: XtCreateManagedWidget, XtIsManaged, XtManageChildren, XtMapWidget,
            XtSetMappedWhenManaged, XtUnmanageChild, XtUnmanageChildren,
            XtUnmapWidget, XtChangeManagedSet

XtManageChildren (R3)

Manages several widgets in a single call

SYNOPSIS

```
void XtManageChildren( widgets, num_children )
        WidgetList                      widgets;
        Cardinal                        num_children;
```

ARGUMENTS

widgets   in   Pointer to a list of widget IDs specifying children to be managed; each
                                must be of class RectObj or any subclass thereof.

num_children   in   Number of widget children to be managed.

DESCRIPTION

XtManageChildren adds the specified children to their parent's managed (displayable) set. If the parent is realized, the children are also realized. By default the childrens' windows are also mapped, making them visible. You may override this behavior by calling XtSetMappedWhenManaged on one or more or the children, specifying a value of False.

If any child is NULL, or all children do not have the same parent, XtManageChildren issues a warning. If the parent widget is not a subclass of Composite, XtManageChildren issues a fatal error.

USAGE

XtManageChildren is used to make normal (not pop-up) widget children visible on the screen, while invoking their parent's geometry management routines to organize them. If several children of the same parent must be managed simultaneously, XtManageChildren is more efficient than multiple calls to XtManageChild. The specific visual effect of XtManageChildren depends on how the parent treats managed children. Generally, the parent displays the newly-managed children and possibly adjusts the geometry of the children and their siblings to make room for them.

A widget may be simultaneously created and managed with XtCreateManagedWidget. A single child may be managed with the routine XtManageChild. A managed widget may be removed from its parent's managed set by calling XtUnmanageChild or XtUnmanageChildren. In the R6 Intrinsics, the routine XtChangeManagedSet can be used to simultaneously manage and unmanage children of the same parent.

CAUTION

Managing or unmanaging a widget that is itself a parent does not change the managed state of its own children. However, a widget is visible only if all of its ancestors are also managed, realized and mapped. So unmanaging a parent removes its children from the screen with it.

XtManageChildren should never be called for pop-up shells, since pop-up widgets do not invoke their parent's geometry management, and are not included in the parent's list of normal children. To make a pop-up shell visible, call XtPopup.

SEE ALSO

Routines: XtCreateManagedWidget, XtIsManaged, XtManageChild, XtMapWidget,
            XtSetMappedWhenManaged, XtUnmanageChild, XtUnmanageChildren,
            XtUnmapWidget, XtChangeManagedSet

XtMapWidget
(R3)

Maps a widget's window without changing whether it is managed

SYNOPSIS

```
void XtMapWidget( w )
      Widget                        w;
```

ARGUMENTS

w   in   The widget whose window should be mapped; must be of class Core or any subclass thereof.

DESCRIPTION

XtMapWidget maps the specified widget's window on the screen. XtMapWidget does not affect the managed state of the widget, so whether the widget is visible will depend on whether its parent has room for it.

USAGE

Mapping a widget makes its window visible. Default toolkit behavior is to map widgets when they are managed, and unmap them when they are unmanaged, so XtManageChild and XtUnmanageChild are the "usual" ways to put a widget on the screen and remove it. However, these routines invoke geometry management, and can sometimes cause undesirable visual effects. For example, a dialog box might shrink, expand or reposition its children to adjust for the sudden management/unmanagement of a child.

In some user interface styles, it is desirable to remove widgets from a layout while still maintaining the space that they occupied. Default behavior can be overridden by calling XtSetMappedWhenManaged to set the widget's *mapped_when_managed* field to False. XtMapWidget and XtUnmapWidget are then used to explicitly map and unmap the widget from the screen while leaving it managed. The parent's geometry management is not invoked, and the parent maintains blank space where the child would normally appear.

If a widget is unmanaged its parent will not make space for it, so the combination of "mapped" but "unmanaged", while possible, is not very useful. Generally, a widget must be both mapped and managed to be visible.

CAUTION

XtMapWidget should only be called after the *mapped_when_managed* field of the specified widget has been set to False with XtSetMappedWhenManaged. Since an unmapped widget is still managed, calls to XtSetValues that affect the geometry of the widget may result in geometry changes in the user interface. If *w* is not realized, calling XtMapWidget may cause a fatal protocol error by referencing a NULL window ID.

SEE ALSO

Routines: XtSetMappedWhenManaged, XtUnmapWidget

XtMergeArgLists (R3)

Combines two ArgLists into one

SYNOPSIS

```
ArgList XtMergeArgLists( args1, num_args1, args2, num_args2 )
        ArgList                     args1;
        Cardinal                    num_args1;
        ArgList                     args2;
        Cardinal                    num_args2;
```

ARGUMENTS

args1	in	Pointer to first array of resource name/value pairs to be merged.
num_args1	in	Number of name/value pairs in *args1*.
args2	in	Pointer to second array of resource/name value pairs to be merged.
num_args2	in	Number of name/value pairs in *args2*.

DESCRIPTION

XtMergeArgLists merges the two specified arglists and returns a single merged arglist. XtMergeArgLists allocates storage for the new merged arglist but does not free the storage associated with the two source arglists.

USAGE

Arglists are supplied to all routines that create widgets, or specify and query resource values. XtMergeArgLists may be used to combine arglists from different sources so as to use them in a single call to a resource management routine.

CAUTION

The returned arglist should be freed with XtFree when it is no longer required.

SEE ALSO

Routines: XtAppCreateShell, XtAppInitialize, XtCreateManagedWidget,
         XtCreatePopupShell, XtCreateWidget, XtGetValues, XtSetArg,
         XtSetValues

XtMoveWidget

(R3)

Moves a widget in response to a geometry request

SYNOPSIS

```
void XtMoveWidget( w, x, y )
        Widget              w;
        Position            x;
        Position            y;
```

ARGUMENTS

w	in	Widget to be repositioned; must be of class RectObj or any subclass thereof.
x	in	New X position of widget in parent's coordinate system.
y	in	New Y position of widget in parent's coordinate system.

DESCRIPTION

XtMoveWidget directly writes the new *x* and *y* values into the specified widget's geometry fields and, if the widget is realized, issues an Xlib XMoveWindow call on the widget's window. If the specified *x* and *y* values are the same as the existing values, XtMoveWidget returns immediately.

USAGE

XtMoveWidget is called only within a manager widget's implementation code to respond to a geometry management directive from its parent, or a request from one of its children. XtMoveWidget is never called by application programs. To reposition a widget, instead call XtSetValues specifying the desired XtNx and XtNy resource values.

CAUTION

Applications never call XtMoveWidget to reposition a widget, as it unilaterally sets the X and Y coordinates of the widget and its window, without giving the parent widget a chance to perform geometry management.

SEE ALSO

Routines: XtConfigureWidget, XtMakeGeometryRequest, XtMakeResizeRequest, XtQueryGeometry, XtResizeWidget

XtName (R4)

Returns the name of a widget

SYNOPSIS

```
String XtName( object )
        Widget                          object;
```

ARGUMENTS

object   in   Widget or object for which resource name is desired; must be of class
                              Object or any subclass thereof.

DESCRIPTION

XtName returns the resource name, specified at creation, of the specified widget or object instance.

USAGE

This routine is often used to retrieve the name of a widget for use in an error or informational message. If the name of a widget is known, its widget ID may be found with XtNameToWidget.

CAUTION

The returned string is owned by the Intrinsics and must not be modified or freed. If the caller needs a private copy, it may be created with XtNewString.

SEE ALSO

Routines: XtNameToWidget

XtNameToWidget

(R3)

Finds a widget with the specified name

SYNOPSIS

```
Widget XtNameToWidget( w, name )
        Widget                  w;
        String                  name;
```

ARGUMENTS

w   in   Widget from which to start the search; must be of class Core or any
                            subclass thereof.

name   in   Partially-qualified name of the desired widget (e.g. "*mywidget").

DESCRIPTION

Given the partially-qualified name of a widget, XtNameToWidget returns the widget ID of the named widget, if found, or NULL if the named widget is not found. The *name* argument is the same as would be used in resource file specification. It may specify a simple object name, or a series of simple object names separated by periods or asterisks. A search for the named widget is started at the specified widget *w*, and proceeds through the tree of descendants of *w*. The search stops at the first widget with the shortest name matching the specified name, and its widget ID is returned.

USAGE

XtNameToWidget is used to get the widget ID of a widget with a known name. Since parameters are supplied to action procedures as strings, XtNameToWidget is often used in an action procedure to convert a string parameter to a widget instance. It can also be used to find the widget ID of a sub-object in a compound widget, if the compound widget documents the names of its children. When searching for the descendant of a widget, the name is often specified starting with an asterisk, in case there are intervening generations:

```
    yes_btn = XtNameToWidget( dialog_box, "*yesButton" );
```

To perform the reverse operation and find the name of a widget when the widget ID is known, call XtName.

CAUTION

XtNameToWidget stops at the first widget with the shortest name matching the specified name. If widgets are created with non-unique names, XtNameToWidget may or may not return the ID of the appropriate widget.

SEE ALSO

Routines: XtName

XtNew   (R3)

Allocates a new instance of a toolkit data structure

SYNOPSIS

```
type *XtNew( type )
        Type                                    type;
```

ARGUMENTS

type   in   Any previously declared storage type.

DESCRIPTION

XtNew is a convenience macro that allocates a block of storage large enough to hold a single instance of the specified data type, and returns a pointer to the allocated storage. The pointer returned by XtNew is automatically cast to the appropriate type. If there is insufficient memory to allocate the new block, XtNew issues a fatal error by calling XtErrorMsg.

USAGE

XtNew is used in widget implementation code to allocate storage when copying data, and for new items added to dynamic arrays and linked lists. It may be used in applications to allocate space when you have to make a private copy of data returned by an Intrinsics routine, or where you want to add a new struct to a linked list.

CAUTION

Memory allocated with XtNew should be freed with XtFree when no longer needed.

SEE ALSO

Routines: XtCalloc, XtFree, XtMalloc, XtNewString, XtRealloc

XtNewString

(R3)

Makes a copy of a NULL-terminated character string

SYNOPSIS

```
String XtNewString( old_string );
        String                          old_string;
```

ARGUMENTS

old_string   in   NULL-terminated string to be copied.

DESCRIPTION

XtNewString is a convenience macro which copies an instance of an existing string. XtNewString allocates sufficient storage for the new string and copies the old contents into it. If there is insufficient memory to allocate the new block, XtNewString issues a fatal error by calling XtErrorMsg.

USAGE

XtNewString is often used to copy a string from storage owned by the Intrinsics to storage owned by the application, e.g. a widget name returned by XtName.

CAUTION

Strings created with XtNewString should be freed with XtFree when no longer required.

SEE ALSO

Routines: XtCalloc, XtFree, XtMalloc, XtNew, XtRealloc

XtNextEvent   (O)

Retrieves the next X event and removes it from the input queue

SYNOPSIS

```
void XtNextEvent ( event )
       XEvent                                   *event;
```

ARGUMENTS

event   in/out   Pointer to event data structure to receive next event.

DESCRIPTION

XtNextEvent fetches the next X event from the server queue associated with the default application context created by XtInitialize. The returned event is removed from the head of the input queue and copied into the specified XEvent data structure.

USAGE

See XtAppNextEvent.

CAUTION

XtNextEvent is an obsolete routine supplied for backwards compatibility with earlier versions of the Intrinsics, and is superseded by XtAppNextEvent in the Release 3 and later Intrinsics. XtNextEvent uses the default application context established by XtInitialize, which must be called first.

SEE ALSO

Routines: XtAppNextEvent, XtInitialize, XtMainLoop

XtNoticeSignal

(R6)

Tells the Intrinsics that a POSIX-style signal has been raised

SYNOPSIS

```
void XtNoticeSignal( signal_id )
        XtSignalId                      signal_id;
```

ARGUMENTS

signal_id in Identifier of signal handler callback registered with `XtAppAddSignal`.

DESCRIPTION

`XtNoticeSignal` causes the Intrinsics to call the specified signal callback as soon as it is safe to do so. Any event dispatch currently in progress, including any callback routines invoked by the dispatch, will complete before the specified signal callback is called. If the toolkit is currently blocking waiting for an event, it will wake up and handle the condition.

USAGE

The Intrinsics cannot invoke a signal callback immediately when a signal is raised, since the signal could interrupt in the middle of any routine. Instead, a signal callback is invoked when it is safe to do so; that it, when any in-progress callback or event dispatch has returned to the main loop. To implement signal handling, the programmer must first register a signal callback with `XtAppAddSignal`. This returns an `XtSignalId` that is used to identify the signal callback/client_data pair. Then, a signal handler should be established with `signal()`. The signal handler should in turn call `XtNoticeSignal` when the signal is raised. The Intrinsics call the specified signal callback as soon as it is safe to do so.

CAUTION

`XtNoticeSignal` is the only toolkit routine that can be called safely within a signal handler. If a signal is raised multiple times before the Intrinsics can dispatch the signal callback, the callback will still only be called once. Also, there is a slight chance that a signal could arrive just after the Intrinsics have marked it as handled, but just before the signal callback is invoked. This will cause an extra callback. Signal callbacks must be prepared to deal with this, if it matters, usually by keeping a count that is synchronized with the signal handler itself.

The best way for pre-R6 clients to handle signals is to create a pipe with `pipe()`, and register one end as an input source with `XtAppAddInput`. Within the signal handler, write to the other end of the pipe. This will force an input callback to be invoked as soon as it is safe to do so. The problem with this method is that if the signal were raised many times in a short space of time, the pipe could potentially fill up and cause a deadlock. The R6 routine avoids this possibility.

SEE ALSO

Routines: `XtAppMainLoop, XtAppNextEvent, XtAppPending, XtAppProcessEvent, XtAppAddSignal, XtRemoveSignal`

XtNumber   (R3)

Returns the number of elements in a fixed-size array

SYNOPSIS

```
Cardinal XtNumber( array )
        Array Variable                  array;
```

ARGUMENTS

array   in   A fixed-size array of any declared type.

DESCRIPTION

XtNumber is a convenience macro that returns the number of elements in a fixed-size array.

USAGE

XtNumber is used to return the number of elements in static ArgLists, XtActionLists, XtResourceLists and other counted arrays. It is handy for specifying the number of items in a statically-declared array when the array must be passed as an argument to an Intrinsics routine. Example:

```
Widget w;
static Arg args[] ={
    { XtNheight, (XtArgVal) 100 },
    { XtNwidth,  (XtArgVal) 100 }
};

XtSetValues( w, args, XtNumber(args));
```

CAUTION

XtNumber cannot be used to calculate the number of elements in a dynamically-allocated array.

SEE ALSO

Routines: None

XtOffset

(R3)

Determines the offset of a field in a structure

SYNOPSIS

```
Cardinal XtOffset( pointer_type, field_name )
        Type                    pointer_type;
        Field                   field_name;
```

ARGUMENTS

pointer_type	in	Type declared as a pointer to a structure.
field_name	in	Structure member for which to calculate the byte offset.

DESCRIPTION

XtOffset is a convenience macro that returns the byte offset, measured from the beginning of the structure, of the specified structure member.

USAGE

XtOffset determines the offset of a specified field from the beginning of a data structure. It is used most often to statically initialize resource lists in widget implementation code, or in application code that fetches application resources with XtGetApplicationResources.

CAUTION

XtOffset is superseded by XtOffsetOf, a more portable routine, in the R4 and later Intrinsics.

SEE ALSO

Routines: XtOffsetOf

XtOffsetOf   (R4)

Determines the offset of a field in a structure

SYNOPSIS

```
Cardinal XtOffsetOf( structure_type, field_name )
        Type                        structure_type;
        Field                       field_name;
```

ARGUMENTS

structure_type	in	Type declared as a structure.
field_name	in	Structure member for which the byte offset is calculated.

DESCRIPTION

XtOffsetOf is a convenience macro that returns the byte offset, measured from the beginning of the structure, of the specified structure member. It is more portable than the older macro, XtOffset.

USAGE

XtOffsetOf determines the byte offset of a specified field from the beginning of a data structure. It is used most often to statically initialize resource lists in widget implementation code, or in application code that fetches application resources with XtGetApplicationResources.

CAUTION

Note that the first argument to XtOffsetOf is a type declared as a structure, while the first argument to the older macro XtOffset is a type declared as a *pointer* to a structure.

SEE ALSO

Routines: XtOffset

XtOpenApplication   **(R6)**

Initialize the toolkit, opens a display and creates a shell to root an application widget tree

SYNOPSIS

```
Widget XtOpenApplication( app_context, app_class, options, num_options,
    argc, argv, fallback_resources, shell_class, args, num_args )
        XtAppContext            *app_context;
        String                  app_class;
        XrmOptionDescList       options;
        Cardinal                num_options;
        Cardinal                *argc;
        String                  *argv;
        String                  *fallback_resources;
        WidgetClass             shell_class;
        ArgList                 args;
        Cardinal                num_args;
```

ARGUMENTS

app_context	in/out	Pointer to a variable to receive new application context.
app_class	in	Resource class of the application instance.
options	in	Pointer to a list of option description records specifying command-line arguments that set resource values.
num_options	in	Number of option descriptors in *options*.
argc	in/out	Pointer to variable specifying the argument count provided to main() at image activation; returns the number of unparsed arguments remaining after XtOpenApplication has parsed *argv*.
argv	in/out	Argument vector provided to main() at image activation; returns all unparsed arguments.
fallback_resources	in	Resource values to be used if the application class resource file cannot be found or opened, expressed as a NULL-terminated list of strings in resource file format. NULL if no fallback resources are to be specified.
shell_class	in	Class pointer specifying type of Shell to create.
args	in	An array of Args that are to override any other resource specifications for the created Shell.
num_args	in	Number of resource name/value pairs in *args*.

DESCRIPTION

XtOpenApplication is a convenience routine that calls XtToolkitInitialize, XtCreateApplicationContext, XtAppSetFallbackResources, XtOpenDisplay and XtAppCreateShell in turn, and returns the widget ID of a new shell. The new shell has no parent, and is used to root a new application widget tree.

Arguments to XtOpenApplication are used as they are in the separate routines which it replaces. The new application context is returned by side-effect in the *app_context* argument. The display pointer is not returned, but may be found by calling XtDisplay and passing the widget ID of the new shell.

XtOpenApplication merges the per-display and per-screen resource databases; for more information on how this is performed, see XtDisplayInitialize. If the display cannot be opened, XtOpenApplication issues a fatal error.

USAGE

XtOpenApplication is used in R6 as a single, blanket initialization routine by applications that require a single application context, display and shell. It supersedes the convenience routine XtAppInitialize used in earlier releases of the Intrinsics. Unlike XtAppInitialize, XtOpenApplication allows you to specify the class of the new shell. The shell should generally be a SessionShell if you intend to participate in session management protocols, or an ApplicationShell if you do not. XtVaOpenApplication is the varargs variant of this routine.

CAUTION

XtOpenApplication calls XtToolkitInitialize, and therefore may only be called once in a program. XtOpenApplication does not allow specification of the application name, which by default is the name of the program itself. This can be overridden by setting the value of the environment variable RESOURCE_NAME, or by passing the desired name after the -name command-line option.

SEE ALSO

Routines: XtAppCreateShell, XtAppSetFallbackResources,
           XtCreateApplicationContext, XtDisplayInitialize, XtOpenDisplay,
           XtToolkitInitialize, XtAppInitialize, XtVaAppInitialize,
           XtVaOpenApplication

XtOpenDisplay   **(R3)**

Opens a server connection and loads the resource databases

SYNOPSIS

```
Display *XtOpenDisplay( app_context, display_string, app_name, app_class,
    options, num_options, argc, argv )
        XtAppContext              app_context;
        String                    display_string;
        String                    app_name;
        String                    app_class;
        XrmOptionDescRec          *options;
        Cardinal                  num_options;
        Cardinal                  *argc;
        String                    *argv;
```

ARGUMENTS

app_context	in	Application context to which display should be added.
display_string	in	Implementation-dependent string specifying the X server connection.
app_name	in	Application name used as root of resource names.
app_class	in	Application class used as root of resource names, and specifying class-specific resource file(s) to merge in resource database.
options	in	Pointer to a list of option description records specifying command-line arguments that set resource values.
num_options	in	Number of option description records in *options*.
argc	in/out	Pointer to integer specifying argument count provided to main() at image activation; returns number of unparsed arguments remaining after XtOpenDisplay has parsed *argv*.
argv	in/out	Argument vector provided to main() at image activation; returns unparsed arguments.

DESCRIPTION

XtOpenDisplay opens a new connection to the specified X server and returns a display pointer used to identify the connection. XtOpenDisplay calls XtDisplayInitialize to merge the per-display and per-screen resource databases, and adds the open display to the specified application context.

The *display_string* argument is implementation-dependent, but on POSIX-based systems is of the form "*node:S.N*", where *node* specifies the node on which the server resides, the colon ":" specifies that the application should connect via a TCP/IP socket, *S* is the number of the server (usually zero), and *N* is the number of the screen (usually zero). If *display_string* is NULL or the empty string "", XtOpenDisplay uses the display specified by the environment variable DISPLAY, or the -*display* command-line argument.

If *app_name* is not specified, XtOpenDisplay uses the name passed via the -name command-line option. If this is not specified, the value of the environment variable RESOURCE_NAME is used. If RESOURCE_NAME is undefined, the name of the program itself (*argv[0]*) is used.

USAGE

XtOpenDisplay is used when you want to open a display connection before you create any widgets, or when you want to open more than one display connection. To build applications that display on more than one screen, you would initialize the toolkit with XtToolkitInitialize, create an application context with XtCreateApplicationContext, and add displays with XtOpenDisplay. To create the first widget on each display, call XtAppCreateShell.

If you want to use a non-default visual, you may also need to call XtOpenDisplay so you can ask the X server which visuals it supports before creating the first shell.

If you only require a single application context, display and application shell, you may use the convenience routines XtAppInitialize or XtOpenApplication (R6) instead. Displays opened with XtOpenDisplay should be closed with XtCloseDisplay when no longer required. All open displays associated with an application context are automatically closed when you call XtDestroyApplicationContext, or when your program exits.

CAUTION

None

SEE ALSO

Routines: XtAppInitialize, XtOpenApplication, XtCloseDisplay, XtDisplayInitialize

XtOverrideTranslations   **(R3)**

Destructively merges new translations with a widget's existing translation table

SYNOPSIS

```
void XtOverrideTranslations( w, translations )
        Widget                      w;
        XtTranslations              translations;
```

ARGUMENTS

w   in   The widget to which the new translations are added; must be of class Core or any subclass thereof.

translations   in   A compiled translation table.

DESCRIPTION

XtOverrideTranslations merges the specified translations into the existing widget translations, ignoring any #replace, #augment or #override directive that may have been specified in the translation string. If a new translation specifies an event sequence that matches one found in the widget's existing translations, the new translation replaces the old one destructively.

USAGE

Every widget has a translation table that defines events or event sequences to be detected, and the actions that are executed in response. Default translations are defined by the widget class, but you can augment these so that the widget will invoke application-defined action procedures. If the actions supplied by a widget are documented, you may also change the translation table to alter the widget's response to input. This is often used to modify the behavior of text widgets to mimic a preferred editing style.

To augment a widget's translations, first define a new translation table in the plaintext format described in Appendix D, and then compile it to its internal format with XtParseTranslationTable. XtOverrideTranslations merges the new table with the existing table, destructively replacing any matching translations. The new behavior is added to the widget, while possibly displacing some or all of its existing behavior.

To resolve the actions referenced in an augmented translation, the toolkit first searches any action tables registered by the widget itself, its superclasses and its ancestors in the widget tree. Action tables registered with XtAppAddActions are searched last.

Translations may be merged non-destructively with XtAugmentTranslations. A widget's translation table may be replaced entirely by calling XtSetValues and passing a compiled table as the new value of the widget's XtNtranslations resource.

CAUTION

Overriding a widget's translations should be done with caution, as it may break the behavior of the destination widget. In most cases, you should try using XtAugmentTranslations first.

SEE ALSO

Routines: XtAppAddActions, XtAugmentTranslations, XtParseTranslationTable, XtUninstallTranslations

XtOwnSelection (R3)

Volunteers a widget to provide the toolkit selection if it is requested

SYNOPSIS

```
Boolean XtOwnSelection( w, selection, time, convert_proc,
    lose_selection_proc, done_proc )
        Widget                      w;
        Atom                        selection;
        Time                        time;
        XtConvertSelectionProc      convert_proc;
        XtLoseSelectionProc         lose_selection_proc;
        XtSelectionDoneProc         done_proc;
```

ARGUMENTS

w	in	The widget volunteering to own the selection; must be of class Core or any subclass thereof.
selection	in	Atom identifying which selection is owned, e.g. XA_PRIMARY for primary selection; XA_SECONDARY to own secondary selection, etc.
time	in	Timestamp specifying when selection ownership should start; must be timestamp of the event that triggered the decision to own selection; the symbolic value CurrentTime is not acceptable.
convert_proc	in	Application-supplied procedure to be called when the selection value is requested.
lose_selection_proc	in	Application-supplied procedure to be called if selection ownership is lost involuntarily, or NULL if the owner is not interested in being notified.
done_proc	in	Application-supplied procedure to be called after a requesting application has successfully received the selection, or NULL if the owner is not interested in being notified.

DESCRIPTION

XtOwnSelection volunteers the calling client as the owner of the specified selection, returning True if the caller receives the selection ownership, or False if it does not. The *convert_proc* argument specifies a callback routine of type XtConvertSelectionProc (see Appendix B) which will be called when the selection value is requested. The selection owner is responsible in this callback routine for converting the selection to the target type or types requested by the receiving application. The selection value will be passed as a single atomic operation.

Two optional routines may be registered. The *lose_selection_proc* argument specifies a callback of type XtLoseSelectionProc (see Appendix B) to be invoked if the selection ownership is lost involuntarily. This happens if another client or widget claims selection ownership by calling XtOwnSelection itself.

The *done_proc* argument specifies a callback procedure of type XtSelectionDoneProc (see Appendix B) which is invoked to let the selection owner know that a selection transfer has completed. The selection owner may use this to provide notification or visual feedback to the user. If *done_proc* is specified, the selection owner also owns the storage allocated to the converted selection value, and is responsible for freeing it.

USAGE

XtOwnSelection is often called in widget implementation code to provide cut-and-paste capabilities without the application having to be explicitly involved. For example, most text widgets acquire the selection ownership when their text is selected with the pointer.

You may also acquire the selection ownership explicitly. In this case you is responsible for providing any visual feedback indicating that the selection is owned, and are also responsible for converting the selection value to the target and type demanded by the requester. You would call XtOwnSelection explicitly if, for example, you allow the user to select objects that you draw in a drawing widget.

If you take selection ownership with XtOwnSelection, you are expected to provide the selection value in a single transfer. If you wish to break the selection transfer into smaller incremental transfers you may establish selection ownership with XtOwnSelectionIncremental. The selection ownership may be surrendered voluntarily by calling XtDisownSelection.

CAUTION

Conversion of the selection to the requested target means that the owner should provide the requested information about whatever is selected. Since there is no restriction on what a requester may ask for, a selection owner must anticipate as many targets as possible that make sense. If you intend to support selection, you should read the ICCCM thoroughly.

SEE ALSO

Routines: XtDisownSelection, XtGetSelectionTimeout, XtGetSelectionValue,
XtGetSelectionValues, XtGetSelectionValueIncremental,
XtGetSelectionValuesIncremental, XtOwnSelectionIncremental,
XtSetSelectionTimeout

XtOwnSelectionIncremental (R4)

Volunteers toolkit incremental selection ownership

SYNOPSIS

```
Boolean XtOwnSelectionIncremental( w, selection, time, convert_proc,
    lose_selection_proc, done_proc, cancel_proc, client_data )
        Widget                          w;
        Atom                            selection;
        Time                            time;
        XtConvertSelectionIncrProc      convert_proc;
        XtLoseSelectionIncrProc         lose_selection_proc;
        XtSelectionDoneIncrProc         done_proc;
        XtCancelConvertSelectionProc    cancel_proc;
        XtPointer                       client_data;
```

ARGUMENTS

w	in	The widget volunteering to own the selection; must be of class Core or any subclass thereof.
selection	in	Atom identifying which selection is owned, e.g. XA_PRIMARY for primary selection; XA_SECONDARY to own secondary selection, etc.
time	in	Timestamp specifying when selection ownership should start; this must be timestamp of the event that triggered the decision to own selection. The symbolic value CurrentTime is not acceptable.
convert_proc	in	Application-supplied procedure to be called when the selection value is requested.
lose_selection_proc	in	Application-supplied procedure to be called if selection ownership is lost, or NULL if the owner is not interested in being notified.
done_proc	in	Application-supplied procedure to be called after a requesting application has successfully received the selection, or NULL if the owner does not wish to be notified.
cancel_proc	in	Application-supplied procedure to be called if a selection request is aborted, or NULL if the owner does not wish to be notified.
client_data	in	Application-supplied data to be passed to each of the specified callback routines when they are executed.

DESCRIPTION

XtOwnSelectionIncremental is similar to XtOwnSelection but volunteers the selection as a series of incremental transfers. The *convert_proc* argument specifies a callback procedure of type XtConvertSelectionIncrProc (see Appendix B) which is called repeatedly to provide segments of a selection transfer. Because several incremental selection transfers may be in progress to different requesters simultaneously, all callback routines registered with XtOwnSelectionIncremental accept a *request_id* argument which uniquely distinguishes separate requests for the selection.

Three optional routines may be registered by XtOwnSelectionIncremental. The *lose_selection_proc* argument specifies a callback of type XtLoseSelectionIncrProc (see Appendix

B) to be invoked if the selection ownership is lost involuntarily. This happens if another client or widget claims selection ownership itself.

The *done_proc* argument specifies a callback procedure of type XtSelectionDoneIncrProc (see Appendix B) which is invoked to let the selection owner know that a selection transfer has completed. The selection owner may use this to provide notification or visual feedback to the user. If *done_proc* is specified, the selection owner also owns the storage allocated to the converted selection value, and is responsible for freeing it.

The *cancel_proc* argument specifies a callback procedure of type XtCancelConvertSelectionProc (see Appendix B) which is invoked to let the selection owner know that a selection transfer in progress has been canceled, possibly due to a timeout. The selection owner must decide what to do with the data associated with a partial transfer.

USAGE

XtOwnSelectionIncremental is often called in widget implementation code to provide cut-and-paste capabilities. For example, most text widgets acquire the selection ownership when their text is selected with the pointer.

You may also acquire the selection ownership explicitly. In this case you is responsible for providing any visual feedback indicating that the selection is owned, and are also responsible for converting the selection value to the target and type demanded by the requester. You would call XtOwnSelection explicitly if, for example, you allow the user to select objects that you draw in a drawing widget.

If you take selection ownership with XtOwnSelectionIncremental, you are expected to provide the selection value as a series of incremental transfers. This makes more sense than a single transfer in cases where the selection value is quite large, or when it represents a number of disjoint pieces of information. If the user selected a group of objects in a drawing, for example, each segment of an incremental transfer might represent one object in the group. The selection ownership may be surrendered voluntarily by calling XtDisownSelection.

CAUTION

Conversion of the selection to the requested target means that the owner should provide the requested information about whatever is selected. Since there is no restriction on what a requester may ask for, a selection owner must anticipate as many targets as possible that make sense. If you intend to support selection, you should read the ICCCM thoroughly.

SEE ALSO

Routines: XtDisownSelection, XtGetSelectionTimeout, XtGetSelectionValue, XtGetSelectionValues, XtGetSelectionValueIncremental, XtGetSelectionValuesIncremental, XtOwnSelection, XtSetSelectionTimeout

XtParent (R3)

Returns the widget ID of a widget's parent

SYNOPSIS

```
Widget XtParent ( w )
        Widget                          w;
```

ARGUMENTS

w in The widget whose parent is requested; must be of class Object or any subclass thereof.

DESCRIPTION

XtParent returns the widget ID of the specified widget's parent.

USAGE

XtParent can be used to traverse the widget tree upward. It is often used in widget implementation code, but may also be useful when using toolkits such as OSF/Motif that create hidden shells. In these toolkits, a convenience routine creates a dialog box and a shell to parent it, but only the widget ID of the dialog box is returned. To set resources on the shell, XtParent must be used to return its widget ID.

CAUTION

The parent of a shell created with XtAppCreateShell, XtAppInitialize or XtOpenApplication is NULL.

SEE ALSO

Routines: None

XtParseAcceleratorTable (R3)

Compiles an accelerator table to its toolkit internal format

SYNOPSIS

```
XtAccelerators XtParseAcceleratorTable( table )
        String                          table;
```

ARGUMENTS

table   in   The plaintext representation of a translation table, as described in Appendix D.

DESCRIPTION

XtParseAcceleratorTable compiles the plaintext representation of an accelerator table into the toolkit internal format and returns a pointer to the compiled table.

USAGE

Accelerators are actions that are bound in the context of one widget, but receive their triggering events through the agency of another widget. The most common use of accelerators is to allow keyboard input trapped by a text widget (for example) to trigger the actions of a button widget in a menu.

An accelerator table is specified in a plaintext format which specifies the mapping of events or event sequences to named actions. Actions specified in the accelerator table must be actions that would be found in the widget that you want to respond to the events (e.g. the button widget). Events must be events that could be trapped by the widget that will be asked to receive the events (e.g. a text widget).

The table is first compiled to an internal format with XtParseAcceleratorTable; then attached with XtSetValues to the widget that is to supply the actions as its XtNaccelerators resource. XtInstallAccelerators or XtInstallAllAccelerators is finally called to alert the widget that will trap the events.

CAUTION

In practice, XtParseAcceleratorTable is rarely called, since most toolkits provide simpler ways to establish keyboard accelerators. For example, the OSF/Motif toolkit exports a resource for "button" widgets which lets you specify the left-hand side (only) of their accelerator table. The right-hand side is assumed to be the activation action of the button. The action names supplied by a given widget class are not always documented, and so may not be known to you. The compiled representation of the accelerator table is considered a toolkit internal format.

SEE ALSO

Routines: XtInstallAccelerators, XtInstallAllAccelerators

XtParseTranslationTable   (R3)

Compiles a translation table to its toolkit internal format

SYNOPSIS

```
XtTranslations XtParseTranslationTable( table )
      String                          table;
```

ARGUMENTS

table   in   The plaintext representation of a translation table, as described in
                                   Appendix D.

DESCRIPTION

XtParseTranslationTable compiles the plaintext representation of a translation table into the toolkit
internal format and returns a pointer to the compiled table.

USAGE

Every widget has a translation table that defines the mapping of events or event sequences to named actions
that are executed when the specified event(s) are detected. The default set of translations is class-specific,
and is defined by the widget programmer when a new widget class is created. These default translations may
be augmented, overridden or replaced to cause the widget to respond to events in new ways, or to invoke
application-defined action procedures.

A new translation table is first specified in plaintext format (described in Appendix D). The table is then
compiled using XtParseTranslationTable.

The compiled table may be merged into the widget's existing translation table with
XtAugmentTranslations or XtOverrideTranslations. A widget's translation table may be
replaced entirely by calling XtSetValues and passing a compiled table as the new value of the widget's
XtNtranslations resource.

CAUTION

The compiled representation of the translation table is considered a toolkit internal format and cannot be
inspected..

SEE ALSO

Routines: XtAppAddActions, XtAugmentTranslations, XtOverrideTranslations

XtPeekEvent   **(O)**

Retrieves the next X event without removing it from the input queue

SYNOPSIS

```
Boolean XtPeekEvent( event )
        XEvent                          *event;
```

ARGUMENTS

event   in/out   Pointer to event data structure to receive the next event.

DESCRIPTION

If an X event is found at the head of the input queue associated with the default application context, XtPeekEvent copies it into *event* and returns True. The event is not removed from the input queue. If no events are found, XtPeekEvent flushes the output buffer and waits for the next event. If any timeouts registered with XtAddTimeOut have expired, their associated callback procedures are called. If the next event received is an X event, XtPeekEvent copies it into *event*, without removing it from the input queue, and returns True. Otherwise, it is assumed to be an event from an alternate input source registered with XtAddInput, and XtPeekEvent returns False.

USAGE

See XtAppPeekEvent.

CAUTION

XtPeekEvent is an obsolete routine supplied for backwards compatibility with earlier versions of the Intrinsics, and is superseded by XtAppPeekEvent in the Release 3 and later Intrinsics. XtPeekEvent uses the default application context established by XtInitialize, which must be called first.

SEE ALSO

Routines: XtAppPeekEvent, XtInitialize

XtPending (O)

Determines which X events, timers or alternate input sources are waiting

SYNOPSIS

XtInputMask XtPending()

ARGUMENTS

None

DESCRIPTION

XtPending returns non-zero if there are any toolkit conditions to be handled in the default application context established by XtInitialize. The returned mask is any bitwise OR of XtIMXEvent, XtIMTimer, XtIMSignal (R6) and XtIMAlternateInput, depending on what type(s) of input are waiting. If there are no conditions pending, XtPending flushes any output buffers and returns zero.

USAGE

See XtAppPending.

CAUTION

XtPending is an obsolete routine supplied for backwards compatibility with earlier versions of the Intrinsics, and is superseded by XtAppPending in the Release 3 and later Intrinsics. XtPending uses the default application context established by XtInitialize, which must be called first.

SEE ALSO

Routines: XtAppPending, XtInitialize

XtPopdown   **(R3)**

Removes a pop-up Shell from the screen

SYNOPSIS

```
void XtPopdown( w )
        Widget                                          w;
```

ARGUMENTS

w   in   Widget to be popped down; must be a subclass of Shell.

DESCRIPTION

XtPopdown unmaps the specified shell's window, removing it from the screen. If the Shell was originally popped up with a *grab_kind* of XtGrabExclusive or XtGrabNonexclusive, XtPopdown calls XtRemoveGrab to remove it from the grab list. Any callback procedures in the pop-up shell's XtNpopdownCallback list are invoked. If *w* is not a subclass of Shell, XtPopdown issues a fatal error.

USAGE

XtPopdown is used to pop down a shell created with XtCreatePopupShell and previously mapped with XtPopup or XtPopupSpringLoaded. Such a shell may be a dialog box, menu or other pop-up user interface tool. Popping down a shell does not unrealize or destroy it, so it may be popped up and down repeatedly with succeeding calls to XtPopup and XtPopdown.

Usually, you'll call XtPopdown from a callback routine attached to a widget inside the pop-up. As a convenience, the Intrinsics supply the predefined callback routine XtCallbackPopdown, which can be added to a widget's callback list and simply calls XtPopdown on a specified shell.

Callbacks added to the XtNpopdownCallback list may be used to free resources or store values after the pop-up is removed from the screen.

CAUTION

Toolkits may substitute alternate methods for handling toolkit-specific shells. The OSF/Motif XmDialogShell pops itself down when its child widget is unmanaged, so in Motif, the shell is controlled by calling XtUnmanageChild on its child. Most toolkits also supply some form of "menu button" widget, which pops up an associated shell (parenting a menu, of course) when the widget is selected with a pointer button. Pull-down menus implemented with such a tool do not need to be explicitly controlled with XtPopup or XtPopdown. Toolkits may also invoke additional callbacks when shells are popped up or down; for example, OSF/Motif calls the XmBulletinBoard XmNunmapCallback when it is popped down.

SEE ALSO

Routines: XtAddGrab, XtCallbackExclusive, XtCallbackNone,
            XtCallbackNonexclusive, XtCallbackPopdown, XtCreatePopupShell,
            XtPopup, XtPopupSpringLoaded, XtRemoveGrab

XtPopup   (R3)

Maps a pop-up Shell to the screen and optionally grabs user input

SYNOPSIS

```
void XtPopup( w, grab_kind )
        Widget                          w;
        XtGrabKind                      grab_kind;
```

ARGUMENTS

w	in	Widget to be popped up; must be a subclass of Shell.
grab_kind	in	XtGrabNone, XtGrabExclusive or XtGrabNonexclusive.

DESCRIPTION

XtPopup maps the specified shell's window, making it appear on the screen. If *grab_kind* is specified as either XtGrabExclusive or XtGrabNonexclusive, XtPopup calls XtAddGrab to place the widget on the grab list with the appropriate grab. Just before the widget is mapped, XtPopup calls any callbacks on the shell's XtNpopupCallback list, and if the shell's *create_popup_child* field is non-NULL, calls its *create_popup_child* procedure. If *w* is not a subclass of Shell, XtPopup issues a fatal error. If *grab_kind* is not one of the allowed values, XtPopup issues a warning and assumes a value of XtGrabNone.

USAGE

XtPopup is used to map a pop-up shell on the screen and optionally force user events within the application to be sent to it. Pop-up shells are used to implement features such as pull-down menus and dialog boxes.

Shells popped up with *grab_kind* equal to XtGrabExclusive or XtGrabNonexclusive are called modal pop-ups, and effectively disable the rest of the application until they are popped down. Non-modal pop-ups, which can be thought of as auxiliary application windows, should be popped up with *grab_kind* equal to XtGrabNone.

Callbacks added to the XtNpopupCallback list may be used to make last-minute changes to the pop-up just before it is displayed. This might include positioning the pop-up at a specific location, or reconfiguring the set of widgets to be displayed in the pop-up tool.

The shell's *create_popup_child* procedure is invoked by XtPopup to give a Shell an opportunity to create its own child if it wants to. The *create_popup_child* proc is specified by the shell's XtNcreatePopupChild resource, usually at widget creation time, and is used to defer the creation of complicated pop-up widget trees until the time that they are first invoked (see XtCreatePopupChildProc, Appendix B).

A Shell popped up with XtPopup may be popped down with XtPopdown. The Intrinsics also supply the built-in callback routines XtCallbackNone, XtCallbackNonexclusive, XtCallbackExclusive and XtCallbackPopdown whose sole function is to pop a specified widget up or down. These may be added to a widget's callback list with XtAddCallback(s). In the rare cases that a shell should be popped up with a "spring-loaded" grab, call XtPopupSpringLoaded.

CAUTION

Toolkits may substitute alternate methods for handling toolkit-specific shells. The OSF/Motif XmDialogShell pops itself up when its child widget is managed, so in Motif, the shell is controlled by calling XtManageChild on its child. Most toolkits also supply some form of "menu button" widget, which pops up an associated shell (parenting a menu, of course) when the widget is selected with a pointer button.

Pull-down menus implemented with such a tool do not need to be explicitly controlled with XtPopup or XtPopdown. Toolkits may also invoke additional callbacks when shells are popped up or down; for example, OSF/Motif calls the XmBulletinBoard XmNmapCallback when it is popped up.

SEE ALSO

Routines: XtAddGrab, XtCallbackExclusive, XtCallbackNone,
            XtCallbackNonexclusive, XtCallbackPopdown, XtCreatePopupShell,
            XtPopdown, XtPopupSpringLoaded, XtRemoveGrab

XtPopupSpringLoaded (R4)

Maps a pop-up Shell to the screen and grabs user input

SYNOPSIS

```
void XtPopupSpringLoaded( w )
        Widget                        w;
```

ARGUMENTS

w   in   Widget to be popped up; must be a subclass of Shell.

DESCRIPTION

XtPopupSpringLoaded pops up the specified shell, setting its *spring_loaded* field to True. XtAddGrab is called for the shell with *exclusive* equal to True and *spring_loaded* equal to True. In all other aspects, XtPopupSpringLoaded performs identically to XtPopup.

USAGE

XtPopupSpringLoaded is called only in a few situations, usually involving pop-up menus. It forces user events to be sent to the pop-up shell (See XtAddGrab) in addition to the widgets inside the shell that would ordinarily get them. The benefit in a menu is that when the user makes a choice, the widget that they select will get the button event and call its callbacks, while the pop-up shell will *also* get the event, so it can know to pop itself down.

There is rarely a need to call XtPopupSpringLoaded in normal applications. Most toolkits endorse other ways to pop up menus, and handle all necessary grabs internally. See Chapters 15 and 16 for how to handle menus in the Athena and OSF/Motif toolkits.

To pop up a spring-loaded shell from a translation table entry, use the Intrinsics built-in action "XtMenuPopup(*shell_name*)". A shell popped up with XtPopupSpringLoaded may be popped down with XtPopdown.

CAUTION

A spring-loaded widget is expected to pop itself down on the "release" event following the "press" event that popped it up in the first place. Generally, XtPopupSpringLoaded is called only if a server-side key or button grab is simultaneously enabled.

SEE ALSO

Routines: XtCreatePopupShell, XtPopup, XtPopdown

XtProcessEvent   **(O)**

Processes the next X event, timer, signal or alternate input source

SYNOPSIS

```
void XtProcessEvent( input_mask )
        XtInputMask                    input_mask;
```

ARGUMENTS

input_mask   in   Bitwise inclusive OR of `XtIMXEvent`, `XtIMTimer`, `XtIMAlternateInput`, `XtIMSignal` (R6 only) or `XtIMAll` specifying acceptable input type(s) to be processed.

DESCRIPTION

`XtProcessEvent` processes the next X event, alternate input event, signal, or expired timeout waiting in the default application context established by `XtInitialize`. Only a single condition matching the specified input mask is processed. If *input_mask* specifies multiple input types, it is undefined which type will be processed. If no input is found matching the input mask, `XtProcessEvent` blocks until a matching event arrives.

    `XtProcessEvent` processes alternate input events by calling the associated callback routine registered with `XtAddInput`. Timeouts are processed by calling the routine registered with `XtAddTimeOut`. Signals are processed by calling the routine registered with `XtAddSignal` (see `XtAppAddSignal`). X events are processed with `XtDispatchEvent`.

USAGE

See `XtAppProcessEvent`.

CAUTION

`XtProcessEvent` is an obsolete routine supplied for backwards compatibility with earlier versions of the Intrinsics, and is superseded by `XtAppProcessEvent` in the Release 3 and later Intrinsics. `XtProcessEvent` uses the default application context established by `XtInitialize`, which must be called first.

SEE ALSO

Routines: `XtAppProcessEvent, XtAddInput, XtAddTimeOut, XtAppAddSignal,`
           `XtDispatchEvent, XtMainLoop, XtNextEvent, XtPeekEvent`

XtProcessLock (R6)

Locks thread access to toolkit global data

SYNOPSIS

void XtProcessLock( )

ARGUMENTS

None

DESCRIPTION

XtProcessLock acquires a process-wide lock that controls access to toolkit global data in multi-threaded applications. XtProcessLock blocks until it acquires the lock. If a thread wishes to lock access to process data and the application context simultaneously, it must call XtAppLock before calling XtProcessLock. When releasing the locks, it should call XtProcessUnlock before calling XtAppUnlock. A thread may assert a lock more than once, and the locks are cumulative. A thread must release a lock as many times as it has acquired it, before it can be acquired by other threads.

USAGE

XtProcessLock and XtProcessUnlock are used to construct thread-safe toolkit programs. Only one thread can hold the lock at a time. Before taking any action that would affect process global data, a thread is expected to call XtProcessLock. After performing any modifications, the thread calls XtProcessUnlock to allow other threads to acquire the lock and access the data. If a thread attempts to acquire the lock while it is held by a different thread, XtProcessLock blocks until the lock can be acquired.

XtProcessLock and XtProcessUnlock are called internally by the Intrinsics routines that access toolkit global data, so there is usually no need for you to call XtProcessLock explicitly. It may be used in the construction of widget internals that need to enforce locking of widget global data. In applications, it could be used to protect access to client data passed between widgets.

CAUTION

Locking is enforced only if participating threads follow the convention of acquiring the lock with XtProcessLock before accessing global data structures. There is really nothing to stop a thread from accessing a structure if it ignores this convention and just accesses it directly. Threads that only access data through the normal Intrinsics routines (XtManageChild, XtSetValues, etc.) do not have to worry about this, because the Intrinsics routines themselves enforce the convention. An application must call XtToolkitThreadInitialize to initialize thread support before calling XtProcessLock or XtProcessUnlock.

SEE ALSO

Routines: XtToolkitThreadInitialize, XtProcessUnlock, XtAppLock, XtAppUnlock

XtProcessUnlock   **(R6)**

Unlocks thread access to toolkit global data

SYNOPSIS

```
void XtProcessUnlock( )
```

ARGUMENTS

None

DESCRIPTION

XtProcessUnlock releases a lock formerly imposed by XtProcessLock. If a thread wishes to lock access to process data and the application context simultaneously, it must call XtAppLock before calling XtProcessLock.   When releasing the locks, it must call XtProcessUnlock before calling XtAppUnlock. A thread may assert a lock more than once, and the locks are cumulative. A thread must be sure to release the lock as many times as it has acquired it.

USAGE

XtProcessLock and XtProcessUnlock are used to construct thread-safe toolkit programs. Only one thread can hold the lock at a time. Before taking any action that would affect process global data, a thread is expected to call XtProcessLock.   After performing any modifications, the thread calls XtProcessUnlock to allow other threads to acquire the lock and access the data. If a thread attempts to acquire the lock while it is held by a different thread, XtProcessLock blocks until the lock can be acquired.

XtProcessLock and XtProcessUnlock are called internally by the Intrinsics routines that access toolkit global data, so there is usually no need for you to call XtProcessLock explicitly. It may be used in the construction of widget internals that need to enforce locking of widget global data. In applications, it could be used to protect access to client data passed between widgets.

CAUTION

Locking is enforced only if participating threads follow the convention of acquiring the lock with XtProcessLock before accessing global data structures. There is really nothing to stop a thread from accessing a structure if it ignores this convention and just accesses it directly. Threads that only access data through the normal Intrinsics routines (XtManageChild, XtSetValues, etc.) do not have to worry about this, because the Intrinsics routines themselves enforce the convention.   An application must call XtToolkitThreadInitialize to initialize thread support before calling XtProcessLock or XtProcessUnlock.

SEE ALSO

Routines: XtToolkitThreadInitialize, XtProcessLock, XtAppLock, XtAppUnlock

XtQueryGeometry   (R3)

Queries a child widget's preferred geometry

SYNOPSIS

```
XtGeometryResult XtQueryGeometry( w, intended, preferred_return )
        Widget                    w;
        XtWidgetGeometry          *intended;
        XtWidgetGeometry          *preferred_return;
```

ARGUMENTS

w	in	The widget to be queried; must be of class RectObj or any subclass thereof.
intended	in	Pointer to structure defining geometry offered by parent.
preferred_return	in/out	Pointer to structure which receives the child widget's geometry preference.

DESCRIPTION

XtQueryGeometry asks a child widget to state its preferred geometry. The *intended* argument specifies a geometry that the parent would like to suggest, so that the child has an idea of what is realistic to ask for.

USAGE

XtQueryGeometry is used in a manager widget's implementation code to ask a child what its preferred geometry would be. The parent does not guarantee that the child will receive this geometry, but well-behaved manager parents try to be as accommodating as their style of geometry management allows. XtQueryGeometry is rarely called directly in applications. It could possibly be used in user interface editors to see what a child's response would be to a proposed change. To query a widget's geometry in ordinary applications, call XtGetValues and specify the appropriate geometry resources.

CAUTION

XtQueryGeometry is a widget internal routine and is not normally called by applications.

SEE ALSO

Routines: XtConfigureWidget, XtMakeGeometryRequest, XtMakeResizeRequest, XtMoveWidget, XtResizeWidget

XtRealizeWidget

(R3)

Creates a widget's window and binds its actions

SYNOPSIS

```
void XtRealizeWidget( w )
        Widget                          w;
```

ARGUMENTS

w   in   The widget to be realized; must be of class Core or any subclass thereof.

DESCRIPTION

XtRealizeWidget realizes the specified widget, and recursively realizes all of its managed descendants. Realization forces widgets to go to the X server and create their windows. After any initial realization, the Intrinsics maintain the rule that if a widget is realized, all managed children of that widget are also realized. This will be true even if the children are managed after their parent has been realized.

Actions named in the widget's translation tables are bound to procedures at realization time. In binding a named action, the Intrinsics search the following action lists in order:

- The widget's class and all superclass action tables, in subclass to superclass order.
- The parent's class and all superclass action tables, in subclass to superclass order; then the grandparent's tables and so on up the widget's instance hierarchy.
- Application-defined action tables registered with XtAppAddActions and XtAddActions, from most recently registered to oldest.

USAGE

Usually you will create and manage your initial widget tree, and then call XtRealizeWidget once on the top-level application shell. The initial realization is performed as a separate step so that widgets will already have determined their final sizes before they go to the server for their windows. This optimizes performance and looks a whole lot nicer to the user. Widgets may be explicitly realized and unrealized (see XtUnrealizeWidget) to control server resource utilization, but this is rarely necessary with modern servers, and places extra computing demands on the client. You can check to see if a widget is realized by calling XtIsRealized.

CAUTION

Widgets must be realized before making any Xlib calls that depend on their windows. This includes all application drawing routines and many resource management routines. For this reason, graphics initialization is commonly done right after the initial widget tree is realized, but before entering the main loop. The order of widget realization can also affect interaction with window managers that use the Window ID of a widget as an icon window, or as the group leader of a window group (see Chapter 11).

Since a widget's XtNtranslations resource can be set in a resource file, any application-supplied action procedures should be registered with XtAppAddActions or XtAddActions before widgets that might reference such actions are realized.

SEE ALSO

Routines: XtCreateWindow, XtIsRealized, XtUnrealizeWidget, XtWindow, XtWindowOfObject

XtRealloc (R3)

Changes the size of a block of memory, allocating more if necessary

SYNOPSIS

```
char *XtRealloc( pointer, size )
        char                            *pointer;
        Cardinal                        size;
```

ARGUMENTS

pointer	in	Pointer to existing block of storage.
size	in	New size requested, in bytes.

DESCRIPTION

XtRealloc changes the size of a block of storage, possibly moving it, then copies the old contents into the new block and frees the old block. If there is insufficient storage available to allocate the space, XtRealloc calls XtErrorMsg to report an error and exit. If *pointer* is NULL, XtRealloc simply calls XtMalloc and allocates a new block of storage.

USAGE

XtRealloc is used to control storage when the contents of an array or string shrink or expand dynamically. XtRealloc is used in numerous places by the Intrinsics, and can be used in applications for the same purposes; a common place is in alternate input callbacks that receive streams of data of unknown length. It is fully compatible and interchangeable with its standard C counterpart, realloc(), but it has the advantage that if called with a NULL pointer, it silently performs an initial allocation. This can simplify algorithms that need to allocate, resize and free memory buffers dynamically.

XtRealloc() should be used in toolkit programs since it is supported even on systems than may not support realloc() directly. To avoid compiler warnings, the pointer returned by XtRealloc should be cast to the appropriate type before use.

CAUTION

Call XtFree to free storage allocated by XtRealloc when it is no longer needed.

SEE ALSO

Routines: XtCalloc, XtFree, XtMalloc, XtNew, XtNewString

XtRegisterCaseConverter (R3)

Registers a KeySym case converter

SYNOPSIS

```
void XtRegisterCaseConverter( display, case_proc, start, stop )
        Display                       *display;
        XtCaseProc                    case_proc;
        KeySym                        start;
        KeySym                        stop;
```

ARGUMENTS

display	in	The display from which Key events will be delivered.
case_proc	in	The case converter to be registered.
start	in	The first keysym for which the specified case converter applies.
stop	in	The last keysym for which the specified case converter applies.

DESCRIPTION

`XtRegisterCaseConverter` registers a new case converter for the inclusive range of keysyms specified by *start* and *stop*. The specified case converter overrides any previous case converter registered for keysyms found in the specified range.

USAGE

A case converter procedure accepts a keysym and returns both the lower-case and upper-case keysym equivalents. The Intrinsics automatically register a default case converter that understands case conversion for all keysyms defined in the core protocol. If you implement your own keycode-to-keysym mapping, or support special keyboards or character sets, you may need to register an application-specific case converter. This is rarely done in ordinary applications.

    `XtRegisterCaseConverter` registers a new case converter for all or part of a keysym table. Multiple converters may be registered for different ranges of keysyms; the converter registered for a given keysym is invoked when you call `XtConvertCase`. Case converters are of type `XtCaseProc` (see Appendix B).

CAUTION

There is no way to unregister a case converter; instead, an identity converter must be registered to replace the converter which is no longer wanted.

SEE ALSO

Routines: `XtConvertCase`

XtRegisterDrawable (R6)

Registers a non-toolkit window with a widget to handle its events

SYNOPSIS

```
void XtRegisterDrawable( display, drawable, widget )
    Display                         *display;
    Drawable                        drawable;
    Widget                          widget;
```

ARGUMENTS

display	in	Display of drawable.
drawable	in	Non-widget drawable to be handled.
widget	in	Widget that will receive the drawable's events.

DESCRIPTION

XtRegisterDrawable assigns a non-widget drawable to a widget. In the future, if XtWindowToWidget is called with the drawable's ID, it will return the ID of the proxy widget. Future events from the drawable will be dispatched as though they belong to *widget*, but will be delivered unchanged to its event handlers or action procedures. The drawable must not be registered with another widget, or belong to another widget in the widget tree, or the results of calling XtRegisterDrawable are undefined.

USAGE

Sometimes you may want to listen for events from drawables that are not associated with a widget in your application. For example, you may want to handle PropertyNotify events on the root window or windows belonging to other applications as a way of communicating. Prior to R6, this meant writing a private main loop that would watch for the "foreign" window's ID and handle the events specially.

In the R6 Intrinsics, XtRegisterDrawable assigns a widget to act as a proxy for the drawable. After you register the drawable, you can add event handlers or action procedures to the widget to handle events coming from the drawable. The events are passed unchanged, so the window ID may be used to distinguish the drawable's events from events generated by the widget's own window. To unregister a drawable when it is no longer important, call XtUnregisterDrawable.

CAUTION

The drawable may not be a window belonging to another widget in the application widget tree, and a drawable may not be registered with two widgets at the same time. The proxy widget should preferably be a widget that does little event processing of its own, and may even be a widget of Core class. The drawable must be unregistered before the widget is destroyed.

SEE ALSO

Routines: XtUnregisterDrawable

XtRegisterExtensionSelector　　　　　　　　**(R6)**

Registers a routine that can select for extension events

SYNOPSIS

```
void XtRegisterExtensionSelector( display, min_event, max_event,
    selector_proc, client_data )
    Display                          *display;
    int                              min_event;
    int                              max_event;
    XtExtensionSelectProc            selector_proc;
    XtPointer                        client_data;
```

ARGUMENTS

display	in	Display for which extension selector is active.
min_event	in	Lower bound for event type ID.
max_event	in	Upper bound for event type ID.
selector_proc	in	Procedure that knows how to select for extension events.
client_data	in	Additional data to be passed to selector proc when it is called.

DESCRIPTION

XtRegisterExtensionSelector registers a function that knows how ask the server to deliver extension events in the specified range.　Future calls to XtInsertEventTypeHandler and XtRemoveEventTypeHandler call *selector_proc*, if they register or unregister handlers for event types that fall within its range. If *display* is NULL, or if the event type range overlaps a range already handled by an extension selector, XtRegisterExtensionSelector issues a fatal error.

USAGE

X server extensions may generate their own kinds of X events.　Since these are not part of the core X protocol, the toolkit does not know what to do with them by default.　You can't select them with the usual event mask, so some other method must be used to ask the server to send extension events.　Usually this is a function or functions provided by the extension library.

　　XtRegisterExtensionSelector registers a function that knows how to select for the extension events in a certain range of integer event types.　Once an extension selector is registered, it is called whenever XtInsertEventTypeHandler and XtRemoveEventTypeHandler are used to establish or cancel extension event handlers.　Extensions always use a contiguous range of event types, so a *selector_proc* could be registered for the entire range of an extension, or for a specified sub-range.

　　An extension selector proc is of type XtExtensionSelectProc (see Appendix B).　The *client_data* is usually specific to the selector proc, and holds information that would affect how the events could be selected.

CAUTION

None

SEE ALSO

Routines:　XtInsertEventTypeHandler, XtRemoveEventTypeHandler

XtRegisterGrabAction **(R4)**

Registers an action procedure that passively grabs keys or buttons

SYNOPSIS

```
void XtRegisterGrabAction( action_proc, owner_events, event_mask,
    pointer_mode, keyboard_mode )
        XtActionProc                    action_proc;
        Boolean                         owner_events;
        unsigned int                    event_mask;
        int                             pointer_mode;
        int                             keyboard_mode;
```

ARGUMENTS

action_proc	in	Action procedure to be registered as a grab action.
owner_events	in	True if pointer events should be reported normally; False if pointer events are to be reported with respect to grab window.
event_mask	in	Event mask specifying which types of pointer events are to be delivered to the application during the grab.
pointer_mode	in	Specifies how pointer events are to be processed during the grab; may be GrabModeSync or GrabModeAsync.
keyboard_mode	in	Specifies how keyboard events are to be processed during the grab; may be GrabModeSync or GrabModeAsync.

DESCRIPTION

XtRegisterGrabAction registers the specified action procedure in a table of *grab actions* known to the translation manager. When a procedure on this list is bound to a translation (at widget realization time, or when a widget's translation tables are modified with XtAugmentTranslations or XtOverrideTranslations), the translation manager examines the event that invokes the action.

If the final or only event in the translation sequence is a KeyPress or ButtonPress event, the translation manager establishes a passive grab on every physical key or button that maps to the triggering event's detail field (see Appendix D). The specified *owner_events, event_mask, pointer_mode* and *keyboard_mode* arguments are passed directly to XtGrabButton or XtGrabKey. If the triggering event is a ButtonPress, the *confine_to* and *cursor* arguments to XtGrabButton are passed as NULL. If the triggering event is a KeyPress, all keycodes that could translate to the detail keysym are grabbed. Modifiers (if any) to be passed to XtGrabKey or XtGrabButton are also determined from the translation.

A passive grab becomes activated when the triggering button or key is pressed (with modifiers, if any), and remains active until the button or key is released (regardless of the state of any modifiers), or until explicitly released with XtUngrabKeyboard or XtUngrabPointer. If the translation that triggers a grab action is modified, any old grab associated with the action is canceled and new grabs are established as appropriate.

USAGE

XtRegisterGrabAction lets you register passive grabs on the keys or buttons associated with an action procedure. Using XtRegisterGrabAction is preferable to calling XtGrabKey or XtGrabButton directly, because it permits the translation that triggers a given action procedure to be changed at any time. If the triggering event is a Key event, this also saves you the trouble of figuring out which physical keys map to the specified keysym.   Grab actions must also be registered with the translation manager via `XtAppAddActions`, before being referenced in a translation table.

CAUTION

Server-side grabs are always tricky, particularly when debugging. If you set a breakpoint in a grab action you may hang your workstation, since the pointer or keyboard may be locked up, preventing you from assigning focus to your debugger window.   Always keep a spare terminal handy while debugging.

SEE ALSO

Routines: `XtAppAddActions, XtGrabKey, XtGrabButton`

XtReleaseGC (R3)

Frees a reference to a shared GC

SYNOPSIS

```
void XtReleaseGC( object, gc )
        Widget                          object;
        GC                              gc;
```

ARGUMENTS

object   in   Widget specifying the display for which the GC is valid; must be of class
                            Object or any subclass thereof.

gc   in   Identifier of shared GC, returned by XtGetGC.

DESCRIPTION

XtReleaseGC frees a reference to a shared GC previously allocated with XtGetGC or XtAllocateGC.
The Intrinsics maintain a reference count for each shared GC, and send a request to the server to free the GC
when the last user releases it. XtReleaseGC replaces the less-portable routine XtDestroyGC.

USAGE

Graphics Contexts (GCs) are server objects that control the attributes of drawing primitives. Shared GCs are
a toolkit optimization which decreases server resource utilization when many widgets use the same graphic
rendition, and could therefore use the same GC. Shared GCs are mainly used in widget implementation code,
when it is likely that many widgets in a toolkit will use the same colors, fonts and patterns to draw their
graphics. Shared GCs may also be used by application programmers in an effort to decrease the number of
server resources required by application graphics code.

You may reserve a shared modifiable GC with XtAllocateGC, or a read-only shared GC with
XtGetGC. Call XtReleaseGC to release a reference to a shared GC when it is no longer needed. When
the last reference to a shared GC is released, the GC is destroyed.

CAUTION

Shared GCs must never be freed directly with XFreeGC. Shared GCs allocated with XtGetGC must never
be directly modified with Xlib routines.

SEE ALSO

Routines: XtDestroyGC, XtGetGC, XtAllocateGC

XtReleasePropertyAtom **(R6)**

Releases an atom used as a property name for parameterized selection

SYNOPSIS

```
void XtReleasePropertyAtom( w, selection )
    Widget                      w;
    Atom                        selection;
```

ARGUMENTS

w	in	Widget that originally reserved the Atom.
Atom	in	Atom identifying a temporary property name.

DESCRIPTION

XtReleasePropertyAtom releases a property name atom for reuse, and deletes the value associated with the property.

USAGE

Certain selection requests don't actually result in the selection being retrieved. Instead, they direct the selection owner to do something with the selection. For example, a request for the selection expressed as the target DELETE tells the selection owner to delete the selection value in its own context. Other targets like INSERT_PROPERTY and INSERT_SELECTION require the requester to pass additional parameters that specify what to insert.

Parameterized selection requests force the requester to name other window properties as parameters. Since property names are identified by atoms (which cannot be freed), it pays not to simply make up a new property name for each request. What you should do instead is reserve an existing atom to use as a property name, create a property of that name for the transfer, and then release the name so that it might be used by other requesters. This cuts down memory utilization on the server.

To temporarily reserve an atom for use as a property name, call XtReservePropertyAtom. When the transfer is complete, call XtReleasePropertyAtom to allow that name to be used again, and to delete the contents of the property. You will use this routine only if you are doing very advanced sorts of selection transfer.

CAUTION

None

SEE ALSO

Routines: XtReservePropertyAtom, XtSetSelectionParameters, XtGetSelectionParameters

XtRemoveActionHook (R4)

Cancels an action hook procedure

SYNOPSIS

```
void XtRemoveActionHook( action_hook_id )
      XtActionHookId             action_hook_id;
```

ARGUMENTS

action_hook_id   in   ID of action hook procedure, assigned when it was registered.

DESCRIPTION

XtRemoveActionHook unregisters an action hook procedure previously registered with XtAppAddActionHook.

USAGE

Just before invoking any named action, the Intrinsics call the list of action hook procedures registered with XtAppAddActionHook. An action hook procedure may be used as a debugging aid, to log or report on action procedures that are executed in response to widget input.

An action hook procedure registered with XtAppAddActionHook may be unregistered at any time with XtRemoveActionHook, after which it will no longer be called. If you were building a "learn" mode into your application, in which actions were recorded by an action hook, you would remove the action hook before playing the actions back with XtCallActionProc. The list of action hook procedures is automatically destroyed when its associated application context is destroyed.

CAUTION

None

SEE ALSO

Routines: XtAppAddActionHook, XtCallActionProc

XtRemoveAllCallbacks   **(R3)**

Removes all callback routines from a widget's callback list

SYNOPSIS

```
void XtRemoveAllCallbacks( w, callback_name )
        Widget                       w;
        String                       callback_name;
```

ARGUMENTS

w	in	The widget from which callbacks are to be removed; must be of class Object or any subclass thereof.
callback_name	in	Name of the callback list from which to remove callbacks, e.g. "destroyCallback" or the symbolic constant XtNdestroyCallback.

DESCRIPTION

XtRemoveAllCallbacks removes all entries in the named callback list belonging to the specified widget. If a callback list of the specified name is not found, XtRemoveAllCallbacks issues a warning.

USAGE

This routine is used only when it is absolutely necessary to stop the specified callback from calling any routines. This is rarely if ever done in application code. Application programmers should instead call XtRemoveCallback or XtRemoveCallbacks to remove specific callback routines.

CAUTION

Calling XtRemoveAllCallbacks will break toolkits in which other widgets (or the Intrinsics themselves) automatically place their own routines on a widget's callback list. This is done quite frequently, so you should avoid XtRemoveAllCallbacks.

SEE ALSO

Routines: XtAddCallback, XtAddCallbacks, XtHasCallbacks, XtRemoveCallback, XtRemoveCallbacks

XtRemoveBlockHook   (R6)

Cancels a block hook procedure

SYNOPSIS

```
void XtRemoveBlockHook( block_hook_id )
        XtBlockHookId                    block_hook_id;
```

ARGUMENTS

block_hook_id   in   ID of block hook procedure/client_data pair, assigned when it was registered with XtAppAddBlockHook.

DESCRIPTION

XtRemoveBlockHook unregisters a block hook procedure previously registered with XtAppAddBlockHook.

USAGE

Just before performing an implementation-dependent wait for something, the Intrinsics call the list of block hook procedures registered with XtAppAddBlockHook. A block hook differs from a work proc in that all block hooks are called when the toolkit prepares to block, whereas only the work procedure at the head of the queue is executed.

A block hook procedure registered with XtAppAddBlockHook may be unregistered at any time with XtRemoveBlockHook, after which it will no longer be called. The list of block hook procedures is automatically destroyed when its associated application context is destroyed.

CAUTION

None

SEE ALSO

Routines: XtAppAddBlockHook, XtAppNextEvent

XtRemoveCallback   (R3)

Removes a callback routine from a widget's callback list

SYNOPSIS

```
void XtRemoveCallback( w, callback_name, callback, client_data )
        Widget                  .       w;
        String                          callback_name;
        XtCallbackProc                  callback;
        XtPointer                       client_data;
```

ARGUMENTS

w	in	The widget from which a callback is to be removed; must be of class Object or any subclass thereof.
callback_name	in	Name of the callback list from which to remove callbacks, e.g. "destroyCallback" or the symbolic constant XtNdestroyCallback.
callback	in	Callback routine to be removed from callback list.
client_data	in	Application-defined data registered with the callback when it was added to the list.

DESCRIPTION

XtRemoveCallback removes a single callback routine from the specified callback list. The *client_data* must match the *client_data* originally registered with the callback, or the callback is not removed. If the same callback routine has also been registered with other *client_data*, those entries remain in the callback list. If the widget does not have a callback list with the specified name, XtRemoveCallback issues a warning.

USAGE

XtRemoveCallback is used to remove a callback routine from a widget when you no longer want it to be called. A callback routine may call XtRemoveCallback from within an event dispatch to remove itself or other routines from a callback list, but the toolkit will still invoke any callbacks on the list currently being executed.

CAUTION

None

SEE ALSO

Routines: XtAddCallback, XtAddCallbacks, XtHasCallbacks,
            XtRemoveAllCallbacks, XtRemoveCallbacks

XtRemoveCallbacks (R3)

Removes multiple callback routines from a widget's callback list

SYNOPSIS

```
void XtRemoveCallbacks( w, callback_name, callbacks )
        Widget                      w;
        String                      callback_name;
        XtCallbackList              callbacks;
```

ARGUMENTS

w   in   The widget for which callbacks are to be removed; must be of class Object or any subclass thereof.

callback_name   in   Name of the callback list from which to remove callbacks, e.g. "destroyCallback" or the symbolic constant `XtNdestroyCallback`.

callbacks   in   Pointer to NULL-terminated list of `XtCallbackRecs` describing callback routine/client_data pairs.

DESCRIPTION

`XtRemoveCallbacks` removes multiple callback routines from the specified callback list. In each entry in *callbacks*, the *client_data* must match that which was originally registered with its corresponding callback, or that callback is not removed. If the same callback routine has been registered with *client_data* not found in *callbacks*, those entries remain in the callback list. If the widget does not have a callback list with the specified name, `XtRemoveCallbacks` issues a warning.

USAGE

`XtRemoveCallbacks` is used to remove a list of callback routines when you no longer want them to be called. The *callbacks* argument is usually a static array of type `XtCallbackRec`. A callback routine may call `XtRemoveCallbacks` from within an event dispatch to remove itself and/or other routines from a callback list, but the toolkit will still invoke any callbacks on the list currently being executed.

CAUTION

The list defined by *callbacks* must be NULL-terminated or an error will occur. This is one of the few places in the toolkit where the number of items in an input list is not specified explicitly.

SEE ALSO

Routines: `XtAddCallback`, `XtAddCallbacks`, `XtRemoveCallback`,
           `XtRemoveAllCallbacks`

XtRemoveEventHandler **(R3)**

Removes an event handler from a widget

SYNOPSIS

```
void XtRemoveEventHandler( w, event_mask, nonmaskable, event_handler,
    client_data )
        Widget                          w;
        EventMask                       event_mask;
        Boolean                         nonmaskable;
        XtEventHandler                  event_handler;
        XtPointer                       client_data;
```

ARGUMENTS

w	in	Widget from which event handler is to be removed; must be of class Core or any subclass thereof.
event_mask	in	Mask specifying event types for which handler is to be unregistered.
nonmaskable	in	True if event handler is to be removed for nonmaskable events (GraphicsExpose, NoExpose, SelectionClear, SelectionRequest, SelectionNotify, ClientMessage, MappingNotify).
event_handler	in	Event handler to be unregistered.
client_data	in	Application-defined data registered with the event handler when it was added to the list.

DESCRIPTION

XtRemoveEventHandler is used to cancel an event handler registered with XtAddEventHandler or XtInsertEventHandler. The call is ignored if the event handler is not registered, or if the specified *client_data* does not match the *client_data* passed in the original call to XtAddEventHandler or XtInsertEventHandler that registered the handler.

    If the widget is realized, XtRemoveEventHandler may call XSelectInput to modify the event mask of the widget's window. However, if other event handlers still require the events specified in *event_mask*, the widget's window will not be updated. If the specified event handler is registered for events other than those specified in the *event_mask*, it remains registered for those events.

USAGE

XtRemoveEventHandler is used to cancel an event handler previously registered with XtAddEventHandler or XtInsertEventHandler, when you are no longer interested in responding to the specified events.

CAUTION

None

SEE ALSO

Routines: XtAddEventHandler, XtAddRawEventHandler, XtInsertEventHandler,
       XtInsertRawEventHandler, XtRemoveRawEventHandler

XtRemoveEventTypeHandler (R6)

Remove an extension event handler from a widget

SYNOPSIS

```
void XtRemoveEventTypeHandler( w, type, select_data, event_handler,
    client_data )
        Widget                    w;
        int                       type;
        XtPointer                 select_data;
        XtEventHandler            event_handler;
        XtPointer                 client_data;
```

ARGUMENTS

w	in	Widget from which handler is to be removed; must be of class Core or any subclass thereof.
event_type	in	Specifies the event type for which the handler is to be canceled.
select_data	in	Data required to deselect events of this type from the server, or NULL.
event_handler	in	Event handler to be unregistered.
client_data	in	Application-defined data originally registered with the event handler by XtInsertEventTypeHandler.

DESCRIPTION

XtRemoveEventTypeHandler unregisters an event handler registered with XtInsertEventTypeHandler. The call is ignored if the specified handler is not registered, or if *client_data* does not match that supplied when the handler was registered. If the event handler is registered for events other than those specified by the *event_type*, it remains registered for those events.

If *event_type* specifies one of the event types in the core protocol, *select_data* must be a pointer to an EventMask (see Table 9-2) specifying the types for which the handler is to be canceled. If the widget is realized, XtRemoveEventTypeHandler may call XSelectInput to modify the event mask of the widget's window.

If *event_type* specifies an extension event, XtRemoveEventTypeHandler calls the extension selector procedure registered for the event range in which *event_type* falls. In that case, *select_data* is whatever is expected by the XtExtensionSelectProc (see Appendix B).

USAGE

XtRemoveEventTypeHandler is usually used to cancel interest in extension events. It can also be used to unregister handlers for ordinary X events, but this is not common. Event handlers registered for ordinary events may be canceled more conveniently with XtRemoveEventHandler.

CAUTION

None

SEE ALSO

Routines: XtInsertEventTypeHandler, XtRegisterExtensionSelector

XtRemoveGrab   **(R3)**

Removes a widget from the grab list

SYNOPSIS

```
void XtRemoveGrab( w )
        Widget                          w;
```

ARGUMENTS

w   in   Widget to be removed from the grab list.

DESCRIPTION

XtRemoveGrab removes widgets from the grab list starting at the most recently registered, and proceeding back to and including the specified widget. If *w* is not on the grab list, XtRemoveGrab issues a warning.

USAGE

The grab list is attached to the application context, and manages a list of widgets called the "modal cascade". Widgets in the modal cascade grab the event stream, remapping user events which would normally be delivered to other widgets in the application. This feature is usually used in popping up modal dialog boxes or menus, which must lock out input to other widgets until the dialog with the pop-up is complete.

A widget is added to the grab list with XtAddGrab and is removed from the grab list with XtRemoveGrab. These are automatically called by XtPopup and XtPopdown, respectively. Since the most common use of the grab list is to support modal pop-ups, most clients call XtPopdown on a pop-up shell rather than calling XtRemoveGrab explicitly. In very rare cases it may be appropriate to add a normal widget to the grab list - for example, to prevent a user from reassigning focus from a password entry field. A widget on the grab list preempts input from the rest of the application, and should be removed with XtRemoveGrab as soon as practical.

CAUTION

The grab list is a client-side mechanism which remaps events within a widget tree, and is not the same as grabs implemented on the server side. Server-side grabs are controlled by the toolkit routines XtGrabButton, XtGrabKey, XtGrabKeyboard and XtGrabPointer.

SEE ALSO

Routines: XtAddGrab, XtDispatchEvent, XtPopdown, XtPopup

XtRemoveInput (R3)

Cancels an alternate input callback

SYNOPSIS

```
void XtRemoveInput( input_id )
        XtInputId                               input_id;
```

ARGUMENTS

input_id   in   Identifier of the alternate input callback to be canceled.

DESCRIPTION

XtRemoveInput unregisters an alternate input callback previously registered with XtAppAddInput or XtAddInput (obsolete). *Input_id* is the identifier returned when the callback was registered. If *input_id* does not specify a valid input callback, XtRemoveInput issues a warning.

USAGE

XtRemoveInput cancels a callback routine that had been registered to read or write an alternate input source. XtRemoveInput does not perform a close() on the associated file descriptor, which may be registered again later with another call to XtAppAddInput.

Any input callbacks registered for a particular file descriptor must be canceled before performing a close() on the file descriptor itself, or XtAppMainLoop will generate many errors. XtRemoveInput is often called inside the input callback that is reading or writing a source when all the data has been written or read.

CAUTION

Disk files usually show as readable even after the end-of-file has been reached. This will cause any related input callback to be called repeatedly even after there is nothing left to read. To avoid handling superfluous callbacks you should watch for the end-of-file and call XtRemoveInput when you see it.

SEE ALSO

Routines: XtAddInput, XtAppAddInput

XtRemoveRawEventHandler   (R3)

Removes an event handler from a widget without updating the widget's event mask

SYNOPSIS

```
void XtRemoveRawEventHandler( w, event_mask, nonmaskable, event_handler,
    client_data )
            Widget                          w;
            EventMask                       event_mask;
            Boolean                         nonmaskable;
            XtEventHandler                  event_handler;
            XtPointer                       client_data;
```

ARGUMENTS

w	in	Widget from which the event handler is to be removed; must be of class Core or any subclass thereof.
event_mask	in	Mask specifying event types for which the handler is to be unregistered.
nonmaskable	in	True if event handler is to be removed for nonmaskable events (GraphicsExpose, NoExpose, SelectionClear, SelectionRequest, SelectionNotify, ClientMessage, MappingNotify).
event_handler	in	Event handler to be unregistered.
client_data	in	Application-defined data supplied with the event handler when it was registered.

DESCRIPTION

XtRemoveRawEventHandler is used to cancel an event handler registered with XtAddRawEventHandler or XtInsertRawEventHandler. The call is ignored if the event handler is not registered, or if the specified *client_data* does not match that which was supplied when the handler was registered. XtRemoveRawEventHandler is similar to XtRemoveEventHandler, but does not modify the event mask of the widget's window. If the specified event handler is registered for events other than those specified by *event_mask*, it remains registered for those events.

USAGE

XtRemoveRawEventHandler is used to cancel an event handler previously registered with XtAddRawEventHandler or XtInsertRawEventHandler, when you are no longer interested in responding to the specified events. Raw event handlers are rarely used, and most applications should call XtAddEventHandler and XtRemoveEventHandler instead.

CAUTION

None

SEE ALSO

Routines: XtAddEventHandler, XtAddRawEventHandler, XtInsertEventHandler,
          XtInsertRawEventHandler, XtRemoveEventHandler

XtRemoveSignal (R6)

Unregisters a signal callback

SYNOPSIS

```
void XtRemoveSignal( signal_id )
        XtSignalId                      signal_id;
```

ARGUMENTS

signal_id   in   Identifier of signal callback to be unregistered.

DESCRIPTION

XtRemoveSignal unregisters a signal callback. *Signal_id* is the identifier returned when the callback was registered with XtAppAddSignal.

USAGE

XtRemoveSignal unregisters a signal callback. Since signal callbacks are only invoked when you call XtNoticeSignal, unregistering one is mainly a way of keeping memory tidy.

CAUTION

Any signal handler that references the specified signal callback in a call to XtNoticeSignal should be canceled before calling XtRemoveSignal. Otherwise, a signal noticed after the call to XtRemoveSignal could reference a stale XtSignalId.

SEE ALSO

Routines: XtAppMainLoop, XtAppNextEvent, XtAppPending, XtAppProcessEvent, XtAppAddSignal, XtNoticeSignal

XtRemoveTimeOut   **(R3)**

Cancels a timeout before it expires

SYNOPSIS

```
void XtRemoveTimeOut( timer_id )
        XtIntervalId                        timer_id;
```

ARGUMENTS

timer_id   in   Identifier of timeout to be canceled.

DESCRIPTION

XtRemoveTimeOut cancels a previously-registered timeout before it expires. *Timer_id* is the identifier returned when the timeout procedure was registered with XtAppAddTimeOut or XtAddTimeOut (obsolete).

USAGE

Timeouts are registered with XtAppAddTimeOut or XtAddTimeOut, and are automatically canceled after they have called their callback routine. XtRemoveTimeOut is used to explicitly cancel a timeout before it has expired. For example, you might start a timeout when you pop up a dialog box, and use it to pop the window down again if the user does not enter some input within the timeout interval. If the user does respond in time, the timeout would be canceled by the widget that receives the user's input.

CAUTION

It is an error to attempt to remove a timeout after it has expired, and will confuse the Intrinsics. The Intrinsics don't supply any method to report which timeouts are still pending; if you expect to cancel timeouts explicitly you should keep a list of active timeouts and update it from the timer callbacks when they are called.

SEE ALSO

Routines: XtAddTimeOut, XtAppAddTimeOut

XtRemoveWorkProc (R3)

Removes a work procedure from the execution queue

SYNOPSIS

```
void XtRemoveWorkProc( work_id )
        XtWorkProcId                    work_id;
```

ARGUMENTS

work_id   in   Identifier of work procedure to be canceled.

DESCRIPTION

XtRemoveWorkProc removes the specified work procedure from the execution queue. *Work_id* is the identifier returned when the work procedure was registered with XtAppAddWorkProc or XtAddWorkProc (obsolete).

USAGE

Work procedures are registered with XtAppAddWorkProc or XtAddWorkProc (obsolete), and are automatically removed from the execution queue when they have completed their work and return True. XtRemoveWorkProc is used to unregister a work procedure before it has completed its work. Often this is called from the callback issued by a "cancel" button, or a timer callback that decides that a work proc has worked long enough. A work procedure may also remove another work procedure, or itself, from the execution queue.

CAUTION

None

SEE ALSO

Routines: XtAddWorkProc, XtAppAddWorkProc

XtReservePropertyAtom (R6)

Reserves an atom to use as a property name for a parameterized selection

SYNOPSIS

```
Atom XtReservePropertyAtom( widget )
    Widget                          widget;
```

ARGUMENTS

widget   in   Widget making the selection request.

DESCRIPTION

XtReservePropertyAtom returns an atom that can be used as the name of a temporary property to hold parameters for a selection request.

USAGE

Certain selection requests don't actually result in the selection being retrieved. Instead, they direct the selection owner to do something with the selection. For example, a request for the selection expressed as the target DELETE tells the selection owner to delete the selection value in its own context. Other targets like INSERT_PROPERTY and INSERT_SELECTION require the requester to pass additional parameters that specify what to insert.

Parameterized selection requests force the requester to name other window properties as parameters. Since property names are identified by atoms (which cannot be freed), it pays not to simply make up a new property name for each request. What you should do instead is reserve an existing atom to use as a property name, create a property of that name for the transfer, and then release the name so that it might be used by other requesters. This cuts down memory utilization on the server.

To temporarily reserve an atom for use as a property name, call XtReservePropertyAtom. When the transfer is complete, call XtReleasePropertyAtom to allow that name to be used again, and to delete the contents of the property. You will use this routine only if you are doing very advanced sorts of selection transfer.

CAUTION

None

SEE ALSO

Routines: XtReleasePropertyAtom, XtSetSelectionParameters,
           XtGetSelectionParameters

XtResizeWidget (R3)

Resizes a widget in response to a geometry request

SYNOPSIS

```
void XtResizeWidget( w, width, height, border_width )
        Widget                          w;
        Dimension                       width;
        Dimension                       height;
        Dimension                       border_width;
```

ARGUMENTS

w	in	Widget to be resized; must be of class RectObj or any subclass thereof.
width	in	New width of widget.
height	in	New height of widget .
border_width	in	New border width of widget.

DESCRIPTION

XtResizeWidget unilaterally sets a new width, height, and border width for the specified widget, without calling its parent's geometry management routines. If the specified widget is realized, XtResizeWidget also issues an XConfigureWindow request to resize the widget's window. XtResizeWidget returns immediately if the specified values are the same as the widget's old values.

USAGE

XtResizeWidget is called only within a manager widget's implementation code to respond to a geometry management directive from its parent or a request from one of its children. XtResizeWidget is never called by application programmers. To resize a child widget in ordinary applications, call XtSetValues, specifying the desired XtNwidth and XtNheight resources.

CAUTION

Never call XtResizeWidget to resize a widget, as it does not give the widget or its parent a chance to respond to the change.

SEE ALSO

Routines: XtConfigureWidget, XtMakeGeometryRequest, XtMakeResizeRequest, XtMoveWidget, XtQueryGeometry, XtResizeWindow

XtResizeWindow   **(R3)**

Resizes a widget's window

SYNOPSIS

```
void XtResizeWindow( w )
        Widget                         w;
```

ARGUMENTS

w   in   Widget whose window must be resized; must be of class Core or any
                               subclass thereof.

DESCRIPTION

XtResizeWindow calls the Xlib routine XConfigureWindow, resizing the specified widget's window
to match the width and height resources in the widget data structures. The widget's *resize* class procedure is
not called.

USAGE

XtResizeWindow is sometimes used in widget implementation code to resize a widget's window without
calling the widget's *resize* class procedure. Widget programmers normally use XtResizeWidget instead.
XtResizeWindow is never called by application programmers. To change the size of a widget's window
in ordinary applications, call XtSetValues, specifying the XtNwidth and XtNheight resources.

CAUTION

Never call XtResizeWidget to resize a widget, as it does not give the widget or its parent a chance to
respond to the change.

SEE ALSO

Routines: XtResizeWidget

XtResolvePathname (R4)

Searches for a file using standard permuted paths

SYNOPSIS

```
String XtResolvePathname( display, type, filename, suffix, path,
    substitutions, num_substitutions, predicate )
            Display                  *display;
            String                   type;
            String                   filename;
            String                   suffix;
            String                   path;
            SubstitutionRec          *substitutions;
            Cardinal                 num_substitutions;
            XtFilePredicate          predicate;
```

ARGUMENTS

display	in	Display identifying a resource database to search for the language spec.
type	in	String specifying the category of the file, e.g. "app-defaults".
filename	in	String specifying a base filename, e.g. "HelloWorld".
suffix	in	String specifying a suffix, e.g. ".xbm", ".dat".
path	in	String specifying a series of potential paths delimited by colons, and including substitution characters.
substitutions	in	Pointer to a list of additional substitution-character/string pairs to be used to permute the path, or NULL if none.
num_substitutions	in	Number of character/string pairs in *substitutions*, or zero if none.
predicate	in	Callback routine that will be invoked to determine whether a synthesized filename is appropriate, or NULL to use the default predicate.

DESCRIPTION

XtResolvePathname searches for a file by name, using a combination of "standard" substitutions and application-supplied substitutions to permute a path. If the file is found, XtResolvePathname returns its complete pathname; otherwise XtResolvePathname returns NULL.

The search is based on the *path* argument. A substitution character in *path* is indicated by a preceding percent sign "%". Each time a substitution character is found, the list specified by *substitutions* is checked for a string to substitute for this character. A list of standard substitutions is also checked:

- %N   Value of the *filename* argument, or if *filename* is NULL, the application class name
- %T   Value of the *type* argument
- %S   Value of the *suffix* argument
- %L   Language string associated with the specified display
- %l   Language part of the display's language string
- %t   Territory part of the display's language string
- %c   Codeset part of the display's language string
- %C   Value of the .customization application resource
- %D   Value of an implementation-specific default path

A path may include any number of substitution characters. In *path*, the string "`%%`" implies a literal percent sign which should not be substituted. The string "`%:`" implies a literal colon which is part of the pathname and should not be interpreted as a delimiter between filenames. If *path* begins with a colon, it will be preceded by `%N%S`. If two adjacent colons are found in *path*, `%N%S` will be inserted between them.

Here's the interesting part: if *path* is `NULL`, `XtResolvePathname` synthesizes a path of its own. This default path is what often drives where applications look for their resource files, and is derived as follows. First, if the environment variable `XFILESEARCHPATH` is defined, it is used as the path. If `XFILESEARCHPATH` is not defined, `XtResolvePathname` synthesizes an implementation-dependent path that contains at least six entries. The entries must be in the following order and must contain the following substitutions. The order of substitutions in a particular entry, however, is implementation-dependent.

%C, %N, %S, %T, %L	or	%C, %N, %S, %T, %l, %t, %c
%C, %N, %S, %T, %l		
%C, %N, %S, %T		
%N, %S, %T, %L	or	%N, %S, %T, %l, %t, %c
%N, %S, %T, %l		
%N, %S, %T		

The idea here is to have files organized by language, type, file suffix, etc. On POSIX systems, some of the substitutions would clearly indicate directories and you would put slashes between them. The X developers suggest the following value for the default path on POSIX systems:

```
/usr/lib/X11/%L/%T/%N%C%S:/usr/lib/X11/%l/%T/%N%C%S:\
/usr/lib/X11/%T/%N/%C%S:/usr/lib/X11/%L/%T/%N%S:\
/usr/lib/X11/%l/%T/%N%S:/usr/lib/X11/%l/%T/%N%S
```

On MS-DOS or OpenVMS systems, the substitutions would still be there, but you would have an implementation-dependent syntax for assembling the substitution strings into a path. On OpenVMS, for example, a path entry might look like "`$%C%:[%L%T]%N%S`"

Whether the path is specified explicitly or `XtResolvePathname` dreams it up, each name in *path* is permuted using the specified substitutions, each time passing the resulting string to *predicate*. The *predicate* routine is of type `XtFilePredicate` (see Appendix B) and returns `True` when the permuted string matches an appropriate filename; the default predicate simply checks to see that the file exists, is readable, and is not a directory. When *predicate* returns `True`, the string specifying the file's full path is returned by `XtResolvePathname`; if no string yields a `True` return from *predicate*, `XtResolvePathname` returns `NULL`.

USAGE

`XtResolvePathname` gives you a way to look up files with stylized file names, organized by language, usage and file type. This is intended to be an aid in organizing Internationalized resource and data files. For example, the equivalent English and French-language resource files for an application might be named "/usr/lib/X11/app-defaults/en_US/Appl" and "/usr/lib/X11/app-defaults/fr_FR/Appl", respectively. `XtDisplayInitialize` calls `XtResolvePathname` to find application class-specific resource files.

CAUTION

The returned string should be freed with `XtFree` when it is no longer required.

SEE ALSO

Routines: `XtFindFile`, `XtDisplayInitialize`

XtScreen   (R3)

Returns a widget's screen pointer

SYNOPSIS

```
Screen *XtScreen( w )
      Widget                        w;
```

ARGUMENTS

w   in   Widget for which screen pointer is desired; must be of class Core or any
                                   subclass thereof.

DESCRIPTION

XtScreen returns a pointer to the Screen data structure associated with the specified widget.

USAGE

XtScreen is used by applications that mix Intrinsics and Xlib routines. Various Xlib routines and macros
take a screen pointer as an argument, and return information about the screen, its size, depth and capabilities
(see Table 12-3). These are important if you will be drawing custom graphics or allocating server resources.
To derive the screen associated with a windowless object, call XtScreenOfObject instead.

CAUTION

The screen pointer should not be confused with the screen number. The screen pointer is a pointer to a
Screen data structure. The screen number is the integer index of the screen being referenced. Both are
used in Xlib information macros.

SEE ALSO

Routines: XtDisplay, XtWindow

XtScreenDatabase

(R5)

Returns the screen-specific resource database

SYNOPSIS

```
XrmDatabase XtScreenDatabase( screen )
    Screen                              *screen;
```

ARGUMENTS

screen   in   Specifies screen with which resources are associated.

DESCRIPTION

XtScreenDatabase returns the fully-merged resource database built by XtDisplayInitialize and associated with the specified screen.

USAGE

A resource database is maintained for each open display and each screen of a display. The contents of these databases are merged from a variety of sources, including resource files, command-line arguments and properties found on the display's root window (see XtDisplayInitialize).

To return the database for a specific screen, use XtScreenDatabase. In general, the screen-specific database is a superset of the per-display database, and holds resources that would be searched by applications displaying on a particular screen. The per-display database holds resources that would be common to all screens of the display, and in releases prior to R5, is used as the sole database for all screens.

Widget resources are automatically initialized at creation time using the contents of their screen-specific database. If you want to explicitly manipulate the database, you can use the "Xrm" routines supplied by Xlib on the XrmDatabase returned by XtScreenDatabase. Though this is rarely necessary, you might do it if you wanted to merge a special application-specific resource file that is not automatically loaded by the toolkit.

CAUTION

The screen-specific database is built by XtDisplayInitialize when the display is initialized. If you call XtScreenDatabase for a screen that is not associated with a display initialized with XtDisplayInitialize, the return value is undefined.

SEE ALSO

Routines: XtAppInitialize, XtDisplayInitialize, XtOpenDisplay, XtDatabase

XtScreenOfObject (R4)

Returns an object's screen pointer

SYNOPSIS

```
Screen *XtScreen( object )
      Widget                          object;
```

ARGUMENTS

object   in   Widget or object for which Screen pointer is desired; must be of class Object or any subclass thereof.

DESCRIPTION

XtScreenOfObject returns a pointer to the Screen data structure associated with the closest windowed relative of the specified widget or object. If the specified object is a widget, XtScreenOfObject is identical in function to XtScreen.

USAGE

XtScreen is used by applications that mix Intrinsics and straight Xlib routines. Various Xlib routines and macros take a screen pointer as an argument, and return information about the screen, its size, depth and capabilities (see Table 12-3). These are important if you will be drawing custom graphics or allocating server resources. XtScreenOfObject is used primarily by widget programmers in the implementation code for windowless objects.

CAUTION

The screen pointer should not be confused with the screen number. The screen pointer is a pointer to a Screen data structure. The screen number is the integer index of the screen being referenced. Both are used in Xlib information macros.

Drawing operations and resource management for windowless objects are greatly complicated by the fact that they must use the window belonging to a relative. You should generally confine any custom drawing to windowed objects (widgets) and will therefore find XtScreen adequate.

SEE ALSO

Routines: XtDisplayOfObject, XtWindowOfObject

XtSendSelectionRequest   (R6)

Sends a bundled selection request

SYNOPSIS

```
void XtSendSelectionRequest( w, selection, time )
    Widget                          w;
    Atom                            selection;
    Time                            time;
```

ARGUMENTS

w	in	Widget requesting the selection; must be of class Core or any subclass thereof.
selection	in	Atom specifying which selection is requested, e.g. XA_PRIMARY.
time	in	Timestamp taken from the event that triggered the decision to request the selection. The value CurrentTime is not acceptable.

DESCRIPTION

XtSendSelectionRequest sends any deferred selection requests as a single request for the MULTIPLE target. The selection request represents all calls to XtGetSelectionValue, XtGetSelectionValues, XtGetSelectionValueIncr, XtGetSelectionValuesIncr and XtSetSelectionParameters undertaken since a previous call to XtCreateSelectionRequest. All deferred requests must be for the same selection and widget.

USAGE

A selection may be requested in multiple targets simultaneously by sending a request for the target MULTIPLE. This guarantees that the selection owner does not change between consecutive requests for different targets. To make requests for ordinary multiple targets, you can use XtGetSelectionValues or XtGetSelectionValuesIncr. Bundled selection requests implemented with XtSendSelectionRequest are required only if you need to make a request with parameterized targets, such as a request for the target INSERT_PROPERTY.

To make a bundled request you bracket ordinary requests for selection values between a call to XtCreateSelectionRequest and another call to XtSendSelectionRequest. If you decide somewhere in this process that you don't really want to send the bundled request, you can call XtCancelSelectionRequest to cancel it.

To make requests for parameterized selections, call XtSetSelectionParameters to supply the appropriate parameters before each call to XtGetSelectionValue that requires parameters. Multiple requests with different parameters can be bundled this way.

CAUTION

XtSendSelectionRequest is used to send a request for multiple selection targets requiring parameter data. To request "ordinary" multiple selections, the routines XtGetSelectionValues or XtGetSelectionValuesIncr are much simpler to use.

SEE ALSO

Routines: XtCreateSelectionRequest, XtCancelSelectionRequest

XtSessionGetToken   (R6)

Accepts a token for a deferred session manager checkpoint operation

SYNOPSIS

```
XtCheckpointToken XtSessionGetToken( widget )
    Widget                              widget;
```

ARGUMENTS

widget   in   Widget ID of the SessionShell managing the session participation.

DESCRIPTION

If called from within a callback responding to a session manager request, XtSessionGetToken returns a pointer to an XtCheckpointTokenRec.   If no checkpoint operation is under way, XtSessionGetToken returns NULL. Checkpoint tokens are cumulative, and all checkpoint tokens accepted with XtSessionGetToken must be returned with XtSessionReturnToken before the checkpoint operation is considered complete.

USAGE

The R6 Intrinsics support session manager protocols through the SessionShell widget. Callbacks of the SessionShell notify your program when it is your turn to save your data, interact with the user, or shut down. These callbacks pass a pointer to an XtCheckpointTokenRec as *call_data*. You fill in return values in this structure to indicate to the session manager what you have done, or what you want to do.

Sometimes you may want to communicate with other agents before confirming that you have taken action. To buy time, you can take out additional checkpoint tokens with XtSessionGetToken. The token is a pointer to a structure of type XtCheckpointTokenRec, described in Chapter 11. When you have handled things to your satisfaction, you return tokens with XtSessionReturnToken. When all tokens have been returned the session manager considers the pending operation complete. The tokens do not have to be returned by the same routine that checked them out.

CAUTION

The conventions for handling checkpoint operations can get complicated; for complete information please see the references listed in Chapter 11, which are available by anonymous FTP from ftp.x.org and other mirror sites on the Internet.

SEE ALSO

Routines: XtSessionReturnToken

XtSessionReturnToken (R6)

Releases the token for a completed session manager checkpoint operation

SYNOPSIS

```
void XtSessionReturnToken( token )
    XtCheckpointToken                       token;
```

ARGUMENTS

token   in   Pointer to XtCheckpointTokenRec previously allocated by XtSessionGetToken, or in some cases, passed as *call_data* to a callback routine.

DESCRIPTION

XtSessionReturnToken returns a checkpoint token to the SessionShell. Checkpoint tokens are cumulative, and all checkpoint tokens reserved with XtSessionGetToken must be returned with XtSessionReturnToken before the save operation is considered complete.

USAGE

The R6 Intrinsics support session manager protocols through the SessionShell widget. Callbacks of the SessionShell notify your program when it is your turn to save your data, interact with the user, or shut down. These callbacks pass a pointer to an XtCheckpointTokenRec as *call_data*. You fill in return values in this structure to indicate to the session manager what you have done, or what you want to do.

In most cases the return from a callback routine passes the checkpoint token back to the SessionShell. Interact callbacks, however, receive a token as *call_data*, but must arrange to return it with XtSessionReturnToken because the interact callback itself usually just pops up a dialog box, and can't know the outcome of the interaction. In this case, the tokens are not returned by the same routine that checked them out.

Sometimes you may want to communicate with other agents before confirming that you have taken action. To buy time, a callback can take out additional checkpoint tokens with XtSessionGetToken. The token is a pointer to a structure of type XtCheckpointTokenRec, described in Chapter 11. When you have handled things to your satisfaction, you return tokens with XtSessionReturnToken. When all tokens have been returned the session manager considers the pending operation complete.

CAUTION

The conventions for handling checkpoint operations can get complicated; for complete information please see the references listed in Chapter 11, which are available by anonymous FTP from ftp.x.org and other mirror sites on the Internet.

SEE ALSO

Routines: XtSessionGetToken

XtSetArg (R3)

Places a resource name/value pair in an Arg

SYNOPSIS

```
void XtSetArg( arg, name, value )
        Arg                             arg;
        String                          name;
        XtArgVal                        value;
```

ARGUMENTS

arg	in	The `Arg` structure in which to place the values.
name	in	Resource name, e.g. "width" or the symbolic constant `XtNwidth`.
value	in	Value of resource, e.g. 100.

DESCRIPTION

`XtSetArg` is a convenience routine or macro that places a resource name/value pair in the specified `Arg` data structure.

USAGE

`XtSetArg` is used to build arglists passed to `XtSetValues`, `XtGetValues` and widget creation routines. Usually, an array of `Args` is declared statically and `XtSetArg` is used to set succeeding name/value pairs in the array:

```
Arg             arglist[10];
Cardinal        i;

i = 0;
XtSetArg( arglist[i], XtNwidth, 100 ); i++;
XtSetArg( arglist[i], XtNheight, 100 ); i++;
XtSetValues( widget, arglist, i );
```

The resource name is usually specified using symbolic constants defined in `<X11/StringDefs.h>` or the toolkit-specific header files. The specified *value* is automatically cast as type `XtArgVal`; if a value is too large to fit in an `XtArgVal`, *value* must be a pointer to the value. Since on many systems an `XtArgVal` is defined as `long`, floating-point numbers must usually be passed by reference to avoid being truncated.

CAUTION

`XtSetArg` does not send any information to a widget; it simply prepares an argument list for a later call to a resource management routine. The notation in which *i* is incremented after `XtSetArg` should be followed, as most versions of the Intrinsics implement `XtSetArg` as a macro that dereferences *i* twice. Be careful when declaring a static array of `Args` to make it as large as will be needed; a common mistake is to increment *i* beyond the end of the array.

SEE ALSO

Routines: XtAppCreateShell, XtCreateManagedWidget, XtCreatePopupShell,
           XtCreateWidget, XtGetValues, XtMergeArgLists, XtSetValues

XtSetErrorHandler (O)

Registers a toolkit low-level error handler

SYNOPSIS

```
void XtSetErrorHandler( error_handler )
        XtErrorHandler                error_handler;
```

ARGUMENTS

error_handler   in   Error handler to be called on fatal error conditions.

DESCRIPTION

XtSetErrorHandler establishes a new error handler within the scope of the default application context created by XtInitialize. When a toolkit fatal error condition is detected (that is, when the application or a toolkit internal routine calls XtError) control is passed to the specified procedure. The error handler is expected to display a message and then exit.

USAGE

See XtAppSetErrorHandler.

CAUTION

XtSetErrorHandler is an obsolete routine supplied for backwards compatibility with earlier versions of the Intrinsics, and is superseded by XtAppSetErrorHandler in the Release 3 and later Intrinsics. XtSetErrorHandler uses the default application context established by XtInitialize, which must be called first.

SEE ALSO

Routines: XtAppSetErrorHandler, XtError, XtInitialize

XtSetErrorMsgHandler (O)

Registers a toolkit high-level error message handler

SYNOPSIS

```
void XtSetErrorMsgHandler( error_msg_handler )
        XtErrorMsgHandler           error_msg_handler;
```

ARGUMENTS

error_msg_handler   in   Error message handler to be called on fatal error conditions.

DESCRIPTION

XtSetErrorMsgHandler establishes a new error message handler within the scope of the default application context created by XtInitialize. When a toolkit fatal error condition is detected (that is, when the application or a toolkit internal routine calls XtErrorMsg) control is passed to the specified procedure. The error message handler is expected to display a message and then exit.

USAGE

See XtAppSetErrorMsgHandler.

CAUTION

XtSetErrorMsgHandler is an obsolete routine supplied for backwards compatibility with earlier versions of the Intrinsics, and is superseded by XtAppSetErrorMsgHandler in the Release 3 and later Intrinsics.   XtSetErrorMsgHandler uses the default application context established by XtInitialize, which must be called first.

SEE ALSO

Routines: XtAppSetErrorMsgHandler, XtErrorMsg, XtInitialize

XtSetEventDispatcher   **(R6)**

Registers a special event dispatcher for extension events

SYNOPSIS

```
XtEventDispatchProc XtSetEventDispatcher( display, event_type,
    dispatch_proc)
    Display                         *display;
    int                             event_type;
    XtEventDispatchProc             dispatch_proc;
```

ARGUMENTS

display	in	Display for which dispatcher is valid.
event_type	in	Event type for which this dispatcher will be called.
dispatch_proc	in	Event dispatcher that will be responsible for the specified event type.

DESCRIPTION

XtSetEventDispatcher registers a custom dispatcher for events of the specified type. Future events of the specified type are forwarded to *dispatch_proc* for handling. The previously-registered dispatcher, or the default dispatcher if none was previously specified, is returned.

USAGE

The usual reason to register a special event dispatcher is to handle extension events, which may need to be delivered to widgets in special ways. Unless you write widgets or applications that expect extension events, you will probably never call XtSetEventDispatcher.

CAUTION

The *dispatch_proc* is expected to perform a certain amount of standard processing on the event. These responsibilities are discussed in Appendix B in the description of XtEventDispatchProc.

SEE ALSO

Routines: XtInsertEventTypeHandler, XtRegisterExtensionSelector,
        XtRemoveEventTypeHandler

XtSetKeyboardFocus (R3)

Remaps keyboard events to a specified widget

SYNOPSIS

```
void XtSetKeyboardFocus( subtree, destination )
        Widget                          subtree;
        Widget                          destination;
```

ARGUMENTS

subtree   in   Widget that roots a subtree of widgets; must be of class Core or any
                              subclass thereof.

destination   in   Normal descendant of *subtree* that should receive keyboard events, or
                              None, to restore ordinary processing of keyboard events.

DESCRIPTION

XtSetKeyboardFocus forwards keyboard input occurring in the widget tree rooted by *subtree* to a
normal (not pop-up) descendant. In the future, Key events occurring in *destination* or one of its normal
descendants are delivered normally, but Key events occurring in other descendants of *subtree* are delivered to
destination. If *destination* is a windowless object, keyboard input is sent to its nearest windowed ancestor.

XtSetKeyboardFocus is a client-side feature that simply remaps events in the widget tree, and is
done before other types of remapping. If there are widgets on the grab list (see XtAddGrab) keyboard input
is first forwarded as specified by XtSetKeyboardFocus. If the destination is in the active set, it receives
the event as planned; otherwise, the event is discarded or remapped to a spring-loaded widget, if any.

If a server-side keyboard grab is established with XtGrabKey or XtGrabKeyboard, the Intrinsics
first remap any Key event as specified by XtSetKeyboardFocus. If the destination turns out to be the
grabbing widget or one of its descendants, the event is then mapped back to the grabbing widget.

USAGE

XtSetKeyboardFocus is used to direct keyboard input in a widget subtree to a particular widget. This
lets the keyboard "stick" to that widget even if the pointer is not located directly over it. It is commonly used
to assign focus to a particular text widget in a data-entry form or a dialog box. Because it does not require
synchronization with the server, XtSetKeyboardFocus is preferable to assigning focus with
XSetInputFocus.

A manager widget may call XtSetKeyboardFocus internally to forward focus to one of its children.
If that child is itself a manager widget, the focus may be forwarded yet again. This can go on to arbitrarily
deep levels. To find out which widget will finally receive keyboard input as a result of any cumulative
forwarding operations, call XtGetKeyboardFocusWidget.

CAUTION

Many toolkits have private methods to direct keyboard focus; for example, if you're using OSF/Motif you do
not call XtSetKeyboardFocus explicitly, but use XmProcessTraversal instead. Since manager
widgets may call XtSetKeyboardFocus internally, focus may be reassigned without your knowledge if
you don't do as a toolkit expects. Other methods for directing keyboard input are contrasted in Chapter 9.

SEE ALSO

Routines: XtCallAcceptFocus, XtAddGrab, XtPopup

XtSetKeyTranslator   **(R3)**

Registers a KeyCode-to-KeySym translator

SYNOPSIS

```
void XtSetKeyTranslator( display, key_proc )
        Display                     *display;
        XtKeyProc                   key_proc;
```

ARGUMENTS

display	in	Display for which translator is to be invoked to interpret key events.
key_proc	in	Keycode-to-keysym translator to be registered.

DESCRIPTION

XtSetKeyTranslator registers a new keycode-to-keysym translator for the specified display.

USAGE

A keycode-to-keysym translator is of type XtKeyProc (see Appendix B), and converts the device-specific keycodes received in Key events to vendor-neutral keysyms. The converter is automatically invoked by the Intrinsics when processing Key events through translation management.

The Intrinsics provide a default key translator named XtTranslateKey, which uses shift, lock and group modifiers with the interpretations defined in the X Protocol specification. XtTranslateKey uses the default mapping tables for each open display to perform the conversion.

You can register a new translator if special keycode-to-keysym translation is needed. This could be used, for example, to simulate alternate-language keyboard layouts. An application-registered XtKeyProc may feel free to consult the default keyboard mapping returned by XtGetKeysymTable or call the default translator, XtTranslateKey. A keycode-to-keysym translator cannot be unregistered, except by setting a new one. The default translator can be restored by calling XtSetKeyTranslator and specifying XtTranslateKey as the *key_proc* argument.

CAUTION

If *key_proc* is set to NULL, your application will not be able to perform translations, and will probably crash. OSF/Motif applications automatically register a special keycode-to-keysym translator to handle Motif "virtual keysyms", so replacing the translator in a Motif program will demand knowledge of Motif internals and keysyms.

SEE ALSO

Routines: XtGetKeysymTable, XtKeysymToKeycodeList, XtTranslateKeycode

XtSetLanguageProc (R5)

Registers a routine that sets the application locale

SYNOPSIS

```
XtLanguageProc XtSetLanguageProc( context, lang_proc, client_data )
        XtAppContext                    context;
        XtLanguageProc                  lang_proc;
        XtPointer                       client_data;
```

ARGUMENTS

context	in	Application context in which language proc will be used, or NULL if it is to be used in all application contexts.
lang_proc	in	Language proc, or NULL to register the default language proc.
client_data	in	Client-specific data to be passed to the language proc when it is called, or NULL if none is required.

DESCRIPTION

XtSetLanguageProc registers a language proc to be called when any subsequent displays are initialized in the specified application context, and returns the previously-registered language proc. Registering a language proc effectively enables internationalized features in applications, if any.

USAGE

Applications that wish to support internationalization must call XtSetLanguageProc before initializing any displays. The language proc is expected to set the locale of the application, and determine the language string used by XtDisplayInitialize to find resource files.

If *lang_proc* is NULL, the Intrinsics register a default language proc which tries to set the locale as requested by the .xnlLanguage application resource; if the requested locale is not supported, it issues warnings and sets the locale to "C". Since the default language proc works just fine for most applications, the most common way to call XtSetLanguageProc is to simply leave all three arguments NULL:

```
main(argc, argv)
int argc; char **argv;
{
  Widget toplevel;
  XtSetLanguageProc(NULL, NULL, NULL);
  toplevel = XtAppInitialize(&context, "International", NULL, 0,
    argc, &argv, NULL, NULL, 0);
```

See XtLanguageProc in Appendix B for more information on the responsibilities of a language proc.

CAUTION

Support for a locale depends on support being built into the operating system, the X libraries, and the toolkit.

SEE ALSO

Routines: XtDisplayInitialize

XtSetMappedWhenManaged   **(R3)**

Sets whether a widget is automatically mapped when it is managed

SYNOPSIS

```
void XtSetMappedWhenManaged( w, value )
        Widget                      w;
        Boolean                     value;
```

ARGUMENTS

w	in	Widget for which *mapped_when_managed* field is set; must be of class Core or any subclass thereof.
value	in	True if widget is to be automatically mapped when managed; False if mapping and management are to be performed separately.

DESCRIPTION

XtSetMappedWhenManaged sets the specified widget's *mapped_when_managed* field to *value*. If the widget is managed when XtSetMappedWhenManaged is called, its window is mapped or unmapped appropriately. XtSetMappedWhenManaged does not affect the managed state of the widget.

USAGE

A normal (not pop-up) widget must be both mapped and managed to be visible. Default toolkit behavior is to map widgets when they are managed, and unmap them when they are unmanaged, so XtManageChild and XtUnmanageChild are the "usual" ways to put a widget on the screen and remove it. However, XtManageChild and XtUnmanageChild invoke the parent's geometry management routines, and can sometimes cause undesirable visual effects. For example, a dialog box might shrink, expand or reposition its children to adjust for the sudden management or unmanagement of a child.

In some user interface styles, it is desirable to remove widgets from a layout while still maintaining the space that they occupied. Default behavior can be overridden by using XtSetMappedWhenManaged to set a widget's *mapped_when_managed* field to False. XtMapWidget and XtUnmapWidget are then used to explicitly map and unmap the widget from the screen without causing its parent to do any geometry adjustments.

CAUTION

Widgets are created by default with their *mapped_when_managed* field set to True. Setting this field to False overrides default toolkit behavior and requires that you explicitly map and unmap the widget's window with XtMapWidget and XtUnmapWidget. Since an unmapped widget is still managed, calls to XtSetValues that affect the geometry of the widget may result in geometry changes in the user interface, even though the widget is not visible.

SEE ALSO

Routines: XtManageChild, XtManageChildren, XtMapWidget, XtUnmanageChild,
            XtUnmanageChildren, XtUnmapWidget

XtSetMultiClickTime   (R4)

Sets the timeout used to distinguish repeated events

SYNOPSIS

```
void XtSetMultiClickTime( display, time )
        Display                         *display;
        int                             time;
```

ARGUMENTS

display	in	Specifies display for which multi-click time is set.
time	in	New multi-click time, expressed in milliseconds.

DESCRIPTION

XtSetMultiClickTime sets the time, expressed in milliseconds, used to determine whether contiguous events of the same type are to be interpreted as a repeated event when matching an entry in a translation table containing a repeat count.

USAGE

The toolkit translation manager distinguishes between a series of single events (e.g. pointer button clicks) and repeated events which should be treated together. This distinction is necessary to allow double-clicks, triple-clicks (and so on) to be defined as translations. Such translations are declared in a translation table by specifying an event with a repeat count. Example; a double-click on button 1:

```
    <Btn1Up>(2):  SelectLine()
```

The "multi-click time" is the period of time within which each succeeding similar event must be processed to be considered part of a repeated event. The routine XtSetMultiClickTime is used to set a new value for the multi-click time so that users with faster or slower fingers can be happy. The multi-click time can also be set using the application resource "multiClickTime" (Class: "MultiClickTime"). The default value for the multi-click time is 200 milliseconds. XtGetMultiClickTime may be used to return the current value of the multi-click time, so that it may be reported to the user or saved as a default.

CAUTION

Multi-click times with very large (>1000 ms.) or small (<100 ms.) values may result in rather eccentric toolkit behavior.

SEE ALSO

Routines: XtGetMultiClickTime

XtSetSelectionParameters   **(R6)**

Stores selection parameters to send to the selection owner

SYNOPSIS

```
void XtSetSelectionParameters( requester, selection, type, value, length,
    format )
    Widget                              requester;
    Atom                                selection;
    Atom                                type;
    XtPointer                           value;
    unsigned long                       length;
    int                                 format;
```

ARGUMENTS

requester	in	Widget ID of selection requester; must be of class Core or any subclass thereof.
selection	in	Atom identifying which selection is being processed, e.g. XA_PRIMARY for primary selection; XA_SECONDARY for secondary selection, etc.
type	in	Atom specifying property type for parameters, e.g. XA_STRING.
value	in	Pointer to list of parameters.
length	in	Length of the parameter list (in *format* units).
format	in	Format (8, 16 or 32-bit) of the parameter data.

DESCRIPTION

XtSetSelectionParameters sets parameters to be sent to the selection owner regarding a selection request.

USAGE

Selection requests for certain targets, such as the targets INSERT_PROPERTY and INSERT_SELECTION, require the requester to pass additional parameters that tell the selection owner more detail about the request. The selection event doesn't have room for such parameters, so they are passed by placing them in a window property where the selection owner can retrieve them. Selection requesters should call XtSetSelectionParameters just before making any selection request that takes additional parameters. The Intrinsics handle the mechanics of getting the parameters from the requester to the owner, and selection owners then call XtGetSelectionParameters to retrieve them. Very few selection targets require parameters, so XtSetSelectionParameters is not used very often.

CAUTION

Parameters, if any, are specific to the target of the request; if you intend to perform parameterized selection, you should read the ICCCM carefully to see what is expected for a particular target. If you want to make multiple parameterized requests for the same selection, you must use XtCreateSelectionRequest and XtSendSelectionRequest.

SEE ALSO

Routines: XtGetSelectionParameters, XtCreateSelectionRequest

XtSetSelectionTimeout (O)

Sets the timeout value used in toolkit selection transfer operations

SYNOPSIS

```
void XtSetSelectionTimeout( timeout )
        unsigned long                  timeout;
```

ARGUMENTS

timeout   in   Selection timeout, in milliseconds.

DESCRIPTION

XtSetSelectionTimeout sets the selection timeout value, expressed in milliseconds. The timeout value set by XtSetSelectionTimeout is valid in the default application context established by XtInitialize.

USAGE

See XtAppSetSelectionTimeout.

CAUTION

XtSetSelectionTimeout is an obsolete routine supplied for backwards compatibility with earlier versions of the Intrinsics, and has been superseded by XtAppSetSelectionTimeout in the Release 3 and later Intrinsics. XtSetSelectionTimeout uses the default application context established by XtInitialize, which must be called first.

SEE ALSO

Routines: XtAppGetSelectionTimeout, XtAppSetSelectionTimeout,
           XtGetSelectionTimeout

XtSetSensitive (R3)

Sets a widget sensitive or insensitive to user input

SYNOPSIS

```
void XtSetSensitive( w, value )
        Widget                    w;
        Boolean                   value;
```

ARGUMENTS

w   in   Widget to be set sensitive or insensitive; must be of class RectObj or any subclass thereof.

value   in   True to set sensitive, False to set insensitive.

DESCRIPTION

XtSetSensitive sets the specified widget sensitive or insensitive. If *w* is a subclass of Composite, it also sets the *ancestor_sensitive* fields of its descendants as follows:

- If *value* is False, XtSetSensitive recursively descends the widget tree of normal (not pop-up) descendants and sets their *ancestor_sensitive* fields to False.

- If *value* is True, and the widget's own *ancestor_sensitive* field is True, XtSetSensitive recursively descends the widget tree of normal (not pop-up) descendants and sets their *ancestor_sensitive* fields to True.

- If *value* is True, but the specified widget's own *ancestor_sensitive* field is False, it does not change its descendants' *ancestor_sensitive* fields.

Widgets set insensitive are not dispatched user events of type KeyPress, KeyRelease, ButtonPress, ButtonRelease, MotionNotify, EnterNotify, LeaveNotify, FocusIn, or FocusOut.

USAGE

Widgets have an "insensitive" state in which they do not respond to user input, and may appear "grayed-out" or stippled. XtSetSensitive is used to set a widget and its descendants sensitive or insensitive.

A widget receives user input only if it and all of its normal ancestors are sensitive. For this reason, widgets have both a *sensitive* and an *ancestor_sensitive* field; both must be True for the widget to be sensitive. Setting a primitive widget insensitive disables only that widget, while setting a manager widget insensitive may be used to block input to an entire section of a user interface, such as a dialog box.

CAUTION

An application will hang if it blocks waiting for input from an insensitive widget or one of its descendants. This could happen if a modal dialog box is popped up with a "press to continue" button, but the dialog box is set insensitive. A pop-up shell will have its *ancestor_sensitive* field set False if its parent is insensitive when the shell is created. XtSetSensitive won't set the shell's *ancestor_sensitive* field, so to make sure that such a shell is sensitive before popping it up with a grab, you should declare a resource of the form:

```
*TransientShell.ancestorSensitive: true
```

in an appropriate resource file, or make sure that the shell's parent is sensitive before creating the shell.

XtSetSensitive should always be used rather than XtSetValues to set a widget's sensitive field, because XtSetSensitive appropriately handles the *ancestor_sensitive* field of descendants. Widgets may or may not visually reflect their sensitivity.

SEE ALSO

Routines: XtIsSensitive

XtSetSubvalues   **(R3)**

Sets values of resources not maintained in a widget instance record

SYNOPSIS

```
void XtSetSubvalues( base, resources, num_resources, args, num_args )
        XtPointer          base;
        XtResourceList     resources;
        Cardinal           num_resources;
        ArgList            args;
        Cardinal           num_args;
```

ARGUMENTS

base	in/out	Base address of data structure to receive resource values.
resources	in	Pointer to list of resource description records declaring names, types and offsets of resource fields.
num_resources	in	Number of resource definitions in *resources*.
args	in	An array of Args specifying resource values.
num_args	in	Number of name/value pairs in *args*.

DESCRIPTION

XtSetSubvalues places the resource values specified in *args* into the data structure pointed to by *base*. The resource list *resources* determines where in the data structure the values are placed and what default values are placed there if no value is found in *args*.

USAGE

XtSetSubvalues is used by widget programmers to set the state of non-widget data structures. It is usually called from a widget's *set_values* class procedure. Normal applications do not use this routine.

The Intrinsics automatically fetch resource values for fields declared in a widget's instance record, but not for fields in other data structures that belong to the widget. Fields not declared in the instance record are considered "non-widget" subparts. If such fields are to be controlled through resources, they must be set by the widget programmer with XtSetSubvalues. When XtSetValues is used on the widget, its *set_values* procedure is called passing the arglist provided by the application programmer. The widget programmer can then forward this arglist to XtSetSubvalues to set any subpart resources. XtVaSetSubvalues is the varargs variant of XtSetSubvalues.

CAUTION

XtSetSubvalues does not fetch resource values from the resource database; it simply puts the values specified by *args* into the destination data stucture. To fetch initial subpart resources from the database call XtGetSubresources.

SEE ALSO

Routines: XtGetSubvalues, XtGetSubresources

XtSetTypeConverter (R4)

Registers a new-format resource type converter

SYNOPSIS

```
void XtSetTypeConverter( from_type, to_type, converter, convert_args,
    num_args, cache_type, destructor )
        String                          from_type;
        String                          to_type;
        XtTypeConverter                 converter;
        XtConvertArgList                convert_args;
        Cardinal                        num_args;
        XtCacheType                     cache_type;
        XtDestructor                    destructor;
```

ARGUMENTS

from_type	in	String identifying the source data type, e.g. "String", or symbolic constant `XtRString`.
to_type	in	String identifying the destination data type, e.g. "Int", or symbolic constant `XtRInt`.
converter	in	Resource type converter to be registered.
convert_args	in	Argument specifying how to compute additional parameters to be passed to converter when it is invoked (see below).
num_args	in	Number of parameters in *convert_args*.
cache_type	in	Specifies whether conversion results are saved for later reference. Possible values: `XtCacheNone`, `XtCacheAll`, `XtCacheByDisplay`. May be modified by ORing with `XtCacheRefCount`.
destructor	in	Procedure called to release this type of resource when the reference count for a particular conversion goes to zero.

DESCRIPTION

`XtSetTypeConverter` registers a new-format resource type converter for use in all application contexts in the current process. The converter is specific to the source and destination types defined by *from_type* and *to_type*. Converters are invoked automatically when the toolkit fetches resources values from resource files.

The results of a conversion may be cached for later reference. This potentially saves trips to the server or computational overhead if the same conversion is requested at a later time. Caching is done if the *cache_type* argument is either `XtCacheAll` or `XtCacheByDisplay`.

If the modifier `XtCacheRefCount` is ORed with either of these values, the Intrinsics keep a reference count for a conversion result. The reference count is incremented each time the converter is called with the same conversion value, and is decremented with `XtAppReleaseCacheRefs`. When the reference count for a given conversion drops to zero, the routine specified by *destructor* is called to release any application or server resources associated with the conversion. If *cache_type* is `XtCacheByDisplay`, *destructor* will also be called if the associated display is closed with `XtCloseDisplay`.

USAGE

A resource converter converts one toolkit data type to another, allocating X server resources if necessary to perform the conversion. The most common converters are those that accept a string and return a toolkit-specific data type. These are used to parse the entries in resource files, which are all simply character strings to start out. For example, a `String-to-Pixel` converter might accept the string "red" and convert it to a valid pixel value by calling `XAllocNamedColor`. A simpler converter that converts strings to integers might just call `sscanf(string, "%i", &int)` to interpret the input string as an integer.

When widget are created, converters are automatically invoked by the Intrinsics to fetch their initial resource values from the resource database. Converters may also be invoked explicitly in C code with the routines `XtConvertAndStore` or `XtCallConverter`.

Type converters are usually registered by widgets to provide for the conversion of widget-specific resource types. You may also register your own converters for application-specific data types fetched with `XtGetApplicationResources`. Converters are usually registered in all application contexts with `XtSetTypeConverter`. If a resource converter is to be registered for just a single application context, you can use `XtAppSetTypeConverter`.

The simple sorts of converters registered by most applications do not require caching, and should be registered with a *cache_type* of `XtCacheNone`. After all, there's really no great benefit in caching the value for a `String-to-int` conversion, since it is easy to recompute and takes no storage other than that for the returned value. Simple converters usually do not require additional arguments, and may be registered with *convert_args* equal to NULL. See Chapter 6 for an example of a simple resource converter.

The implications of caching are far-reaching. Caching is usually reserved for resource types that involve a server resource (Pixmap, Cursor, Font, Pixel, Colormap, etc.) and require a round-trip to the server to perform the conversion. The idea here is that if two (or more) agents request a conversion with the same input value, they could use the same result, so the resource converter will simply save the result the first time it is called and give the saved answer to all subsequent callers.

For example, if two widgets are created that both have their `XtNbackground` resource set to "red" in a resource file, the String-to-Pixel converter will call `XAllocNamedColor` when the first widget is created, and will simply give the same pixel value to the next widget. This strategy can be applied equally well to pixmaps, fonts, etc. and saves server memory as well as network traffic. *However, this also means that the server object must continue to exist as long as anything that called for the conversion still references it.*

So how does the toolkit know when it is safe to release a server resource? The simple answer is: it never does, so any server object allocated by a converter will stay allocated until the display connection is terminated. This is what you get if you register a converter with a *cache_type* of `XtCacheAll`.

Of course, this could leave the server fairly bulging with extra Pixmaps and Fonts, etc. if widgets using lots of different renditions were created and destroyed dynamically. A more complicated form of caching is done if the `XtCacheRefCount` bit is ORed with the *cache_type*. In this case, a *destructor* procedure of type `XtDestructor` (see Appendix B) must also be registered along with the type converter. This is a routine that knows how to release the server (or other) resource when it is safe to do so. To decide when it is safe, the toolkit keeps a reference count for each unique conversion source and destination. The reference count is incremented each time the conversion is performed. But when does the reference count get decremented?

Usually the caller of a converter is a widget that is being created. By default, the toolkit binds a callback routine to the `XtNdestroyCallback` of the widget when a reference counted conversion is performed. This is also done when you invoke a converter with `XtConvertAndStore`, or use a varargs resource routine with `XtVaTypedArg` resource specifications. The callback routine calls `XtAppReleaseCacheRefs` when the widget is destroyed, telling the toolkit that this widget, at least, doesn't intend to reference the server resource anymore. When the cache reference count drops to zero, the destructor is called to free the server resource. This is why Pixels and other server resources that you allocate with `XtConvertAndStore` are not freed until the widget associated with the conversion is destroyed.

However, if you call a converter explicitly with XtCallConverter, there is no widget for the toolkit to deal with. If the converter expects to perform caching, you are expected to accept the cache reference and call XtAppReleaseCacheRefs yourself when you no longer require the conversion value. Otherwise it will never be freed.

The value of the *convert_args* argument is a list of XtConvertArgRecs. These generally do not provide conversion arguments directly, but tell the Intrinsics how to compute the required arguments when the converter is invoked. As an example, consider the following XtConvertArgRec list defined by the Intrinsics:

```
XtConvertArgRec colorConvertArgs[] = {
    {XtWidgetBaseOffset, (XtPointer)XtOffset(Widget, core.screen),
        sizeof(Screen *)},
    {XtWidgetBaseOffset, (XtPointer)XtOffset(Widget, core.colormap),
        sizeof(Colormap)}
};
```

These definitions ask the Intrinsics to fetch the Screen pointer and colormap belonging to the widget for which resources are being fetched. Unfortunately, they demand some knowledge of widget internals. See the definition of XtConvertArgRec in Appendix A for more information.

CAUTION

Converters are not a perfect solution to resource utilization. Often it pays to use Xlib routines to deal with server resources, particularly if you use lots of them and dynamically create and destroy them. Since server resources allocated with XtConvertAndStore are not released until the widget that you reference is destroyed, it is not a great way to allocate large numbers of colors or fonts. If you call XtCallConverter, you have to know what additional arguments the converter expects so you can pass them explicitly.

SEE ALSO

Routines: XtAppReleaseCacheRefs, XtAppSetTypeConverter,
            XtCallbackReleaseCacheRef, XtCallbackReleaseCacheRefList,
            XtCallConverter, XtConvertAndStore

XtSetValues

(R3)

Sets widget resource values

SYNOPSIS

```
void XtSetValues( w, args, num_args )
        Widget                      w;
        ArgList                     args;
        Cardinal                    num_args;
```

ARGUMENTS

w	in	Widget for which to set resource values; must be of class Object or any subclass thereof.
args	in	An array of Args specifying new resource values for the widget.
num_args	in	Number of name/value pairs in *args*.

DESCRIPTION

XtSetValues sets the state of the specified widget while allowing it to override disallowed values, and invoking geometry management and a graphics redisplay if required. Valid resource names are widget class-dependent. If *args* holds a resource name that the widget does not support, that name/value pair is simply ignored. Other valid resource name/value pairs in *args* are still accepted. If a widget's parent is a subclass of Constraint, XtSetValues sets the values of any constraint resources attached to the child. If a NULL arglist is passed, but *num_args* is greater than zero, XtSetValues issues a fatal error.

USAGE

XtSetValues is the primary mechanism for modifying the state or appearance of a widget. The input arglist is usually declared as a static array of Args; XtSetArg is called repeatedly to fill in values. To query a widget's resource values, call XtGetValues. XtVaSetValues and XtVaGetValues are the varargs variants of these routines, and are easier to use in many cases.

CAUTION

You may not always get exactly what you expect when you call XtSetValues. For one thing, resources are not always orthogonal, so setting one may affect others that were not explicitly set. For another, a widget may override or modify the requested values to conform to its parent's geometry management policy or its own visual style.

If a call to XtSetValues results in a graphics redisplay, the Intrinsics generate an Expose event for the widget's window, which is handled some time after the call to XtSetValues returns. If bad resource values were assigned, they may show up as protocol errors when the widget redisplays.

If *num_args* does not match the number of name/value pairs actually set in *args*, unpredictable errors may result. XtSetValues should not be used to set callback resources, since it replaces the entire callback list rather than adding callback routines to the end of it.

SEE ALSO

Routines: XtGetValues, XtSetArg, XtVaGetValues, XtVaSetValues

XtSetWarningHandler (O)

Registers a toolkit low-level warning handler

SYNOPSIS

```
void XtSetWarningHandler( warning_handler )
        XtErrorHandler              warning_handler;
```

ARGUMENTS

warning_handler   in   New warning handler to be established.

DESCRIPTION

XtSetWarningHandler establishes a new warning handler within the scope of the default application context created by XtInitialize. When a toolkit non-fatal error condition is detected (that is, when the application or a toolkit internal routine calls XtWarning) control is passed to the specified procedure. The handler is expected to display a message, perform any application-specific fixups, and then return.

USAGE

See XtAppSetWarningHandler.

CAUTION

XtSetWarningHandler is an obsolete routine supplied for backwards compatibility with earlier versions of the Intrinsics, and is superseded by XtAppSetWarningHandler in the Release 3 and later Intrinsics. XtSetWarningHandler uses the default application context established by XtInitialize, which must be called first.

SEE ALSO

Routines: XtAppSetWarningHandler, XtWarning

XtSetWarningMsgHandler   **(O)**

Registers a toolkit high-level warning message handler

SYNOPSIS

```
void XtSetWarningMsgHandler( warning_msg_handler )
       XtErrorMsgHandler              warning_msg_handler;
```

ARGUMENTS

warning_msg_handler in   New warning message handler to be established.

DESCRIPTION

XtSetWarningMsgHandler establishes a new warning message handler within the scope of the default application context created by XtInitialize. When a toolkit non-fatal error condition is detected (that is, when the application or a toolkit internal routine calls XtWarningMsg) control is passed to the specified procedure. The handler is expected to display a message, perform any application-specific fixups, and then return.

USAGE

See XtAppSetWarningMsgHandler.

CAUTION

XtSetWarningMsgHandler is an obsolete routine supplied for backwards compatibility with earlier versions of the Intrinsics, and is superseded by XtAppSetWarningMsgHandler in the Release 3 and later Intrinsics. XtSetWarningMsgHandler uses the default application context established by XtInitialize, which must be called first.

SEE ALSO

Routines: XtAppSetWarningMsgHandler, XtWarning, XtWarningMsg

XtSetWMColormapWindows   (R4)

Sets the WM_COLORMAP_WINDOWS property on a Shell window

SYNOPSIS

```
void XtSetWMColormapWindows( w, widget_list, count )
        Widget                      w;
        WidgetList                  widgets;
        Cardinal                    count;
```

ARGUMENTS

w	in	Widget on whose window the WM_COLORMAP_WINDOWS property should be placed; must be of class Core or any subclass thereof.
widgets	in	List of widgets whose windows should be listed in the WM_COLORMAP_WINDOWS property.
num_widgets	in	Number of widgets in *widgets*.

DESCRIPTION

XtSetWMColormapWindows sets the WM_COLORMAP_WINDOWS property on the specified widget's window. The value of this property is a list of windows requiring different colormaps, and is constructed from the supplied list of widgets. The widget *w* must be a subclass of WMShell. If *w* is not realized, or *num_widgets* is zero, XtSetWMColormapWindows returns immediately. A widget specified in *widgets* is ignored if it is unrealized or employs a non-unique colormap.

USAGE

Window managers communicate with applications primarily through the use of window properties. Most properties examined by window managers are exported as resources on WMShell widgets, and are set by calling XtSetValues on the shell and specifying the resource name/value corresponding to the property.

The WM_COLORMAP_WINDOWS property, however, is set explicitly with XtSetWMColormapWindows. The list of widgets represents a prioritized list of windows referencing separate colormaps. A window manager may implement ways to traverse multiple colormaps required by an application or, on hardware that supports it, may install more than one colormap.

CAUTION

Setting the WM_COLORMAP_WINDOWS property does not guarantee that the workstation hardware or window manager will be able to support multiple colormaps. It should be viewed as a hint only. On most workstations, it is not possible to load more than one colormap into hardware, so it is inconvenient to have widgets in the same application use different colormaps.

SEE ALSO

Routines: None

XtStringConversionWarning   **(R3O)**

Logs an error message in response to a string conversion error

SYNOPSIS

```
void XtStringConversionWarning( source, dest_type )
        String                      source;
        String                      dest_type;
```

ARGUMENTS

source	in	String specifying source data which could not be converted.
dest_type	in	String specifying destination data type, e.g. "Int" or the symbolic constant XtRInt.

DESCRIPTION

XtStringConversionWarning is a convenience routine that displays a message indicating that a resource converter failed to convert a string value to the appropriate type. It simply calls XtWarningMsg with name="conversionError", type="string", class="XtToolkitError" and the message "Cannot convert string *source* to type *dest_type*".

USAGE

XtStringConversionWarning was used to report conversion errors in R3 built-in resource converters, and is maintained solely for the use of old-format resource converters that convert from strings. It is no longer used by the Intrinsics, which now call XtDisplayStringConversionWarning or XtAppWarningMsg.

CAUTION

XtStringConversionWarning is an obsolete routine provided for backwards compatibility with earlier releases of the Intrinsics. It is superseded by XtDisplayStringConversionWarning. XtStringConversionWarning uses the default application context established by XtInitialize, which must be called first.

SEE ALSO

Routines: XtAppWarningMsg, XtDisplayStringConversionWarning

XtSuperclass (R3)

Returns the class pointer of a widget's superclass

SYNOPSIS

```
WidgetClass XtSuperclass( w )
        Widget                          w;
```

ARGUMENTS

w   in   The widget whose superclass is requested; must be of class Object or any subclass thereof.

DESCRIPTION

XtSuperclass returns a pointer to the class record of *w*'s immediate superclass.

USAGE

This function is used within the toolkit Intrinsics to implement the inheritance of resources and procedures. It is generally not used by application programmers.

CAUTION

The superclass of a widget's class should not be confused with the parent of a widget instance (see Chapter 3).

SEE ALSO

Routines: XtClass, XtIs<*Class*>, XtIsSubclass

XtToolkitInitialize

(R3)

One-time toolkit initialization function

SYNOPSIS

void XtToolkitInitialize()

ARGUMENTS

None

DESCRIPTION

XtToolkitInitialize is a one-time toolkit initialization routine that registers Intrinsics built-in type converters and initializes toolkit internal data structures.

USAGE

XtToolkitInitialize is called once at the beginning of a toolkit application. The only Intrinsics routines that may precede a call to XtToolkitInitialize are XtSetLanguageProc and XtToolkitThreadInitialize. Some toolkits, however, may provide other initialization routines which must be called before or after XtToolkitInitialize (or both).

To start an application and create an application shell, XtToolkitInitialize is usually followed by calls to XtCreateApplicationContext, XtAppSetFallbackResources, XtOpenDisplay and XtAppCreateShell. In applications requiring only a single application context and application shell, the convenience routines XtAppInitialize or XtOpenApplication (R6) may be used to accomplish all of these in a single call.

CAUTION

XtToolkitInitialize may be called only once in an application program. The effects of calling it more than once are undefined.

SEE ALSO

Routines: XtAppCreateShell, XtAppInitialize, XtAppSetFallbackResources,
XtCreateApplicationContext, XtOpenDisplay

XtToolkitThreadInitialize   (R6)

One-time initialization for toolkit thread support

SYNOPSIS

```
Boolean XtToolkitThreadInitialize()
```

ARGUMENTS

None

DESCRIPTION

XtToolkitThreadInitialize initializes toolkit support for threaded applications, returning True if the Intrinsics support mutually exclusive thread access and False if they do not.

USAGE

Multi-threaded applications must call XtToolkitThreadInitialize before calling XtAppInitialize, XtOpenApplication, XtCreateApplicationContext or XtSetLanguageProc. XtToolkitThreadInitialize may be called more than once, but you must ensure that it is not called simultaneously by two separate threads. If your application is not multi-threaded, you do not need to call XtToolkitThreadInitialize.

CAUTION

None

SEE ALSO

Routines: XtAppLock, XtAppUnlock, XtProcessLock, XtProcessUnlock,
           XtAppSetExitFlag, XtAppGetExitFlag

XtTranslateCoords   **(R3)**

Translates widget X and Y positions to root window coordinates

SYNOPSIS

```
void XtTranslateCoords( w, x, y, rootx_return, rooty_return )
        Widget                  w;
        Position                x;
        Position                y;
        Position                *rootx_return;
        Position                *rooty_return;
```

ARGUMENTS

w	in	The widget in which X and Y are measured; must be of class RectObj or any subclass thereof.
x	in	X position in specified widget coordinate system.
y	in	Y position in specified widget coordinate system.
rootx_return	in/out	Pointer to variable in which root X coordinate is returned.
rooty_return	in/out	Pointer to variable in which root Y coordinate is returned.

DESCRIPTION

XtTranslateCoords translates a position measured in the coordinate system of widget *w* to a position in root window coordinates. It is similar to the Xlib function XTranslateCoordinates, but does not require a round trip to the X server. Instead, it uses the geometry information stored in the client-side widget data structures.

USAGE

This routine is most often used to calculate a position for a pop-up dialog box or menu relative to another widget or to the pointer. In these cases, the coordinates of the pop-up must be specified in root window coordinates, while the desired position is known in the coordinate system of some widget.

CAUTION

Key, Button and Motion events report a root X and Y location explicitly, and may save a call to XtTranslateCoords if what you really want is the root pointer position.

SEE ALSO

Routines: None

XtTranslateKeycode (R3)

Translates a KeyCode and modifiers to a KeySym

SYNOPSIS

```
void XtTranslateKeycode( display, keycode, modifiers, modifiers_return,
    keysym_return )
        Display                         *display;
        KeyCode                         keycode;
        Modifiers                       modifiers;
        Modifiers                       *modifiers_return;
        KeySym                          *keysym_return;
```

ARGUMENTS

display	in	Display with which keycode-to-keysym translator is associated.
keycode	in	Keycode to be converted.
modifiers	in	Modifiers supplied with the keycode.
modifiers_return	in/out	Pointer to a variable to receive a mask indicating which modifiers were actually inspected by the translator.
keysym_return	in/out	Pointer to a variable to receive the returned keysym.

DESCRIPTION

XtTranslateKeycode calls the keycode-to-keysym translator currently registered for the specified display, or the default translator if none has been registered.

USAGE

Key events contain a keycode that tells which physical key (e.g. top row, third key) was pressed or released. The mapping of physical keys to keycodes is fixed and specific to a keyboard make and model. Prior to further processing, a keycode is usually translated into a keysym, which is a vendor-neutral encoding that describes the symbol or function associated with the key (e.g. the symbol "A" - see <X11/keysymdef.h>). As a Key event is parsed through translation management, the Intrinsics convert keycodes to keysyms by calling a keycode-to-keysym translator.

You can invoke the current translator directly with XtTranslateKeycode. You might do this to parse raw Key events delivered by event handlers. The default translator is named XtTranslateKey, and uses shift, lock and group modifiers with the interpretations defined in the X Protocol specification. You can register a new translator with XtSetKeyTranslator if special keycode-to-keysym translation is to be done. This could be used, for example, to simulate alternate-language keyboard layouts.

CAUTION

Toolkits may register private keycode-to-keysym translators, so the keysym you get by calling XtTranslateKeycode may not be the same as you would get by calling XLookupString, which only uses the default mapping tables. In particular, OSF/Motif registers a special converter to convert keycodes to Motif-specific keysyms.

SEE ALSO

Routines: XtGetKeysymTable, XtSetKeyTranslator

XtUngrabButton **(R4)**

Releases a passive server-side grab on a pointer button

SYNOPSIS

```
void XtUngrabButton( w, button, modifiers )
        Widget                          w;
        unsigned int                    button;
        Modifiers                       modifiers;
```

ARGUMENTS

w	in	Widget specifying grab window; must be of class Core or any subclass thereof.
button	in	Pointer button to ungrab, e.g. AnyButton, Button1, Button2, etc.
modifiers	in	Key modifiers associated with button. AnyModifier, or any bitwise OR of: ShiftMask, LockMask, ControlMask, Mod1Mask, Mod2Mask, Mod3Mask, Mod4Mask, Mod5Mask.

DESCRIPTION

XtUngrabButton cancels a passive button grab previously established with XtGrabButton. If the specified widget is realized, XtUngrabButton calls XUngrabButton specifying the widget's window as the grab window. If the widget is not realized, XtUngrabButton cancels a deferred XtGrabButton request, if any, for the specified widget, button and modifiers. If the specified button is not grabbed, XtUngrabButton issues a warning and returns.

USAGE

Passive button grabs are used to control the delivery of pointer events so that they go to a specific client, or in some cases, to keep them from being sent until a client is ready to process them. You will rarely need to ask for a grab explicitly, since most widgets that require one take care of it internally. Please see Section 9.9 for a discussion of grabs and the situations in which they are useful.

In the rare cases where a passive button grab is needed, the toolkit routines XtGrabButton and XtUngrabButton should be used instead of their Xlib equivalents, since the Intrinsics routines handle the request properly whether the widget is realized or not.

CAUTION

Grabs established by XtGrabButton are implemented in the X server, and should not be confused with grabs implemented on the client side via the grab list and XtAddGrab. Server-side grabs should only be employed when it is absolutely necessary to control the delivery of events to the exclusion of other clients.

SEE ALSO

Routines: XtGrabButton, XtGrabKey, XtGrabKeyboard, XtGrabPointer, XtUngrabKey, XtUngrabKeyboard, XtUngrabPointer

XtUngrabKey   (R4)

Releases a passive server-side grab on a key

SYNOPSIS

```
void XtUngrabKey( w, keycode, modifiers )
        Widget                          w;
        KeyCode                         keycode;
        Modifiers                       modifiers;
```

ARGUMENTS

w   in   Widget specifying grab window; must be of class Core or any subclass thereof.

keycode   in   Specifies the physical key to be ungrabbed.

modifiers   in   Key modifiers associated with key. AnyModifier, or any bitwise OR of: ShiftMask, LockMask, ControlMask, Mod1Mask, Mod2Mask, Mod3Mask, Mod4Mask, Mod5Mask.

DESCRIPTION

XtUngrabKey cancels a passive key grab previously established with XtGrabKey. If the specified widget is realized, XtUngrabKey calls XUngrabKey specifying the widget's window as the grab window. If the widget is not realized, XtUngrabKey cancels a deferred XtGrabKey request, if any, for the specified widget, keycode and modifiers. If the specified key is not grabbed, XtUngrabKey issues a warning and returns.

USAGE

Passive key grabs are used to control the delivery of keyboard events so that they go to a specific client, or in some cases, to keep them from being sent until a client is ready to process them. You will rarely need to ask for a grab explicitly, since most widgets that require one take care of it internally. However, passive key grabs are sometimes used to reserve function keys. Please see Section 9.9 for a discussion of grabs and the situations in which they are useful.

In the rare cases where a passive key grab is needed, the toolkit routines XtGrabKey and XtUngrabKey should be used instead of their Xlib equivalents, as the Intrinsics routines handle the request properly whether the widget is realized or not.

CAUTION

Grabs established by XtGrabKey are implemented in the X server, and should not be confused with grabs implemented on the client side via the grab list and XtAddGrab. Server-side grabs should only be employed when it is absolutely necessary to control the delivery of events to the exclusion of other clients.

SEE ALSO

Routines: XtGrabButton, XtGrabKey, XtGrabKeyboard, XtGrabPointer,
            XtUngrabButton, XtUngrabKeyboard, XtUngrabPointer

XtUngrabKeyboard   **(R4)**

Releases an active server-side grab of the keyboard

SYNOPSIS

```
void XtUngrabKeyboard( w, time )
        Widget                          w;
        Time                            time;
```

ARGUMENTS

w	in	Widget specifying grab window; must be of class Core or any subclass thereof.
time	in	Server time at which to ungrab keyboard; an event timestamp or the symbolic value CurrentTime.

DESCRIPTION

XtUngrabKeyboard cancels an active keyboard grab established with XtGrabKeyboard. XtUngrabKeyboard calls XUngrabKeyboard passing the specified widget's window ID. If *w* is not realized, XtUngrabKeyboard simply returns.

USAGE

Active keyboard grabs are sometimes used to ensure security when entering sensitive data such as passwords. The grab forces all keyboard events to the grabbing client and prevents other clients from eavesdropping. Please see Section 9.9 for a discussion of grabs and the situations in which they are useful.

In the rare cases where a grab is needed, XtGrabKeyboard and XtUngrabKeyboard should be used rather than their Xlib equivalents, as the Intrinsics routines handle the request whether the widget is realized or not. The Intrinsics routines also cause the toolkit to restore keyboard events to the grabbing widget if keyboard focus has been remapped with XtSetKeyboardFocus. An active pointer grab remains in effect until the grab window is unmapped or your client calls XtUngrabPointer; to avoid impacting other clients, you must call XtUngrabPointer as soon as the grab is no longer required.

CAUTION

Grabs established by XtGrabKeyboard are implemented in the X server, and should not be confused with grabs implemented on the client side via the grab list and XtAddGrab. Server-side grabs should only be employed when it is absolutely necessary to control the delivery of events to the exclusion of other clients.

SEE ALSO

Routines: XtGrabButton, XtGrabKey, XtGrabKeyboard, XtGrabPointer,
        XtUngrabButton, XtUngrabKey, XtUngrabPointer

XtUngrabPointer (R4)

Releases an active server-side grab of the pointing device

SYNOPSIS

```
void XtUngrabPointer( w, time )
        Widget                          w;
        Time                            time;
```

ARGUMENTS

w   in   Widget specifying grab window; must be of class Core or any subclass thereof.

time   in   Server time at which to ungrab pointer; an event timestamp or the symbolic value CurrentTime.

DESCRIPTION

XtUngrabPointer cancels an active pointer grab established with XtGrabPointer. XtUngrabPointer calls XUngrabPointer passing the specified widget's window ID. If w is not realized, XtUngrabPointer simply returns.

USAGE

Active pointer grabs are used to ensure delivery of motion or button events when the pointer is going to be over another client's window. The xwd utility, for example, lets you select another client's window, and establishes an active pointer grab to make sure that it gets the button click no matter where the pointer is positioned. Please see Section 9.9 for a discussion of grabs and the situations in which they are useful.

In the rare cases where a grab is needed, XtGrabPointer and XtUngrabPointer should be used rather than their Xlib equivalents, XGrabPointer and XUngrabPointer, since the Intrinsics routines handle the request properly whether the widget is realized or not. An active pointer grab remains in effect until the grab window is unmapped or your client calls XtUngrabPointer; to avoid impacting other clients, you must call XtUngrabPointer as soon as the grab is no longer required.

CAUTION

Grabs established by XtGrabPointer are implemented in the X server, and should not be confused with grabs implemented on the client side via the grab list and XtAddGrab. Server-side grabs should only be employed when it is absolutely necessary to control the delivery of events to the exclusion of other clients.

SEE ALSO

Routines: XtGrabButton, XtGrabKey, XtGrabKeyboard, XtGrabPointer,
            XtUngrabButton, XtUngrabKey, XtUngrabKeyboard

XtUninstallTranslations

(R3)

Removes a widget's translation table completely

SYNOPSIS

```
void XtUninstallTranslations( w )
      Widget                    w;
```

ARGUMENTS

w   in   Widget from which translations are to be removed; must be of class Core or any subclass thereof.

DESCRIPTION

XtUninstallTranslations removes the specified widget's entire translation table.

USAGE

Each widget has a translation table that it uses to determine how to respond to events or sequences of events. XtUninstallTranslations is used in widget implementation code only when it is necessary to completely reset the translation table. Application programmers should not call XtUninstallTranslations.

CAUTION

Removing the translation table from a widget may cause it to cease functioning in part or completely.

SEE ALSO

Routines: XtAugmentTranslations, XtOverrideTranslations, XtParseTranslationTable

XtUnmanageChild (R3)

Unmanages a normal widget child and removes it from the screen

SYNOPSIS

```
void XtUnmanageChild( w )
        Widget                          w;
```

ARGUMENTS

w   in   Child widget to be unmanaged; must be of class RectObj or any subclass
                                thereof.

DESCRIPTION

XtUnmanageChild removes the specified child from its parent's managed set and, if it is mapped, unmaps
it from the screen. If the child is NULL, XtUnmanageChild issues a warning. If the parent widget is not a
subclass of Composite, XtUnmanageChild issues a fatal error.

USAGE

XtUnmanageChild is used to make a normal widget disappear from the screen, while invoking the
parent's geometry management routines. The specific visual effect of XtUnmanageChild depends on how
the parent treats its remaining managed children, if any. The parent may adjust itself or the remaining
children to take up the extra space.

    Since the toolkit internally grants any geometry a widget wants when it is unmanaged, children are
sometimes unmanaged so that their geometry can be reset. When they are managed again, the parent is often
more likely to grant their new geometry than if they requested geometry changes while managed.

    Unmanaging a parent removes its children from the screen with it, and can be used to remove entire
portions of a user interface from the screen. This does not change the managed state of the children, so if the
parent is once again managed the children will become visible again.

    A child may be managed again with XtManageChild or XtManageChildren. If several children
of the same parent must be unmanaged simultaneously, XtUnmanageChildren is more efficient than
multiple calls to XtUnmanageChild. In the R6 Intrinsics, the routine XtChangeManagedSet can be
used to simultaneously manage and unmanage children of the same parent.

CAUTION

XtUnmanageChild should never be called for pop-up shells, since pop-up widgets do not receive
geometry management from their parents, and are not included in the parent's list of normal children. To
remove a pop-up shell from the screen, call XtPopdown.

SEE ALSO

Routines: XtManageChild, XtManageChildren, XtUnmanageChildren,
            XtChangeManagedSet

XtUnmanageChildren **(R3)**

Unmanages multiple children of the same parent

SYNOPSIS

```
void XtUnmanageChildren( widgets, num_widgets )
        WidgetList              widgets;
        Cardinal                num_children;
```

ARGUMENTS

widgets	in	Pointer to a list of widgets to be unmanaged; each must be of class RectObj or any subclass thereof.
num_children	in	Number of widgets in widget list.

DESCRIPTION

XtUnmanageChild removes the specified children from their parent's managed set and, if they are mapped, unmaps them from the screen. If any child is NULL, or if all children do not have the same parent, XtUnmanageChildren issues a warning. If the parent widget is not a subclass of Composite, XtUnmanageChildren issues a fatal error.

USAGE

XtUnmanageChildren is used to make normal widgets disappear from the screen, while invoking their parent's geometry management routines. If several children of the same parent must be unmanaged simultaneously, XtUnmanageChildren is more efficient than multiple calls to XtUnmanageChild. The specific visual effect of XtUnmanageChildren depends on how the parent treats its remaining managed children (if any). The parent may adjust itself or the remaining children to take up the extra space.

Since the toolkit internally grants any geometry a widget wants when it is unmanaged, children are sometimes unmanaged so that their geometry can be reset. When they are managed again, the parent is often more likely to grant their new geometry than if they requested geometry changes while managed.

Unmanaging a parent removes its children from the screen with it, and can be used to remove entire portions of a user interface from the screen. This does not change the managed state of the children, so if the parent is once again managed the children will become visible again.

Children may be managed again with XtManageChild or XtManageChildren. In the R6 Intrinsics, the routine XtChangeManagedSet can be used to simultaneously manage and unmanage children of the same parent.

CAUTION

XtUnmanageChildren should never be called for pop-up shells, since pop-up widgets do not receive geometry management from their parents, and are not included in the parent's list of normal children. To remove a pop-up shell from the screen, call XtPopdown.

SEE ALSO

Routines: XtManageChild, XtManageChildren, XtUnmanageChild, XtChangeManagedSet

XtUnmapWidget   (R3)

Unmaps a widget's window without changing whether the widget is managed

SYNOPSIS

```
void XtUnmapWidget( w )
        Widget                          w;
```

ARGUMENTS

w   in   Widget whose window is to be unmapped; must be of class Core or any
                                     subclass thereof.

DESCRIPTION

XtUnmapWidget unmaps the specified widget's window, and any of its window descendants.
XtUnmapWidget does not affect the managed state of the widget, and white space is maintained where it
would normally appear.

USAGE

Unmapping a widget makes its window invisible. Default toolkit behavior is to map widgets when they are
managed, and unmap them when they are unmanaged, so XtManageChild and XtUnmanageChild are
the "usual" ways to put a widget on the screen and remove it. However, these routines invoke geometry
management, and can sometimes cause undesirable visual effects. For example, a dialog box might shrink,
expand or reposition its children to adjust for the sudden management/unmanagement of a child.

In some user interface styles, it is desirable to remove widgets from a layout while still maintaining the
space that they occupied. Default behavior can be overridden by using XtSetMappedWhenManaged to
set the widget's *mapped_when_managed* field to False. XtMapWidget and XtUnmapWidget are then
used to explicitly map and unmap the widget from the screen while leaving it managed. The parent's
geometry management is not invoked, and the parent maintains blank space where the child would normally
appear.

If a widget is unmanaged its parent will not make space for it, so the combination of "mapped" but
"unmanaged", while possible, is not very useful. Generally, a widget must be both mapped and managed to
be visible.

CAUTION

Before calling XtUnmapWidget you must call XtSetMappedWhenManaged to set the
mapped_when_managed field of the widget to False. An unmapped widget is still managed, so calls that
affect the geometry of the widget may change the geometry of the user interface. If *w* is not realized, calling
XtUnmapWidget may cause a fatal protocol error by referencing a NULL window ID.

SEE ALSO

Routines: XtMapWidget, XtSetMappedWhenManaged

XtUnrealizeWidget   **(R3)**

Destroys a widget's window and frees its server resources

SYNOPSIS

```
void XtUnrealizeWidget( w )
        Widget                      w;
```

ARGUMENTS

w   in   Widget to be unrealized; must be of class Core or any subclass thereof.

DESCRIPTION

XtUnrealizeWidget destroys the window(s) associated with the specified widget and all of its normal descendants. If *w* is managed, it is automatically unmanaged before its window is destroyed. The widget itself is not destroyed, and is automatically realized again if it is managed at a future time by a realized parent.

USAGE

This routine can be used to free the server resources associated with a widget to conserve memory on small X servers. However, repeatedly realizing and unrealizing widgets adversely impacts performance, since it demands numerous round trips to the X server. This routine is rarely called by application programmers.

CAUTION

You must be careful not to reference the widget's window ID in any subsequent Xlib drawing or resource allocation routines. XtWindow or XtWindowOfObject return NULL if called for an unrealized widget; to see if a widget is realized before fetching its window ID, call XtIsRealized. Naturally, unrealized widgets are not visible on the display, nor are their normal children.

SEE ALSO

Routines: XtRealizeWidget, XtWindow

XtUnregisterDrawable   (R6)

Remove a non-widget drawable from event dispatches

SYNOPSIS

```
void XtUnregisterDrawable( display, drawable )
    Display                        *display;
    Drawable                       drawable;
```

ARGUMENTS

display	in	Display of drawable.
drawable	in	Non-widget drawable to be unregistered.

DESCRIPTION

XtUnregisterDrawable removes the specified drawable from consideration by the toolkit event dispatcher. Future events from the drawable, if any, will be discarded.

USAGE

Sometimes you may want to listen for events from drawables that are not associated with a widget in your application. For example, you may want to handle PropertyNotify events on the root window or windows belonging to other applications as a way of performing inter-client communication. Prior to R6, this meant writing a private main loop that would watch for the "foreign" window ID and handle the events specially.

In the R6 Intrinsics, XtRegisterDrawable assigns a widget to act as a proxy for the drawable. After you register the drawable, you can add event handlers or action procedures to the widget to handle events coming from the drawable. The events are passed unchanged, so the window ID may be used to distinguish the drawable's events from events generated by the widget's own window. When the drawable is no longer important, you can unregister it with XtUnregisterDrawable.

CAUTION

The drawable may not be a window belonging to another widget in the application widget tree, and a drawable may not be registered with two widgets at the same time. The drawable should be unregistered with XtUnregisterDrawable before its proxy widget is destroyed.

SEE ALSO

Routines: XtRegisterDrawable

XtVaAppCreateShell   **(R4)**

Varargs form of XtAppCreateShell

SYNOPSIS

```
Widget XtVaAppCreateShell( app_name, app_class, widget_class, display,
    ... )
        String                          app_name;
        String                          app_class;
        WidgetClass                     widget_class;
        Display                         *display;
        varargs                         ...
```

ARGUMENTS

app_name	in	Resource name of the application instance to be rooted by the new Shell.
app_class	in	Resource class of the application instance to be rooted by the new Shell.
widget_class	in	Class pointer specifying type of Shell to create. Must specify a subclass of Shell - usually `applicationShellWidgetClass`.
display	in	Display on which new Shell is to be created.
...	in	Variable-length argument list of resource name/value pairs to override values found in database.

DESCRIPTION

XtVaAppCreateShell is identical in function to XtAppCreateShell, except that it uses an ANSI C varargs interface to pass the list of resource name/value pairs that sets the initial state of the shell. The ArgList and varargs form of this routine may be used interchangeably. For a discussion of the format of the varargs argument list, please see the description of XtVaCreateArgsList.

USAGE

See XtAppCreateShell.

CAUTION

See XtAppCreateShell.

SEE ALSO

Routines: XtAppCreateShell, XtVaCreateArgsList

XtVaAppInitialize   (R4O)

Varargs form of XtAppInitialize

SYNOPSIS

```
Widget XtVaAppInitialize( app_context_return, app_class, options,
    num_options, argc, argv, fallback_resources, ... )
        XtAppContext              *app_context_return;
        String                    app_class;
        XrmOptionDescList         options;
        Cardinal                  num_options;
        int                       *argc;
        String                    *argv;
        String                    *fallback_resources;
        varargs                   ...
```

ARGUMENTS

app_context	in/out	Pointer to variable to receive the new application context.
app_class	in	Resource class of the application.
options	in	Pointer to a list of option description records specifying command-line options that set resource values.
num_options	in	Number of option descriptors in *options*.
argc	in/out	Pointer to variable specifying argument count provided to main() at image activation; returns number of unparsed arguments left after XtVaAppInitialize has parsed *argv*.
argv	in/out	Argument vector provided to main() at image activation; returns unparsed arguments.
fallback_resources	in	Resource values to be used if the application defaults file cannot be found or opened, expressed as a NULL-terminated array of strings in resource file format. NULL if no fallback resources are to be specified.
...	in	Variable-length argument list of resource name/value pairs to override values found in database.

DESCRIPTION

XtVaAppInitialize is identical in function to XtAppInitialize, except that it uses an ANSI C varargs interface to pass the list of resource name/value pairs that sets the initial state of the shell. The ArgList and varargs form of this routine may be used interchangeably. For a discussion of the format of the varargs argument list, please see the description of XtVaCreateArgsList. As of R6, XtVaAppInitialize is superseded by XtVaOpenApplication.

USAGE

See XtAppInitialize.

CAUTION

See XtAppInitialize.

SEE ALSO

Routines: XtAppInitialize, XtVaCreateArgsList, XtOpenApplication

XtVaCreateArgsList (R4)

Creates a nested varargs argument list

SYNOPSIS

```
XtVarArgsList XtVaCreateArgsList( unused, ... )
        NULL                          unused;
        varargs                         ...
```

ARGUMENTS

unused	in	Reserved for future use. Must be NULL.
...	in	Variable-length argument list of resource name/value pairs.

DESCRIPTION

`XtVaCreateArgsList` accepts a varargs argument list of resource name/value pairs, returning a pointer which may itself be referenced as a resource value in a varargs list.

USAGE

A varargs argument list is a comma-separated list of resource name/value pairs. Each resource name is of type `String`, and is followed by a value of type `XtArgVal`. The end of the list is indicated by a name entry containing `NULL`:

```
XtVaSetValues( w, XtNwidth, 100, XtNheight, 200, NULL );
```

If a resource name in the list is the special value `XtVaTypedArg`, the next four arguments are interpreted as a name,type,value,size tuple where *name* and *type* are Strings, *value* is of type `XtArgVal`, and *size* is of type `int`. When the `XtVaTypedArg` is processed, a resource converter is called to convert the value from the specified type to the type associated with the resource name. If the data size is less than or equal to `sizeof(XtArgVal)`, *value* should be the data itself cast to the type `XtArgVal`. Otherwise, *value* is a pointer to the data. If the specified *type* is `XtRString`, *value* should be a pointer to the NULL-terminated character buffer and *size* should be the length of the buffer in bytes. If the type conversion fails, a warning message is issued and the entry is skipped.

```
XtVaSetValues( w,
    XtNwidth, 200,
    XtVaTypedArg, XtNbackground, XtRPixel,(XtArgVal)"red", 4,
    NULL );
```

If a resource name in the list is the special value `XtVaNestedList`, the next argument is interpreted as a nested `XtVarArgsList` to be inserted into the list at that point. A nested varargs list is created with `XtVaCreateArgsList`.

```
XtVarArgsList args;
args = XtVaCreateArgsList( XtNwidth, 100, XtNheight, 200, NULL );
XtVaSetValues( w, XtNborderWidth, 2, XtVaNestedList, args, NULL );
```

This way, an entire list of resource name/value pairs may be condensed into a single reference in a varargs list. Lists may be nested as deep as desired. Lists created with `XtVaCreateArgsList` should be freed with `XtFree` when no longer needed.

CAUTION

All the varargs routines eventually call their ArgList counterparts. There is a slight performance penalty in the extra call overhead and the time spent composing the ArgList. However, the varargs routines are usually easier to read and less subject to coding errors than repeated calls to XtSetArg.

SEE ALSO

Routines: XtVaAppCreateShell, XtVaAppInitialize, XtVaOpenApplication,
XtVaCreateManagedWidget, XtVaCreatePopupShell, XtVaCreateWidget,
XtVaGetApplicationResources, XtVaGetSubresources, XtVaGetSubvalues,
XtVaGetValues, XtVaSetSubvalues, XtVaSetValues

XtVaCreateManagedWidget (R4)

Varargs form of XtCreateManagedWidget

SYNOPSIS

```
Widget XtVaCreateManagedWidget( name, widget_class, parent, ... )
        String                          name;
        WidgetClass                     widget_class;
        Widget                          parent;
        varargs                         ...
```

ARGUMENTS

name	in	Resource name for new widget.
widget_class	in	Class pointer specifying type of widget to be created.
parent	in	Parent of new widget; must be of class Composite or any subclass thereof.
...	in	Variable-length argument list of resource name/value pairs to override values found in database.

DESCRIPTION

XtVaCreateManagedWidget is identical in function to XtCreateManagedWidget, except that it uses an ANSI C varargs interface to pass the list of resource name/value pairs that sets the initial state of the widget. The ArgList and varargs form of this routine may be used interchangeably within an application. For a discussion of the format of the varargs argument list, please see the description of XtVaCreateArgsList.

USAGE

See XtCreateManagedWidget.

CAUTION

See XtCreateManagedWidget.

SEE ALSO

Routines: XtCreateManagedWidget, XtVaCreateArgsList

XtVaCreatePopupShell   **(R4)**

Varargs form of XtCreatePopupShell

SYNOPSIS

```
Widget XtVaCreatePopupShell( name, widget_class, parent, ... )
        String                          name;
        WidgetClass                     widget_class;
        Widget                          parent;
        varargs                         ...
```

ARGUMENTS

name	in	Resource name for new widget.
widget_class	in	Class pointer specifying type of widget to be created. Must be a subclass of Shell.
parent	in	Parent of new widget; must be of class Core or any subclass thereof.
...	in	Variable-length argument list of resource name/value pairs to override values found in database.

DESCRIPTION

XtVaCreatePopupShell is identical in function to XtCreatePopupShell, except that it uses an ANSI C varargs interface to pass the list of resource name/value pairs that sets the initial state of the shell. The ArgList and varargs form of this routine may be used interchangeably within an application. For a discussion of the format of the varargs argument list, please see the description of XtVaCreateArgsList.

USAGE

See XtCreatePopupShell.

CAUTION

See XtCreatePopupShell.

SEE ALSO

Routines: XtCreatePopupShell, XtVaCreateArgsList

XtVaCreateWidget (R4)

Varargs form of XtCreateWidget

SYNOPSIS

```
Widget XtVaCreateWidget( name, widget_class, parent, ... )
        String                          name;
        WidgetClass                     widget_class;
        Widget                          parent;
        varargs                         ...
```

ARGUMENTS

name	in	Resource name for new widget.
widget_class	in	Class pointer specifying type of widget to be created.
parent	in	Parent of new widget; must be of class Object or any subclass thereof.
...	in	Variable-length argument list of resource name/value pairs to override values found in database.

DESCRIPTION

XtVaCreateWidget is identical in function to XtCreateWidget, except that it uses an ANSI C varargs interface to pass the list of resource name/value pairs that sets the initial state of the widget. The ArgList and varargs form of this routine may be used interchangeably within an application. For a discussion of the format of the varargs argument list, please see the description of XtVaCreateArgsList.

USAGE

See XtCreateWidget.

CAUTION

See XtCreateWidget.

SEE ALSO

Routines: XtCreateWidget, XtVaCreateArgsList

XtVaGetApplicationResources   **(R4)**

Varargs form of XtGetApplicationResources

SYNOPSIS

```
void XtVaGetApplicationResources( object, base, resources, num_resources,
    ... )
        Widget                          object;
        XtPointer                       base;
        XtResourceList                  resources;
        Cardinal                        num_resources;
        varargs                         ...
```

ARGUMENTS

object	in	Specifies root of resource names. The database associated with this object will be searched; must be of class Object or any subclass thereof.
base	in/out	Base address of application data structure to receive resource values.
resources	in	Pointer to a list of resource description records.
num_resources	in	Number of resource definitions in *resources*.
...	in	Variable-length argument list of resource name/value pairs to override values found in database.

DESCRIPTION

XtVaGetApplicationResources is identical in function to XtGetApplicationResources, except that it uses an ANSI C varargs interface to pass the list of resource name/value pairs. The ArgList and varargs form of this routine may be used interchangeably within an application. For a discussion of the format of the varargs argument list, please see the description of XtVaCreateArgsList.

USAGE

See XtGetApplicationResources.

CAUTION

See XtGetApplicationResources.

SEE ALSO

Routines: XtGetApplicationResources, XtVaCreateArgsList

XtVaGetSubresources (R4)

Varargs form of XtGetSubresources

SYNOPSIS

```
void XtVaGetSubresources( w, base, name, class, resources, num_resources,
    ... )
        Widget                  w;
        XtPointer               base;
        String                  name;
        String                  class;
        XtResourceList          resources;
        Cardinal                num_resources;
        varargs                 ...
```

ARGUMENTS

w	in	Widget which owns the subresources to be set; must be of class Object or any subclass thereof.
base	in/out	Base address of subresource data structure to receive values.
name	in	Resource name of widget subpart.
class	in	Resource class of widget subpart.
resources	in	Pointer to a list of resource description records.
num_resources	in	Number of resource definitions in *resources*.
...	in	Variable-length argument list of resource name/value pairs to override values found in database.

DESCRIPTION

XtVaGetSubresources is identical in function to XtGetSubresources, except that it uses an ANSI C varargs interface to pass the list of resource name/value pairs. The ArgList and varargs form of this routine may be used interchangeably within an application. For a discussion of the format of the varargs argument list, please see the description of XtVaCreateArgsList.

USAGE

See XtGetSubresources.

CAUTION

See XtGetSubresources.

SEE ALSO

Routines: XtGetSubresources, XtVaCreateArgsList

XtVaGetSubvalues   **(R4)**

Varargs form of XtGetSubvalues

SYNOPSIS

```
void XtVaGetSubvalues( base, resources, num_resources, ... )
        XtPointer              base;
        XtResourceList         resources;
        Cardinal               num_resources;
        varargs                ...
```

ARGUMENTS

base	in	Base address of widget subpart data structure from which to retrieve resource values.
resources	in	Pointer to a list of resource description records.
num_resources	in	Number of resource definitions in *resources*.
...	in/out	Variable-length argument list of resource name/value pairs.

DESCRIPTION

XtVaGetSubvalues is identical in function to XtGetSubvalues, except that it uses an ANSI C varargs interface to pass the list of resource name/value pairs. The ArgList and varargs form of this routine may be used interchangeably within an application. For a discussion of the format of the varargs argument list, please see the description of XtVaCreateArgsList.

USAGE

See XtGetSubvalues.

CAUTION

See XtGetSubvalues.

SEE ALSO

Routines: XtGetSubvalues, XtVaCreateArgsList

XtVaGetValues (R4)

Varargs form of XtGetValues

SYNOPSIS

```
void XtVaGetValues( w, ... )
        Widget                          w;
        varargs                         ...
```

ARGUMENTS

w   in   Widget from which resource values are to be retrieved; must be of class Object or any subclass thereof.

...   in/out   Variable-length argument list of resource name/value pairs.

DESCRIPTION

XtVaGetValues is identical in function to XtGetValues, except that it uses an ANSI C varargs interface to pass the list of resource name/value pairs. The ArgList and varargs form of this routine may be used interchangeably within an application. For a discussion of the format of the varargs argument list, please see the description of XtVaCreateArgsList.

USAGE

See XtGetValues.

CAUTION

See XtGetValues.

SEE ALSO

Routines: XtGetValues, XtVaCreateArgsList

XtVaOpenApplication (R6)

Varargs form of XtOpenApplication

SYNOPSIS

```
Widget XtVaOpenApplication( app_context, app_class, options, num_options,
    argc, argv, fallback_resources, shell_class, ... )
        XtAppContext            *app_context;
        String                  app_class;
        XrmOptionDescList        options;
        Cardinal                num_options;
        Cardinal                *argc;
        String                  *argv;
        String                  *fallback_resources;
        WidgetClass             shell_class;
        varargs                 ...
```

ARGUMENTS

app_context	in/out	Pointer to a variable to receive new application context.
app_class	in	Resource class of the application.
options	in	Pointer to a list of option description records specifying command-line options that set resource values.
num_options	in	Number of option descriptors in *options*.
argc	in/out	Pointer to variable specifying the argument count provided to main() at image activation; returns the number of unparsed arguments remaining after XtVaOpenApplication has parsed *argv*.
argv	in/out	Argument vector provided to main() at image activation; returns all unparsed arguments.
fallback_resources	in	Resource values to be used if the application class resource file cannot be found or opened, expressed as a NULL-terminated array of strings in resource file format. NULL if no fallback resources are to be specified.
shell_class	in	Class pointer specifying what kind of Shell to create.
...	in	Variable-length argument list of resource name/value pairs.

DESCRIPTION

XtVaOpenApplication is identical in function to XtOpenApplication, except that it uses an ANSI C varargs interface to pass the list of resource name/value pairs that sets the initial state of the shell. The ArgList and varargs form of this routine may be used interchangeably. For a discussion of the format of the varargs argument list, please see the description of XtVaCreateArgsList.

USAGE

See XtOpenApplication.

CAUTION

See XtOpenApplication.

SEE ALSO

Routines: `XtOpenApplication, XtVaCreateArgsList`

XtVaSetSubvalues   **(R4)**

Varargs form of XtSetSubvalues

SYNOPSIS

```
void XtVaSetSubvalues( base, resources, num_resources, ... )
        XtPointer                       base;
        XtResourceList                  resources;
        Cardinal                        num_resources;
        varargs                         ...
```

ARGUMENTS

base	in/out	Base address of widget subpart data structure to receive values.
resources	in	Pointer to a list of resource description records.
num_resources	in	Number of resource definitions in *resources*.
...	in	Variable-length argument list of resource name/value pairs.

DESCRIPTION

XtVaSetSubvalues is identical in function to XtSetSubvalues, except that it uses an ANSI C varargs interface to pass the list of resource name/value pairs. The ArgList and varargs form of this routine may be used interchangeably within an application. For a discussion of the format of the varargs argument list, please see the description of XtVaCreateArgsList.

USAGE

See XtSetSubvalues.

CAUTION

See XtSetSubvalues.

SEE ALSO

Routines: XtSetSubvalues, XtVaCreateArgsList

XtVaSetValues   **(R4)**

Varargs form of XtSetValues

SYNOPSIS

```
void XtVaSetValues( w, ... )
        Widget                          w;
        varargs                         ...
```

ARGUMENTS

w   in   Widget for which resource values are being set; must be of class Object or any subclass thereof.

...   in   Variable-length argument list of resource name/value pairs.

DESCRIPTION

XtVaSetValues is identical in function to XtSetValues, except that it uses an ANSI C varargs interface to pass the list of resource name/value pairs. The ArgList and varargs form of this routine may be used interchangeably within an application. For a discussion of the format of the varargs argument list, please see the description of XtVaCreateArgsList.

USAGE

See XtSetValues.

CAUTION

See XtSetValues.

SEE ALSO

Routines: XtSetValues, XtVaCreateArgsList

XtWarning   (O)

Calls the toolkit low-level warning handler

SYNOPSIS

```
void XtWarning( message )
        String                          message;
```

ARGUMENTS

message   in   NULL-terminated string specifying a warning message to be displayed.

DESCRIPTION

XtWarning calls the low-level warning handler installed in the default application context. The warning handler is expected to display the message, perform any application-specific fixups, and return. The default handler registered by the toolkit simply prints the message to stderr and returns.

USAGE

XtWarning is called by toolkit internal routines that cannot derive the application context of the caller, and do not need it. Application programmers should call XtAppWarning instead.

CAUTION

XtWarning is an obsolete routine supplied for backwards compatibility with earlier versions of the Intrinsics, and is superseded by XtAppWarning in the Release 3 and later Intrinsics. XtWarning uses the default application context established by XtInitialize, which must be called first.

SEE ALSO

Routines: XtAppWarning, XtInitialize, XtSetWarningHandler

XtWarningMsg (O)

Calls the toolkit high-level warning message handler

SYNOPSIS

```
void XtWarningMsg(name, type, class, default, params, num_params)
        String                          name;
        String                          type;
        String                          class;
        String                          default;
        String                          *params;
        Cardinal                        *num_params;
```

ARGUMENTS

name	in	Resource name of message, e.g. "invalidChild".
type	in	Secondary resource name of message, e.g. "xtManageChildren".
class	in	Resource class of message, e.g. "XtToolkitError".
default	in	Default message to display if no match is found.
params	in	Pointer to a list of string values to be substituted in the warning message.
num_params	in	Pointer to variable specifying number of string values in parameter list.

DESCRIPTION

XtWarningMsg calls the high-level warning message handler installed in the default application context. The warning message handler displays the message generated from the arguments, and then returns. The default warning message handler constructs a message by consulting the error database (usually merged from /usr/lib/X11/XtErrorDB). String parameters specified by *params* and *num_params* are substituted in the output message wherever the substitution characters "%s" appear in the message text.

USAGE

XtWarningMsg is called by toolkit internal routines that cannot derive the application context of the caller, and do not need it. Application programmers should call XtAppWarningMsg instead.

CAUTION

XtWarningMsg is an obsolete routine supplied for backwards compatibility with earlier versions of the Intrinsics, and is superseded by XtAppWarningMsg in the Release 3 and later Intrinsics. XtWarningMsg uses the default application context established by XtInitialize, which must be called first.

SEE ALSO

Routines: XtAppWarningMsg, XtInitialize, XtSetWarningMsgHandler, XtWarning

XtWidgetToApplicationContext   **(R3)**

Returns the application context associated with a specified widget

SYNOPSIS

```
XtAppContext XtWidgetToApplicationContext( w )
       Widget                          w;
```

ARGUMENTS

w   in   Widget for which application context is desired; must be of class Object
                                       or any subclass thereof.

DESCRIPTION

`XtWidgetToApplicationContext` returns the application context in which the specified widget was created.

USAGE

`XtWidgetToApplicationContext` is often used in callback routines to derive the application context from the widget ID passed as the first callback argument. The application context is required to register certain other kinds of callbacks, including input callbacks, timeouts, signal callbacks, action procedures and work procedures.

CAUTION

None

SEE ALSO

Routines: `XtCreateApplicationContext, XtDestroyApplicationContext`

XtWindow (R3)

Returns the window ID belonging to a specified widget

SYNOPSIS

```
Window XtWindow( w )
      Widget                       w;
```

ARGUMENTS

w   in   Widget whose window ID is requested; must be of class Core or any
                                  subclass thereof.

DESCRIPTION

Returns the specified widget's window ID. If *w* is not realized, XtWindow returns NULL.

USAGE

XtWindow is used to supply a window ID for Xlib graphics and resource allocation routines. You will often call it when drawing custom graphics in widgets such as the OSF/Motif XmDrawingArea widget.

CAUTION

You should make sure that the specified widget is realized before calling XtWindow, or be careful to check for a non-zero return value before depending upon it in Xlib calls. Except in very specific cases, you should not manipulate window attributes directly with Xlib routines, but should instead call XtSetValues on the associated widget, passing the appropriate resource values.

SEE ALSO

Routines: XtDisplay, XtIsRealized, XtRealizeWidget, XtScreen,
           XtUnrealizeWidget, XtWindowOfObject

XtWindowOfObject (R4)

Returns the window ID of an object's nearest windowed relative

SYNOPSIS

```
Window XtWindowOfObject( object )
        Widget                          object;
```

ARGUMENTS

object   in   Object or widget for which a window ID is desired; must be of class Object or any subclass thereof.

DESCRIPTION

XtWindowOfObject returns the window ID associated with the specified widget or object. If *object* is a windowless object, XtWindowOfObject returns the window ID associated with its nearest widget ancestor. If the nearest windowed ancestor is not realized, XtWindowOfObject returns NULL. If *object* is a windowed object, XtWindowOfObject performs identically to XtWindow.

USAGE

XtWindowOfObject is used to supply a window ID for Xlib graphics and resource allocation routines. XtWindowOfObject is used mainly by widget programmers in the implementation code for windowless objects. Ordinary programs should draw only in widgets, and should use XtWindow instead.

CAUTION

You should make sure that the nearest windowed ancestor is realized before calling XtWindowOfObject, or check for a non-zero return value from XtWindowOfObject before depending upon it in Xlib calls. Drawing operations and resource management for windowless objects are complicated by the fact that they must use the window belonging to a relative in the window tree (usually the parent).

SEE ALSO

Routines: XtDisplayOfObject, XtIsRealized, XtRealizeWidget, XtScreenOfObject, XtUnrealizeWidget, XtWindow

XtWindowToWidget   (R3)

Returns ID of widget that owns a specified window

SYNOPSIS

```
Widget XtWindowToWidget( display, window )
        Display                         *display;
        Window                          window;
```

ARGUMENTS

display	in	Display on which window is created.
window	in	Window ID valid on the specified display.

DESCRIPTION

XtWindowToWidget returns the widget ID (if any) associated with the specified window and display. If no matching widget is found, XtWindowToWidget returns NULL.

USAGE

This routine is used internally by the Intrinsics to determine the mapping of events to widgets, and is seldom needed by ordinary applications. You would use it if you wrote your own event dispatcher (see XtEventDispatchProc, Appendix B) or if you traverse a window tree with Xlib calls, searching for a window belonging to widget that you recognize. To make the opposite transformation and return the window ID associated with a known widget, call XtWindow.

CAUTION

XtWindowToWidget cannot return the IDs of widgets in other applications.

SEE ALSO

Routines: XtWindow, XtRegisterDrawable

Appendix D

TRANSLATION TABLE SYNTAX

A *translation table* is used to specify how sequences of X events are interpreted by a widget. Each unique sequence of events may trigger one or more named *actions*.

A translation table is specified in a plaintext format, which is then compiled to a toolkit internal representation with `XtParseTranslationTable` or `XtParseAcceleratorTable`. In a program, the plaintext representation is usually declared as a static `String`. A translation table may also be declared in a resource file with the resource name "translations", and is automatically converted to the appropriate internal type when the resource is fetched.

A translation table consists of a series of translation table entries. Each entry has a *left-hand side* and a *right-hand side*, separated by a colon. The left-hand side specifies an event or series of events, while the right-hand side specifies the action or actions to invoke when that event sequence is detected:

```
event-list : action-list
```

Translation tables may contain multiple lines separated by the symbolic newline characters backslash-n ("\n"). An optional *directive* may be placed at the beginning of a translation table, to indicate whether the translation table should be merged destructively or non-destructively with a widget's existing translations.

```
/* C language program */
/* Example translation table */
static String mytranslations =
            "#augment                 \n\
            <Btn3Down> : PopMenu()    \n\
            <Btn1Up>(2)  : Select()   ";


! Resource File
! Example translation table
XmDraw*graphics.translations:    \
        #augment                 \n\
        <Btn3Down> :  PopMenu()   \n\
        <Btn1Up>(2)   :   Select()
```

Events may be specified with keyboard or button *modifiers*. Depending on the event type, a *detail* field may also be provided, which allows the required events to be identified very specifically. For instance, the following translation is only satisfied by pressing the letter "K" on the keyboard, modified by the "shift" and "control" keys simultaneously:

```
!Shift Ctrl <KeyPress>K:   Select()
```

A count field may be placed in parentheses after an event specification to indicate a repeated event. For example, the following specification represents a double click on pointer button 1:

```
<Btn1Up>(2):  DoubleClick()
```

The right-hand side of a translation specifies the actions to be invoked. Parameters to be passed to the action procedures are specified inside parentheses as quoted or unquoted strings. Strings must be placed inside double-quotes to pass embedded blanks or the special characters tab, comma, newline or paren. The following translation passes two string to the action named PopMenu.

```
<Btn3Down>: PopMenu(drawAreaMenu, "Drawing Functions")
```

The following sections describe the various parts of a translation table in more detail.

D.1 Directive

The *directive*, if any, is specified as the first line in the translation table, and is followed by a symbolic newline "\n". A directive is only meaningful when a translation table is declared in a resource file. The value #override implies that translations specified in the table override any matching translations found in the widget's existing translation table. The value #augment implies that matching translations do not replace existing translations. The value #replace (the default) specifies that the new table completely replaces the widget's default translations.

D.2 Event Specification (left-hand side)

An *event* is specified by name between pointy braces ("<>"). Events in a series are separated by commas. Besides the canonical event types, the toolkit also accepts the abbreviations shown in Table D-1. The abbreviations make it easier to specify the desired events.

Table D-1   Event Type Specifications

X EVENT	ABBREVIATIONS	MEANING
<KeyPress>	<Key>	Keyboard key was pressed (Detail field tells which one)
	<KeyDown>	Synonym for KeyPress
	<Ctrl>	Key pressed with "Ctrl" modifier
	<Shift>	Key pressed with "Shift" modifier
	<Meta>	Key pressed with "Meta" modifier

Table D-1 Event Type Specification (continued)

X EVENT	ABBREVIATIONS	MEANING
<KeyRelease>	<KeyUp>	Keyboard key was released
<ButtonPress>	<BtnDown>	Pointer button was pressed
	<Btn1Down>	Pointer button 1 was pressed
	<Btn2Down>	Pointer button 2 was pressed
	<Btn3Down>	Pointer button 3 was pressed
	<Btn4Down>	Pointer button 4 was pressed
	<Btn5Down>	Pointer button 5 was pressed
<ButtonRelease>	<BtnUp>	Pointer button was released
	<Btn1Up>	Pointer button 1 was released
	<Btn2Up>	Pointer button 2 was released
	<Btn3Up>	Pointer button 3 was released
	<Btn4Up>	Pointer button 4 was released
	<Btn5Up>	Pointer button 5 was released
<MotionNotify>	<Motion>	Pointer moved
	<PtrMoved>	Synonym for MotionNotify
	<MouseMoved>	Synonym for MotionNotify
	<BtnMotion>	Pointer moved while any pointer button was held down
	<Btn1Motion>	Pointer moved while pointer button 1 was held down
	<Btn2Motion>	Pointer moved while pointer button 2 was held down
	<Btn3Motion>	Pointer moved while pointer button 3 was held down
	<Btn4Motion>	Pointer moved while pointer button 4 was held down
	<Btn5Motion>	Pointer moved while pointer button 5 was held down
<EnterNotify>	<Enter>	Pointer entered widget's window
	<EnterWindow>	Synonym for EnterNotify
<LeaveNotify>	<Leave>	Pointer left widget's window
	<LeaveWindow>	Synonym for LeaveNotify
<FocusIn>	<FocusOut>	Server assigned keyboard focus to widget's window
<KeymapNotify>	<Keymap>	Keyboard state changed
<Expose>	<Expose>	Widget's window exposed by window reconfiguration
<GraphicsExpose>	<GrExp>	Widget's window was exposed due to graphics operation
<NoExpose>	<NoExp>	Operation expected to produce an exposure didn't
<VisibilityNotify>	<Visible>	Visibility of window changed
<CreateNotify>	<Create>	Window was created
<DestroyNotify>	<Destroy>	Window was destroyed
<UnmapNotify>	<Unmap>	Window was unmapped
<MapNotify>	<Map>	Window was mapped
<MapRequest>	<MapReq>	Client requests that a window be mapped
<ReparentNotify>	<Reparent>	Window was reparented
<ConfigureNotify>	<Configure>	Window was reconfigured
<ConfigureRequest>	<ConfigureReq>	Client requests that window be reconfigured
<GravityNotify>	<Grav>	Window gravity changed
<ResizeRequest>	<ResReq>	Window was resized
<CirculateNotify>	<Circ>	Window stacking order changed

Table D-1 Event Type Specification (continued)

X EVENT	ABBREVIATIONS	MEANING
\<CirculateRequest\>	\<CircReq\>	Client requests that stacking order be changed
\<PropertyNotify\>	\<Prop\>	Property value changed
\<SelectionClear\>	\<SelClr\>	Selection ownership lost
\<SelectionRequest\>	\<SelReq\>	Another client requests the current selection value
\<SelectionNotify\>	\<Select\>	Current selection value is ready for retrieval
\<ColormapNotify\>	\<Clrmap\>	Colormap changed or was installed or uninstalled
\<ClientMessage\>	\<Message\>	Client message received
\<MappingNotify\>	\<Mapping\>	Keyboard mapping changed

D.2.1 Detail Field

An event specification may be followed by an optional *detail* field, which provides more information about the event. The detail corresponds to a field in the event structure; the field used depends on the event type. For example, if the event is a ButtonPress, the detail corresponds to the *button* field of the XButtonPressedEvent structure, and specifies which button changed state. Detail specifications are valid for the event types listed in Table D-2.

Table D-2   Detail Field Specification by Event Type

EVENT TYPE	EVENT FIELD	EXAMPLE
KeyPress	KeySym from *keycode* field	\<Key\>D
KeyRelease	KeySym from *keycode* field	\<KeyUp\>KP_F1
ButtonPress	*button* field	\<BtnDown\>Button1
ButtonRelease	*button* field	\<BtnUp\>Button2
MotionNotify	*is_hint* field	\<Motion\>NotifyNormal
EnterNotify	*mode* field	\<Enter\>NotifyNormal
LeaveNotify	*mode* field	\<Leave\>NotifyGrab
FocusIn	*mode* field	\<FocusIn\>NotifyNormal
FocusOut	*mode* field	\<FocusOut\>NotifyNormal
PropertyNotify	*atom* field	\<Prop\>WM_NAME
SelectionClear	*selection* field	\<SelClr\>PRIMARY
SelectionRequest	*selection* field	\<SelReq\>PRIMARY
SelectionNotify	*selection* field	\<Select\>PRIMARY
ClientMessage	*message_type* field	\<Message\>WM_PROTOCOLS
MappingNotify	*request* field	\<Mapping\>MappingKeyboard

The detail field for a Key event specifies the keysym of the translated event. The keysym may be specified by any of the following:

- Any standard KeySym name defined in `<X11/keysymdef.h>`, but with the "XK_" prefix removed:

  `<Key>KP_F1:  ClearText()`

- Any KeySym name defined in `/usr/lib/X11/XKeysymDB`:

  `<Key>osfDelete: DeleteObj()`

- A Latin-1 literal character:

  `<Key>L:  SelectLine()`

- A hexadecimal number, prefixed with "0x" or "0X":

  `<KeyUp>0xFF08:  Delete()`

- An octal number, prefixed with "0":

  `<KeyUp>0177410:  Delete()`

- A string of characters in double quotes means a sequence of Latin-1 characters

  `"quit":  Quit()`

D.2.2 Repeated events

Repeated events may be specified with a *repeat count* in parentheses immediately after the event specification. For example, the following translation implies a double-click on pointer button 2:

`<Btn2Up>(2):   Select()`

Events are considered repeated if they follow each other within the time period specified by the application resource "multiClickTime" (Class: "MultiClickTime"). The multi-click timeout value may be set and queried within a program with the Intrinsics routines `XtSetMultiClickTime` and `XtGetMultiClickTime`, respectively. To match multiple events greater than or equal to a number, use the plus sign "+" after the repeat count:

`<Btn2Up>(3+):   Count()`

The specified actions in this example would be invoked on the third click, and again on each subsequent click arriving within the multi-click timeout period.

D.2.3 Modifiers

Modifiers are logical keys or buttons that are pressed while another event is generated. To specify a modifier in a translation table, place the modifier symbol before the event specification. Modifiers may be applied to events of type <KeyPress>, <KeyRelease>, <ButtonPress>, <ButtonRelease>, <MotionNotify>, <EnterNotify> and <LeaveNotify>. Modifier specifications are listed in Table D-3.

Table D-3   Modifiers

MODIFIER	ABBREVIATIONS	MEANING
None		No modifiers
Any		Any combination of modifiers
Ctrl	c or ^	Control modifier bit
Shift	s	Shift modifier bit
Lock	l	Lock modifier bit
Meta	m or $	Meta modifier bit
Hyper	h	Hyper modifier bit
Super	su	Super modifier bit
Alt	a	Alt modifier bit
Mod1		Mod1 modifier bit
Mod2		Mod2 modifier bit
Mod3		Mod3 modifier bit
Mod4		Mod4 modifier bit
Mod5		Mod5 modifier bit
Button1		Button1 modifier bit
Button2		Button2 modifier bit
Button3		Button3 modifier bit
Button4		Button4 modifier bit
Button5		Button5 modifier bit
@keysym		Any keysym used as modifier

The mapping of physical keys to modifiers is performed by the server, and is therefore on a per-display basis. The default mapping is implementation-dependent. Modifier mapping may be changed with the xmodmap utility or the Xlib function XSetModifierMapping. Zero or more modifiers may be specified before an event. The following rules define how a list of modifiers is parsed:

- If no modifiers are specified it means "don't care" about modifiers

- If "None" is specified, no modifiers may be asserted

- A modifier preceded by a tilde ("~") must *not* be asserted

- An exclamation point ("!") at the start of the list implies that all listed modifiers must be exactly in the state specified, and no other modifiers are allowed

- If an exclamation point is *not* specified at the start of a list, it implies that all listed modifiers must be in the specified state, and "don't care" about other modifiers

- A colon (":") preceding the modifier list specifies that standard Shift and Lock modifiers are applied to translate the event to a keysym. This lets you encode case-sensitive translations - ":<Key>A" is distinct from ":<Key>a" - or symbols that appear as shifted characters on keys. For example, the symbols "#", "$", "&", etc. often appear over the number keys. Using the colon notation, ":<Key>&" is distinct from ":<Key>7" on keyboards where the number 7 and the ampersand are on the same key.

- If no colon (":") is specified, standard modifiers are not applied to the translation of a keycode to a keysym. Thus, "<Key>A" and "<Key>a" are equivalent, but "<Key>&" and "<Key>7" are also the same on keyboards where the number 7 and the ampersand are on the same physical key.

- If a colon (":") and an exclamation point ("!") are both specified at the start of the modifier list, it implies that *only* standard modifiers (Shift and Lock) may be asserted

Note that certain buttons or keys may be interpreted as either detail or modifiers, depending on how they are specified in the translation table.

D.3 Action Specification (right-hand side)

The right-hand side of a translation table defines the actions to be invoked by the translation. Actions are specified as a list of action names. After each action name, a pair of parentheses is required, which enclose a list of optional parameters. Parameters in the list are separated by commas, and are delivered to the action proc as an array of Strings. Example:

```
<KeyPress> : Action1() Action2(always, never) Action3()     \n\
```

D.4 Conventions

Always place more specific events in the table before more general ones:

```
Shift <Btn1Down>: Pick()
<Btn1Down>:       Choose()
```

Overlapping translations are OK. That is, if two translations both start with the same event, they will both get invoked when their full sequences are entered. Given the following translations, entering the string "gone" would invoke the first translation after the characters "go", and the second translation after the characters "gone".

```
"go" : GoAction()
"gone" : GoneAction()
```

Embedded translations are not invoked. That is, if an event sequence is a non-initial part of another sequence, it is not taken as a translation if the received events occur in the context of the longer sequence. Given the following translations, entering the string "gone" would invoke only the first translation. The translation for "one" would only be invoked if "one" was preceded by a key other than "g", or another event type entirely.

```
"gone" : GoneAction()
"one" : OneAction()
```

Double-clicks are often specified with a count field:

```
<Btn1Up>(2):   DoubleClick()
```

This introduces its own problems. The translation shown above is actually understood by the toolkit to mean:

```
<Btn1Down>,<Btn1Up>,<Btn1Down>,<Btn1Up>: DoubleClick()
```

In the following case, the translation for a single <Btn1Up> would be a non-initial fragment of the double-click translation. The translation would be taken only if the button release were not preceded by a button press, or if other (non-motion) events intervene between the press and release.

```
<Btn1Up>:      SingleClick()
<Btn1Up>(2):   DoubleClick()
```

The solution is to specify the single click as follows:

```
<Btn1Down>,<Btn1Up>:    SingleClick()
<Btn1Up>(2):            DoubleClick()
```

If not explicitly specified, MotionNotify events are disregarded when they occur between two events. This allows the pointer to move slightly between Button events, for example:

```
<Btn1Down>,<Btn1Up>:   Highlight()
```

Similarly, <MotionNotify> stands for any number of motion events, as it would be very hard for the user to control pointer motion so as to generate only one. If a motion event is the last event in a translation sequence, and causes an action to be invoked, the action is invoked repeatedly after each subsequent motion event

```
<Btn1Motion>:      Drag()
```

Called repeatedly on motion with Btn1Down and Shift, and don't care about other modifiers:

```
Shift <Btn1Motion>: Rubberband()
```

These conventions make sense, but they also make it impossible to define motion and double-click events in the same translation table. As soon as the toolkit honors implicit motion events between button events, it is forced to treat explicit motion events as an embedded sequence. Finally, here are some examples of key translations. First, some case-sensitive translations:

```
:Ctrl <Key>u:  Undo(last)
:Ctrl <Key>U:  Undo(all)
```

and keyboard "A" pressed with Shift and Ctrl modifiers, and no others:

```
!Shift Ctrl <Key>A:  Restart()
```

Index

A

N

O

S

X

Z

—